BEYOND THE GLITTER

Everything You Need to Know to
Buy . . . Sell . . . Care For . . . and Wear
Gems and Jewelry Wisely

By Gerald L. Wykoff

Adamas Publishers
P.O. Box 5504
Washington, D.C. 20016

Library of Congress: 81-69981
ISBN 0-9607892-1-9

To my wife, Margaret,
for Confidence and Faith.

Contents

BEYOND THE GLITTER
THERE MUST BE UNDERSTANDING

A controversy currently embroils the jewelry industry.

One side of this controversy holds that it is improper to go into too much detail about precious gemstones because it will tend to confuse an already suspicious customer who is usually buying only for emotional reasons.

The other side of the controversy contends that it is not only useful but vital that any gemstone or jewelry customer be given the basic facts because that individal will be more likely to buy gems of known higher quality.

As one with a deep and abiding love for precious gems, I find neither argument to be particularly inspiring.

I believe that in any sales transaction all parties to the transaction must gain their desires—or the transaction should be cancelled. That may be idealistic, but I've been pretty much able to achieve that goal in the more than 30 years I've spent as a diamond cutter, lapidary, goldsmith, manufacturer, and salesman fo fine gems.

What made my goal easier—in almost every case—was the confirmation I received in those face-to-face encounters with customers who were gemstone knowledgeable. A moment's reflection will reveal the why.

We both spoke the same language. We had the ability to communicate.

Most important, I did not have to overcome the suspicion and hostility that a normal person projects as a result of self-awareness that he or she is virtually at the mercy of someone who is far more knowledgeable. Perhaps many sales people need the additional assurance that they know something the other person doesn't know.

I find it a bit boring. How much more exciting and enjoyable it is for me to discuss these miracles of nature with a compatriot than the alleged potential victim of an "insider's information."

I believe that an informed buyer is the best buyer. This kind of buyer will go immediately to the transfer of information and involve the whole process in a higher level of exchange, of ethics, and of appreciation.

This book is designed to provide the kind of information which will help you become that better customer. If you are a jewelry salesman, it is designed to bring to you—quickly and reliably—a level of gemstone expertise that will enable you to provide a better service to customers.

i

Above all, it is a book whose intent is to provide guidelines, a confident path through what has been for centuries a maze for mystics into whose carefully nurtured and hidden gardens only a chosen few could enter. There is no great mystery about gemstones.

At the same time, this is not a book wherein will be found the various descriptions and specifications of the various groups, species, and varieties of gems. The area of gem testing is left to other books and other authors—and the available inventory in this field of inquiry is splendid.

This is a book about people and how to evaluate buy, sell, care for, and wear gemstones to your and their fullest potential. Some hard gemology is unavoidable.

Given the information provided here, I believe a reader can—at his or her own convenience and ambition—go on to a greater study of gemology, one of the truly fascinating areas of inquiry.

Gerald L. Wykoff

INTRODUCTION

Gems!

From the time perhaps of creation itself they have held the attention of men and women. Because of their intensity and integrity of color; because of their ability to endure, and because of their relative rarity, gems have come to represent all that is important and central to the idea of beauty and value.

Fortunately or unfortunately, the thrilling mystique attached to precious gemstones has produced flaws in the crown of understanding. The complexities of gems—their colors, clarities, rarities, proportions, values, and the like—seem restricted to the translations of an elite.

It is an incredible—but rather obvious—facet of human nature that some of the most costly investments earn from the buyer the least attention, knowledge and caution. In a single transaction involving a significant amount of money, an individual may finalize a gemstone purchase with little true awareness of what is being bought—or how out-of-balance the transaction might be.

The gemstone business is a magnificent business. Most jewelers sincerely want to fulfill their role while maintaining the highest level of integrity and trust. Many, too, would much rather deal with a customer who brings to the process a substantial fund of existing gemstone awareness.

But, this isn't the case most of the time. Men and women have other obligations and demands on their available time. As much as they want—and purchase—valuable gems and jewelry, they rely heavily on a jeweler for expertise on the somewhat justifiable grounds that one can't possibly be an expert in everything one does.

Still, though, there is some obligation. When a person intends to spend a large amount of money for a gem, whether for investment or adornment, it is a good idea to have some buyer intelligence.

The gemstone business is renowned for the level of trust that exists—on the wholesale level. It is true that cutters and wholesale merchants will send an extraordinarily valuable memo of gems to a dealer based only on a verbal promise to pay if the latter decides to buy.

That is business ethics on the wholesale level. Such honor and accuracy is not so prevalent when it comes to the retail buyer—the consumer. Caveat emptor (let the buyer beware) works in the retail jewelry business as well.

Dealing with a reputable jeweler and preferably known to you is the major defense against unhappiness. But having some gemstone knowledge is equally as good—and your jeweler should brighten to the task of dealing with an informed customer. Next to selling gems, jewelers like to talk about them.

But not all jewelers are well grounded in gemology—or in business ethics. It should therefore come as no great surprise that many jewelry sellers press the distinct advantage they have over an uninformed buyer.

One does not need to become a professional gemologist to gain an acceptable and competent skill level in judging and evaluating gems. While much of the vocabulary of gemology may seem strange and exotic, enough can be learned in a minimal amount of time.

This book does not seek to provide a minimal amount. It has been written with the full intent to give you a superior understanding of the elements involved in gems and jewelry.

An understanding of the ideas and concepts presented throughout these pages should enable a person with little or no previous gemology experience to be able to discern fine gem grade stones from the ordinary—and to be able to assign realistic dollar values to these different grades.

Venturing into the world of gems can be an inspirational experience as well as an imposing one. There are more than 20 color grades in diamonds alone. There are some 10 clarity grades, running from "Flawless" to the bottom values of "Included."

As for cuts and proportions, there are thousands of variations . . . and the same thing holds true in colored stones.

Is it any wonder that a resourceful jeweler can locate virtually any gemstone of any given grade, color, or cut to match any given pocketbook?

For all the seeming complexity and myriad opportunities to go intellectually astray, the heart of gemological understanding can be reduced to a manageable set of principles—all easily remembered and, just as easily, applied.

The need for knowledge is increasingly important as the level of sophistication grows in man-made gems. Many of the known gemstone deposits throughout the world are nearing exhaustion. The number of large gems newly discovered each year is decreasing.

This has provided a stimulant to "doctor" gems that would have been commercially unacceptable a few years ago—as well as to open the market for man-made synthetic gems. With new technology and processes, man has been able to duplicate natural gemstones in every physical, chemical and optical way.

Just a few short years ago the promoters of synthetics boasted, "Only your jeweler can tell." Today, not even the jeweler is certain; even he needs instruments—and sometimes the backup assistance of a professional gemological laboratory.

In most cases, this book will enable you to stroll interesting, exciting gemological pathways with confidence. For those rare instances where laboratories and instruments are the only safe way—you'll, at least, know when you're in that kind of situation.

Confidence in what you do and should know—and knowing when you need help—that's what knowledge is all about.

CHAPTER ONE

GEMS: The Monarchs of Nature

Who knows how long ago it happened?

But somewhere about 7000 years ago a man or woman probably bent over and picked up a glistening pebble. For one or perhaps a number of reasons that pebble had something different about it.

Then came other pebbles like it and soon the ancients began to find even other stones with more qualities. Each possessed something unique and with the power to fascinate. In an understandably ignorant but profound need to explain why certain pebbles were more desirable than others—men and women—invested the pebbles with near magical powers. They wore them, of course.

But they also began to regard them with awe, worship and avarice. From historical records, we now know that the first pebbles of value included amethyst, amber, rock crystal, garnet, jade, jasper, lapis lazuli, pearl, coral, emerald and turquoise.

That early civilizations treated these early gems with such reverence should come as no surprise. Of the 92 natural elements in the universe, science has now identified their combination into some 2,000 different minerals.

From this huge number about 90 possess the beauty and durability to qualify as gemstones. Of this 90, only about 20 are particularly useful in the jewelry industry.

As a result, gems soon came under the reservation of the wealthy and powerful as symbols of their special station in life. Rulers formalized documents with jewel-encrusted seals.

There isn't much doubt that the art of carving gems existed long before the art of faceting them was developed. Excavations have revealed that the first carved gems were made about 4000 B.C.

These were not the cameos and intaglios of today but rather cylinders and seals used primarily for the purpose of placing signatures to contracts as well as for messages and identity.

Later, of course, gems found use as amulets, as talismans, and as money. They were also used as protection against ghosts, and could be relied upon to provide a wearer with special favors from angels and saints.

They likewise could repulse evil, preserve health, ward off poisons and plagues.

Additionally, gems could make princes gracious (especially if you gave a prince a gem) and led sailors home. Amethysts (from the Greek word

"Amathos" meaning non-drunkenness) for example, is famous for its protection against becoming drunk.

Up to the beginning of the 19th century, gemstones were often utilized as medicine. For the most part, gems were used medicinally in three ways: one, the presence of the stone was deemed sufficient to effect a cure; two, the afflicted part of the body was touched by the gem, and three, the gem was powdered and eaten.

While success may be contributed more to the positive thought processes of the sufferer, failures were explained away as attributable to the fact that the stones used were not "genuine."

Lest there be any doubt as to the lingering power of belief in the magical healing powers of gemstones, it should be noted that even today low-grade pearls in Japan are ground up and made into calcium tablets for sale to many Japanese as medicine.

Fig. 1-1 The hardness of gemstone materials was useful for carving durable seals and cylinders which could affix signatures and marks on ancient documents and clay tablets.

Seals, Cylinders Among First . . .

In the beginning, though, it appears that early man and woman were restricted to the use of river-worn, i.e., tumble polished stones.

Later, when the ability to carve was developed the first uses apparently were in the construction of seals and cylinders for use by the elite.

The digs in Sumer, a territorial division of Babylonia (Iraq) uncovered cylinder-type seals used in 4000 B.C. for pressing impressions into the clay writing tablets. The logical extension of cylinder carving undoubtedly came from the tribal customs of cutting individual markings into arrows which were pressed into clay to indicate ownership.

In any event, the custom of using seals as signature marks was followed in Babylon, Syria, Assyria and Persia.

By the time the custom spread to ancient Egypt, the cylinder was supplanted by the scarab seal. The Egyptians wrote on papyrus, not on clay, and thus had no need for an impression instrument such as the cylinder-seal.

But the rise of the sacred beetle about 2500 B.C. as a symbol for the Egyptian god Khepera led to the development of what has become known as the scarab.

Fig. 1-2 Egyptians attributed powerful significance to the scarab or kheper symbol which has held its sacred meaning for more than 2000 years.

In Egyptian the beetle is called 'Kheper'' (pronounced "Kee-per''). The Greeks translated the heiroglyphics first, and used their word, "scarab," for "Kheper" or "beetle."

What is behind the incredible popularity of the scarab symbol is the deep esoteric significance given it by the Egyptians who saw in the Kheper the same symbolic power that Christians see in the cross.

Cherished as an all-powerful amulet, it carried a sacred power for more than 2000 years. Nearly every Egyptian owned a Kheper which is why so many of them exist today.

From Egypt, the art of gem carving spread to the Greek empire. By the 7th and 6th centuries, B.C., trade and commerce stimulated the production of signature gem seals. Possession of a copy of another's seal, under Solon's laws, carried a death penalty.

In the continuing line of cultural transfer, the Greek gem seals retained the scarab form, gradually transitioning to the use of cameo-like satyr heads and other renditions of Greek mythology.

Characteristics of Gemstones . . .

Despite the practical and symbolic early use of gemstones, most people began to recognize objectively the essentials that comprise a true gem.

The qualities—without which a species or variety cannot truthfully be categorized as gemstone—include:

BEAUTY:

In all of nature's incredible spectrum of beauty, few elements can equal or surpass the pure, pristine beauty of a gemstone, its spectacular purity of hue, tone and intensity, or the awesome transparency of the river white gems such as diamonds, quartz and topaz.

Is it any wonder that ancient peoples looked upon such creations with such awe?

To be a gem, a specimen must have the unique appearance of color quality and depth, even when clear. Opaque stones, of course, depend mostly on color richness alone.

The point is: a specimen must yield up its potential beauty in response to cutting fashioning or polishing or it can never take its place among the gemological wonders.

This is a good point to remember the next time you come across a newspaper or magazine advertisment offering TRUE, GENUINE EMERALDS FOR ONLY $5 PER CARAT, OR $5 DIAMONDS.

Emeralds of legitimate value run into the thousands of dollars per carat, because of their spectacular green color. The $5/carat stones lack this color; they lack beauty and that's why they can't provide gemological value.

The same may be true of $5 diamonds. They are specimens of carbon crystallized in the cubic form. That makes them genuine diamonds. But for the most part they are uncuttable, of extremely low color or clarity (or low in both) and can not be cut or fashioned into items of *beauty.*

Potential beauty is the key.

The sad examples above demonstrate the lack of potential beauty. What is not there cannot be released: beauty.

Go to an estate sale—as many gem collectors do. Don't be turned away too quickly because that Imperial Topaz is so badly abraded on the facet joins, making the gem look ugly.

Look into the gem—use a penlight if you have one—and evaluate the inside. Does it have potential beauty? A quick re-cutting or re-polishing may produce a majestic gem as the potential beauty is released . . . probably at a fraction of the cost of a new Imperial Topaz.

RARITY:

In general, the rarer the gem the higher will be its value.

Quartz is one of the most plentiful minerals on earth. Its ready availability as well as the ease in mining it account for the relatively low value of quartz gems.

These include Amethyst (a violet colored quartz), Citrine (a light yellow to gold-brown quartz) or Prasiolite (a leek-green quartz). Incidentally, Prasiolite is produced by heating amethyst, and most Citrine is heat treated amethyst as is smokey quartz (the latter is sometimes also called Smoky Topaz).

Even flawless, fine specimens of the above gems are relatively inexpensive because fine material is not all that rare.

Now consider Emerald. The best emerald come from Columbia, South America, and in the finer qualities is most rare.

Ruby is swiftly becoming more rare.

Today, as a result of rarity, fine emeralds and rubies command greater prices per carat than colorless diamonds often do.

Too much of a good thing is not good, though. Many beautiful gems are so rare that they have never had the chance for exposure adequate enough to develop a demand among gem buyers.

Benitoite is a beautiful corn flower blue gem—similar to the color of the most expensive sapphire—which is found only in San Benito county, California, and then only in small pieces. It will probably never have a market because the available supply is just too small.

Sphene occurs as a yellow, brown, or green gem of great brilliance and fire. But it is not a well-known gem and its rarity suggests that it perhaps never will be sufficiently abundant to develop and hold popular demand.

DEMAND:

Popular demand is the third of the vital necessities for gemstone value.

At any given time, some gemstones are in demand, while others are climbing or slipping.

The big four (Diamond, Ruby, Sapphire, Emerald) have held their popularity for centuries. Other gems bask in the public's favor for a limited time and then give way to other contenders.

In the 20s, it was amber. Then the so-called "Baltic Gold" went into eclipse. Pearls were the rage in the 30s, then slipped a bit—with a noticeable resurgence in the late 70s.

Aquamarine—the cold, brilliant blue beryl—has been popular for 5 decades. In the 80s, it began slipping a bit—due to the growing problem of rarity—and has stimulated the rise in popularity of Precious Blue Topaz as an alternate.

Precious Blue Topaz bears essentially the same coloration as fine Aquamarine.

DURABILITY:

A gemstone does not need to be indestructible, but it does need to possess sufficient durability to accomodate the wear and tear that is to be expected from use.

Admittedly, some gemstones are much harder and tougher than others and can resist the loss of beauty to a greater degree. The advertising slogan, "Diamonds Are Forever," is nearly accurate. Diamonds can retain their qualities for centuries—much longer than many other materials.

The durability difference between a diamond and, say, an Opal are extreme. Opal is a much softer gem material. As a matter of fact, Opals are so fragile that special care must be accorded them less they chip, break, craze, or simply lose their luster.

Pearls, being organic, are generally given a life of 100 to 150 years. By that time, usually, their composition has broken down.

TRADITION:

No treatment of the characteristics of gemstones would be complete without some mention of tradition.

Since the first polished pebble found its way into the human value system, tradition has been the major shaping force in the assignment of value.

Not everyone found a polished pebble. It seems reasonable that the first man or woman announced the find by using the pebble as an ornament.

That could have begun the use of gems to symbolize accomplishment. It is human nature to want that which is largely unobtainable or which is most difficult to acquire.

By obtaining it, a man or woman can demonstrate accomplishment. That's why gems quickly became the exclusive property of the powerful and wealthy. They symbolized position in life, wealth, power, authority, accomplishment.

Succeeding generations continued the custom. Tradition became a powerful influence in the establishment of exquisite gemstones as symbolizng the elevation of individuals in the church, business, family and other groups.

If beauty alone was the criterion the synthetics and imitations would have gained prominence since in most cases man-made stones are far superior in color and clarity to natural gems.

If rarity alone was the criterion, simple marketing restrictions could have achieved this goal. Restrictions do have a powerful influence as witnessed by the beneficial economic influence of the pervasive De Beers monopoly in diamonds, or the limitations on the sapphire-blue gem, Tanzanite, which comes from Tanzania.

If durability alone was the criterion, the man-made element called Borozon—next only to a diamond in hardness—would be far more valuable.

Tradition is the binding agent. Accomplishment is rare and beautiful and durable. So this trait traditionally is symolized by the rare, beautiful and durable—the precious gemstone—flaws and all.

In the United States, perhaps far more than in other countries, men and women desire the genuine. Synthetics has never made a deep or lasting penetration into the American gem buying consciousness.

This may change in coming years because of the apparent drying up of many gem sources. For the present, tradition is too strongly in the forefront for the man-mades to ever threaten a large replacement.

To the American mind gemstones, becoming increasingly rare, will simply become increasingly more valuable.

Some individuals, particularly the supporters of gems as investment, herald portability as one of the vital attributes of gemstones.

Perhaps.

Certainly, some gems have the wherewithal to concentrate a great deal of value into a small object. It is true that many people have saved their fortunes by putting gems into a small pouch and crossing into a safer country.

On the other hand, portability is limited to a small segment of the gemstone group. Only a few gemstones have the ability to store great values into small pouches.

Most gemstones do not have that capability—and to decry the desirability of a magnificent gemstone on the shaky basis that it doesn't sufficiently concentrate value is to apply a somewhat questionable judgement.

What's Precious . . . Semi-Precious?

Depending on portability to function as a reliable component of gemstone value, is almost as questionable as maintaining an attitude that some gemstones are precious and some are semi-precious.

We may thank a French gentleman, Jerome Cardan, for authoring this unfortunate distinction, just prior to the Renaissance. Most gemstone experts give little credence to this absurdity anymore.

If a gemstone has value—regardless of its station on the value scale—it is a precious gemstone. Cardan classified all rare, small, brilliant-appearing stones as precious gems.

Of course, Cardan's opinions were influenced by the animism of the previous centuries. He assumed precious stones to be living things which ". . . suffer illness, old age, and death."

Unfortunately, the designations are still used in the jewelry trade despite the obvious fact that many gemstones, under the semi-precious category, are more valuable than some of the precious ones.

Gemstones might be a better term to indicate the precious from the non-precious.

Even the word gemstone can have its uneasy definitional moment, though. One should remember that not all gemstones are minerals. Some precious gems are of organic origin—amber, coral, pearl.

Even fossils have been used as ornaments or jewelry.

7

No specific line of demarcation for value exists and precious ornaments are as apt to come from minerals or organic processes as they are to come from a factory or laboratory.

So that you may become familiar with some of the words, here are the generally accepted definitions for gemological terms that are heavily used:

A *gemstone* is a collective name for all ornamental stones. It is a synonym for all precious stones and is convenient to avoid the difficulty of more or less valuable stones.

A *mineral* is an inorganic, natural, solid element of the earth. Most minerals form into definite crystals but not always. Minerology is the branch of science which deals with minerals.

A *stone* is a popular name and usually serves as a synonym for mineral. A jeweler often calls a gem a stone; an architect refers to building materials and gravel as stone, and sculptors carve out of stone. In geology, one talks of minerals and rock—not stones.

A *rock* is an aggregate of natural minerals, sometimes combining a number of minerals in one large unit. Sand and gravel are also considered rocks. Petrography is the science of rocks.

A *crystal* is a uniform body of a mineral that has developed in strict accordance with its own peculiar atomic lattice. The different geometric shaped habits into which the various gems form are dependant on the varying physical properties of the atomic structure. The colors of various crystals come from chemical impurities included in the basic mineral. Crystallography is the science of crystals.

A *jewel* is a personal ornamental piece. It can be any material —gemstone, metal, wood, plastic, glass, etc. It can refer equally to a piece of jewelry set or unset with gems and with cut and uncut gems.

Where the Gems' Names Come From . . .

If there is unfortunate confusion between what gems are precious and what gems are semi-precious, then the names of gems themselves can be a quagmire.

Most of this difficulty is traceable to the Greek and Latin, both languages having left an enormous stamp on the language of gems. Gems have been named after special characteristics, after the place of occurrence and after people.

Then, too, we must consider a most reprehensible reason for naming gems—a deliberate effort to confuse a less valuable stone with one of greater value and thus stimulate sales. Foreign sounding names is the favorite tactic. A geographic qualifier attached to a real gem name runs a close second.

It is difficult enough to keep track of gem names without the addition of "marketing names." A number of governments have moved into this area in an effort to correct the obvious abuses. But the promoters are still hard at work fanning up markets with misleading and confusing names.

Probably the practice can never be stamped out completely, but a wary buyer can take reasonable steps for self-protection.

Originally, most gem names referred to the special characteristics of the stones. The Greek "prase" means green, so it is easy to see that Chrysoprase came to mean an opaque, translucent green gem.

Diamond is derived from the Greek word "adamas" meaning unconquerable. Adamas was usually a name for iron or iron alloy, but Ovid probably intended it to mean diamond when he wrote. At least the French interpreted Ovid that way and it was a quick shift from the French word, "diamant," itself a derivation from the Latin and the Greek adamas.

Agate is named after the famous river in Sicily, and other examples of gems named after places of occurrence are Tanzanite, the magnificent sapphire-blue form of heat-treated Zoisite which comes from Tanzania, Africa, and the Benitoite, which comes from San Benito County, California.

Considerable controversy surrounds mineral names that are based on occurrences. Different languages mean different spellings.

Take the mineral Vesuvianite which was named after Mount Vesuvius in Italy. Understanding the origin of this mineral's name wasn't helped by the fact that today Vesuviante is also found in Canada, the U.S. and Russia. To eliminate confusion, the mineral has received a new name—idocrase (after its crystal form)—with the result that the industry now has two names . . . or perhaps three. Vesuvius or idocrase has recently been found in Siberia and it has been named after a river there—wiluite. Other similar examples exist.

Naming minerals after people has created even more confusion. Kunzite, the lavender colored variety of Spodumene, was named after Dr. G.E. Kunz who discovered it—which, presumably, is reasonable.

But many minerals have been named after princes, politicians, wives and others who have little to do with gemology.

Add to this confusion the readiness of individuals interested in developing a market for slow moving or inexpensive minerals, and the unwary can quickly become ensnared.

Beware of Two-Word Gem Names . . .

Gem or mineral names that are more trustworthy generally consist of one word to identify a species or variety, or, if two words are used, the first word is a color followed by a well-known mineral or gem name.

A good rule, though, is: beware of two-worded gem names.

The commercial names, that is, names used to permit minerals of lesser character to attract value by "riding" on the names and reputations of more popular gems, often contain a place or geographical location as the first word, followed by the well-known mineral's name.

A couple of examples will demonstrate this technique of "boosting" a gem name. Red Sea Pearls are not pearls at all: they are coral beads, and Paris pearls are out-and-out imitation pearls. A Montana ruby is not a ruby; it is a red garnet. Swiss Lapis is not Lapis Lazuli; it is dyed jasper.

Here is a list of some commercial names. It is not a recommendation against their purchase; the listing is merely so you will know the true identity of some of the gems and minerals with which you are really dealing:

Commercial Name	What It Really Is
African Jade	green garnet, opaque
Amazon Jade	green feldspar
Arkansas Diamond	clear quartz (although there are genuine diamonds in Arkansas)
Atlas Pearls	white satin spar
Black Amber	jet
Cape Emerald	Prehnite
Cape Ruby	red garnet
California Moonstone	chaledony (quartz)
Citrine Topaz	yellow quartz
Ceylon Diamond	white zircon
Colorado Ruby	red garnet
Herkimer Diamond	clear quartz
Indian Jade	green quartz
Indian Topaz	yellow sapphire
Madiera Topaz	yellow quartz
Nassau Pearl	pink conch shell
Oriental Amethyst	purple sapphire
Oriental Topaz	yellow sapphire
Oriental Emerald	green sapphire
Rose Kunzite	synthetic pink sapphire
Smoky Topaz	brown-grey quartz
Rubolite	common red Opal
Star Topaz	yellow star sapphire
Vienna turquoise	imitation turquoise

The Link With Astrology . . .

The fact that people have long been fascinated by gems, by their enduring qualities, by their remarkable purity and beauty, and by their presumed supernatural powers led ultimately to a link-up with astrology.

This, of course, led to the idea of birthstones, the selection of certain gems as a symbol of protection for those born under certain signs of the Zodiac, for certain months, days, weeks, seasons, etc.

The movement toward astrological significance probably originated as a result of the instructions to Moses in Exodus, Chapter 28, to make a breastplate of judgement set with four rows of stones.

From this, the New Testament (Revelation XXI) listed the Foundation Stones of the New Testament. So much commentary and speculation have been written of the spin-off symbolism of the Breastplate for Aaron, brother of Moses and High Priest of Israel, that it is beyond the scope of this chapter.

What is noteworthy, is that use of gems as birthstones did not commence until a relatively later date, in the mid 1500s.

The order of gems and months did evolve even then from the Foundation Stones. Over the years, of course, the gems were changed from their traditional order.

Here is the present birthstone list as well as the list of birthstones that was originally based on the best available translation of the Foundation Stones:

Month	Present List of Birthstones	List of Birthstones Originally From Foundation Stones
January	Garnet	Garnet
February	Amethyst	Amethyst
March	Aquamarine, Bloodstone	Jasper
April	Diamond	Diamond
May	Emerald	Emerald
June	Pearl, Alexandrite, Moonstone	Agate
July	Ruby	Turquoise
August	Peridot, Sardonyx	Carnelian
September	Sapphire	Chrysolite
October	Opal, Pink Tourmaline	Beryl
November	Topaz	Topaz
December	Blue Zircon, Turquoise	Ruby

The wearing of a birthstone is supposed to bring luck to its owner. But there are other stones which can be worn as special talismans, symbolic of angels, zodiacal signs and apostles.

For those individuals unhappy or unattracted to their own birthstone, a consideration can be given to one of these alternates.

Here are the gems for the Zodiacal signs.:

Zodiacal Sign	Gem
Aquarius (Jan. 21-Feb. 21)	Garnet
Pisces (Feb. 21-Mar. 21)	Amethyst
Aries (Mar. 21-Apr. 20)	Bloodstone
Taurus (Apr. 20-May 21)	Sapphire
Gemini (May 21-June 21)	Agate
Cancer (June 21-July 22)	Emerald
Leo (July 22-Aug. 22)	Onyx
Virgo (Aug. 22-Sep. 22)	Carnelian
Libra (Sep. 22-Oct. 23)	Chrysolite
Scorpio (Oct. 23-Nov. 21)	Beryl
Sagittarius (Nov. 21-Dec. 21)	Topaz
Capricorn (Dec. 21-Jan. 21)	Ruby

Here are the gems for Guardian Angels:

Month	Gem	Guardian Angel
January	Onyx	Gabriel
February	Jasper	Barchiel
March	Ruby	Malchediel
April	Topaz	Asmodel
May	Carbuncle	Ambriel
June	Emerald	Muriel
July	Sapphire	Herchel
August	Diamond	Humatiel
September	Jacinth	Zuriel
October	Agate	Barbiel
November	Amethyst	Adnachiel
December	Beryl	Humiel

While the translations do not all agree, medieval writers made a determined effort to associate a gemstone with each of the apostles. Judas has been eliminated on most lists and substituted by St. Paul, who was not one of the original twelve.

This list is useful for men who may have a Christian name after one of the apostles. Here are the Apostles and their associated gems:

Apostle	Gem
St. Peter	Jasper
St. Andrew	Garnet
St. James & John	Emerald
St. Philip	Carnelian
St. Bartholomew	Chrysolite
St. Thomas	Beryl
St. Matthew	Topaz
St. James	Sardonyx
St. Thaddeus	Chrysoprase
St. Simeon	Jacinth
St. Matthew	Amethyst
St. Paul	Sapphire

Here are other lists for birthstones from which a selection may be made:

Birthstones Based On The Hour of Birth

1 AM	Smokey Quartz	1 PM	Zircon
2	Hematite	2	Emerald
3	Malachite	3	Beryl
4	Lapis-Lazuli	4	Topaz
5	Turquoise	5	Ruby
6	Tourmaline	6	Opal
7	Chrysolite	7	Sardonyx
8	Amethyst	8	Chalcedony
9	Kunzite	9	Jade
10	Sapphire	10	Jasper
11	Garnet	11	Lodestone
12	Diamond	12	Onyx

Birthstones Based on Week Day of Your Birth	Day	Phenomenal Birthstone Based on Week Day of Your Birth
Topaz	SUNDAY	Sunstone
Pearl, Rock Crystal	MONDAY	Moonstone
Ruby, Emerald	TUESDAY	Star Sapphire
Amethyst, Lodestone	WEDNESDAY	Star Ruby
Sapphire, Carnelian	THURSDAY	Cat's Eye
Emerald, Cat's Eye	FRIDAY	Alexandrite
Turquoise, Diamond	SATURDAY	Labradorite

Finally, here are the birthstones for the Seasons:

Spring	Emerald
Summer	Ruby
Autumn	Sapphire
Winter	Diamond

Given such an imposing list—and a selection that will certainly fall somewhere for every individual on earth—it may be somewhat simpler to understand why the powerful superstitions attached to gemstones gave way to a more realistic, scientific acceptance.

Still, the mystical, magical bond between gemstones and people is as strong as ever—and it can withstand this happy little arena of birthstone madness.

CHAPTER TWO

GEM CARE: . . . A General Knowledge

One of the great diamonds of the world, the Pigott, a fine-quality, oval-shaped 49-carat river white diamond no longer exists—following one of history's most famous demonstrations that diamonds aren't tough.

The Pigott was deliberately crushed under the heel of a Persian soldier of fortune, upon the order of his commander and owner of the gem, the 80-year-old Ali Pasha. Dying of wounds inflicted after the Sultan of Turkey, resentful of the Pasha's growing power in Albania had sent an emissary demanding his surrender, the Pasha ordered the Pigott diamond destroyed and his other most precious possession, his beautiful wife, Vasilikee, put to death lest any other man enjoy them.

His faithful officer, Captain d'Anglas, placed the huge diamond under his heel and, in one single twist, shattered it. Because the Pasha succumbed to his wounds before Vasilikee could be executed she managed to avoid a similar fate.

Fig. 2-1 The beautiful 49-carat Pigott diamond is no more. It was destroyed under the grinding heal of a palace guard at the owners's insistence—proving that diamonds may be hard . . . but they are not tough.

The theme of this is: it doesn't take much more than a little pressure or unfortunate knock to destroy a diamond—because a diamond isn't very tough.

That's right: a diamond isn't tough. Hard, yes—but not tough.

You might remember the story of the Pigott diamond the next time you see someone pound a perfectly good diamond against something in what could easily become an ill-fated demonstration of a presumed characteristic that, in reality, doesn't exist.

Because a diamond is merely hard—and not tough—diamonologists avoid inflicting harsh treatment or rough handling to diamonds ... and they also avoid scratch tests whenever possible.

You see, hardness is a measure of the ability to scratch. Toughness is the ability to accomodate impact or hard blows.

Because of its hardness—and diamonds are the hardest substance on earth—a diamond tends to be quite brittle. The readiness with which a diamond will chip or break astonishes people. That's why, under magnification you often see little chips or abraded marks on the facets edges. It's standard practice for diamond dealers and merchants to place a number of diamonds together in a paper envelope and this allows them to strike and chip each other.

Besides their brittleness, diamonds have a very distinctive cleavage plane and will split abruptly along that plane if enough pressure or a sharp blow is applied.

Splitting or cleaving a diamond according to plan is one thing; doing the same thing accidentally—or by pounding it after the diamond has been cut—is something else entirely.

Whether you're dealing with a diamond or another gemstone is unimportant.

Careless handling means the difference often between one intact gemstone and two or three fragments of gem material following an unfortunate—and often avoidable—incident.

Care, Maintenance of Gemstones . . .

The atomic composition of different gemstones causes them to vary in hardness, toughness, cleaving or splitting potential, as well as their reaction to heat, light, acids, etc. The challenge of proper care and maintenance of gems confronting a jewelry owner can thus be quite substantial.

Similar to almost all other things, some gems are hardy and can absorb nearly any level of abuse or negligence without the slightest loss of beauty. Other gems are very sensitive even to the extent of losing their color if exposed to sunlight for a few hours (Kunzite—the rich, lavender colored variety of spodumene—is just such a gemstone).

It's not enough to delegate the care of your gems to your jeweler. You can, and should, accept the major responsibility for your gems. You don't need to be a professional gemologist to care for them expertly. Despite the fact that the matter of care and maintenance of gemstones appears formidable, a few general rules will produce a maximum of beautiful results—plus maximum safety.

So far as cleaning gems is concerned most gems—not all of them—can be brought to their full brilliance simply by using a mild detergent in warm water and a soft brush (not a toothbrush). Most of the commercially prepared jewelry cleaners are safe—but you do need to be a bit careful with some which contain ammonia or chemicals capable of damaging sensitive gems such as pearl or amber.

In the absence of a total understanding of gemology and which cleaning techniques are suitably compatible with which gems you would be as well advised to stick to the sudsy warm water-detergent solution, leaving difficult cleaning jobs to a jeweler.

Such a strategy will serve you satisfactorily 99% of the time. In the balance of cases when you are unable to dislodge accumulated dirt or grease a jeweler has the necessary equipment, and liability insurance should his efforts with your gem end in disaster.

The real key to lifting a transparent faceted gemstone to its best brilliance level is the careful cleaning of the portion below the stone's girdle (called the pavilion).

Fig. 2-2 Some gem materials are heat sensitive; some are not. Some materials react violently to chemicals; some do not. Some are weakened by inclusions; some are not. Warm water, a mild detergent and a soft brush is the safest cleaning medium for almost all gems—with the least danger of inflicting harm on gems with which you aren't familiar.

Unfortunately, the pavilion—or bottom—of the gem is where most dirt accumulates. Often, too, the setting makes it the most difficult spot to get at. Be especially watchful around prongs. In cutting out the notches on the prongs, most gem setters don't polish the notches and any roughened metal is quick to gather dirt and debris.

As for a safe, acceptable cleaning procedure first let the entire jewelry piece soak for a few moments in the solution, whether it's the warm water-detergent or a commercial preparation. Scrub gently with the brush. A very soft brush is quite useful. So, too, is a fine camel hair artist's brush; it's narrow and fits better through the setting and inbetween prongs. A shaved matchstick or toothpick is quite good at picking out accumulations, but don't be too harsh. Patience pays off.

When you're finished with the scrubbing, dip the jewelry piece back into the solution for one last wetting. Then rinse in warm running water, preferably about the same temperature as your solution. Radical temperature changes are dangerous and should be avoided.

A good shake—or blowing on the item—will remove excess liquid. Then gently polish with a soft lint-free cloth or chamois (leather). Many jewelers, to avoid any liquid stains on a gem or precious metal setting, dispense with the cloth drying and immerse the jewelry piece in a bed of dry maple wood chips. Once dry, the chips can be blown away and the piece is free of water spots. If interested, you'll find the wood chip technique best for large gems.

Cleaning jewelry after it gets dirty is only part of proper care. Pre-use care is also important.

For example, apply your perfumes, colognes, and hairsprays BEFORE you put on your gems. Not only will these chemicals reduce gem brilliance, they are highly destructive to pearls which react violently to acid and alcohol.

For much of the same reason, try to wear your perfumes in areas where they won't come in contact with gems. Again, in the case of pearls, try to keep the pearls out of contact with the skin whether you're wearing perfume or not; perspiration is inimical to pearls, too. That's, of course, impossible in the case of a choker or bracelet—but the pearls should be wiped clean with a damp cloth immediately after wearing.

Mechanical Cleaning Can Be Dangerous . . .

Have you noticed that in the comments thus far on gemstone care no mention has been made of mechanical cleaning processes? There's a reason for this: no mechanical system is without danger.

There's no desire here to demean these systems but nearly every jeweler who has used or currently uses the various mechanical systems—ultrasonic, steam, or boiling—is aware of some rather sad experiences related to mechanical cleaning.

Stone upon stone can be successfully cleaned with one or more of these

Fig. 2-3 Pearls react to chemicals and even perspiration. Under the best conditions, they should be worn over cloth material. If worn against the skin, try to keep pearls away from perfume and cosmetics. It's a good idea to apply perfume and other sprays before putting on pearls.

systems—and then abruptly and inexplicably a stone shatters. The reason could have been an inclusion, a fracture, undetected pressure or stress. Whatever, a jeweler has a stone to replace or must call on his own insurance to make good.

It's the internal personality of the gemstone that holds the key to mechanical cleaning success or failure. Even with gemological experience and training you can't predict with absolute accuracy the outcome.

An emerald is a green colored beryl. Beryl is normally a rather hardy gem mineral. But the heavy inclusions in an emerald weaken the normal strength of the mineral, and the unique stresses that mechanical cleaning exerts can ruin—even shatter—an emerald.

A topaz can appear perfectly flawless, even under magnification. But a topaz has a very distinct cleavage plane which is perpendicular to the gemstones' crystallographic axis. The best color is yielded by a topaz when the cutter aligns the top of the finished gem nearly parallel with this cleavage plane so that the CA (crystallographic axis) runs from the top of the finished gem (the table facet) to the bottom (the culet).

The cutter faces a serious challenge with each topaz. If the cutter attempts to place a polished facet on the same plane as the cleavage plane it will be impossible to polish the facet. Therefore, the cutter tries to tip the rough gem material so that no facet angle will be closer than 10° to the cleavage plane.

In most cases, this means that ultimately a gem setter is faced with the task of pressing the setting prongs directly against the cleavage plane—or at least very close to this critical plane. Unknown to you or to a jeweler, one of the prongs could be exerting undue pressure on the cleavage plane —and the gemstone is just waiting for a physical contribution to create a split as neatly as a slice of bread. Vibrations or sudden temperature change might be all that is necessary.

The same danger is lurking in a diamond—although diamonds may not cleave as readily as a topaz. But there are incidents where one lovely diamond went into a mechanical cleaning system—and out came two or three diamonds. Recent research indicates some of these strange and unpredictable accidents may be due to unseen liquid inclusions. The high temperature caused by a mechanical system causes the liquid to heat, then expand and then zap!

So that you'll better appreciate why mechanical cleaning systems are more appropriate for the jeweler and his work bench and why the slower, safer hand wash systems should be reserved for your use, here are some capsule commentaries on the various mechanical systems:

ULTRA SONIC: These units usually consist of a stainless steel tank with milllions of microscopic frequency waves bouncing around in a special liquid. The implosion (inward collapse) of the bubbles against the piece of jewelry function as tiny vacuums which siphon off dirt and grime.

Unfortunately or fortunately, the frequency impulses concentrate on the hardest element in the liquid. When you have a diamond in the bath you may imagine where all the energy is focused. Should the diamond —or any other gemstone—have an incipient cleave or pressure point the energy could aggravate the weakness to the point of destruct.

If you have placed one of the gems that are notorious for being treated with oil to improve color, i.e., emeralds, rubies, sapphires, the tiny bubbles could drive out the oil. What went into the ultrasonic as a brilliantly colored gemstone could come out a sad, sorry version sorely in need of another oil bath.

Despite the criticisms and the assurances on both sides of this cleaning system, it's pretty much agreed that you *never* allow the ultrasonic to give a bubble cleaning to *opal, pearl, emerald, tanzanite, coral, turquoise, malachite,* and *amber.*

Unless you are certain that your ruby or sapphire hasn't been oiled you should avoid placing them in an ultrasonic, too.

Many jewelers and repairmen use ultrasonic cleaners extensively for clean-up on metals and watch parts. They are quite efficient devices for removing the jeweler rouges and abrasives used in metal work and polishing.

If you do elect to use an ultrasonic cleaner there are a few safeguards to keep in mind:

1) Don't let the jewelry piece lay on the bottom of the stainless steel tank; keep it suspended so it floats in the liquid without touching or vibrating or hitting the tank;

2) Check the temperature of the liquid. Prolonged use of an ultrasonic cleaner can run the temperature of the bath up to unsafe levels, exposing your gems to thermal shock and causing a liquid filled inclusion to literally "blow" the gem apart.

3) Check the stones in your jewelry item before and after cleaning. The vibrations can dislodge a loose stone so that it falls to the bottom of the tank.

4) Use commercially prepared cleaners intended for use in an ultrasonic cleaner: they're more effective and do the job in a much shorter time.

Steam Cleaning: Not too many consumers have a steam cleaner. They're more efficient for large scale cleaning tasks. In any event, they create some thermal dangers by elevating the temperature of a gemstone quickly. The too rapid return to a normal gem temperature creates serious problems as well.

Nonetheless, steam is highly efficient for melting grease and oil and blowing it away with other dirt. A quick squirt of high temperature steam is about all the average cleaning job requires.

Boiling: Of the three major mechanical cleaning systems, boiling is the one most used by non-professionals. It is used often enough by professionals as well. It's simple; can be done quickly—and is dangerous enough that care must be exercised.

You just put the jewelry pieces into a pot of water, add some detergent, and turn on the heat. After a boiling period, the pieces are removed, perhaps scrubbed with a soft brush, rinsed, and dried.

In actuality, it's almost the same as the warm water-detergent-soft brush routine except done at a much higher temperature.

You might wonder—accurately—why all the extra bother since temperature extremes are chancey for all gemstones including the champs at taking heat—diamonds, rubies, and sapphires. Even a diamond can be ruined if the water boils out and the stone is left in a heated, dry pan bottom.

If it appears that an excessive amount of attention is being placed on temperature, the appearance is quite deliberate. Rapid temperature changes can create structural havoc in even the strongest of gemstones.

Often the so-called flaws in a certain gemstone consist of an included crystal of an entirely different mineral. The two could have different heating coefficients—and a rapid jump, or drop, in the host gem's temperature could produce stresses that cause a split. A liquid inclusion is the more dangerous because it takes only a small heat increase to expand a liquid which produces critical pressures.

If ever you intend to expose one of your gems to a high heat, prepare the gem first. Pre-warm it by immersing it in warm and then warmer water. All three mechanical cleaning techniques have the potential to elevate a stone's temperature too quickly.

If you made it to a high temperature safely without pre-warming, realize that coming back down again poses an equal challenge. You might not be as fortunate this time. Put the gem in warm water. Avoid taking it directly, say, outside in the cold air, or exposing it to a cold draft both of which can produce an unhappy end.

Trusting your jeweler to know and exercise appropriate treatment of your gems is a good policy. It's not a perfect policy, though; they make mistakes like everyone else.

In many cases, too, incompetent sales personnel—who have a disturbing talent for feigning gemological wisdom where it simply doesn't exist —err on the stone's take-in policy. They don't have a sound knowledge of gems and fail to write careful, explicit instructions on the envelope.

What happens then is that a repairman or bench worker or someone else, whose specialty may not include gemstone characteristics, may go off on their own and give your gemstone cleaning a treatment to end all treatments. A good rule of thumb when dealing with a jewelery store is: deal with the owner or manager since he or she would be the one to have a firmer grip on proper take-in procedures. If you're dealing with an employee, talk with that individual a bit; ask a few gemological questions and analyze the answer. They should give you a firm lead on what to do: either turn in your jewelry for the servicing you want or wait and talk to the owner, or go elsewhere.

A good knowledge of your gems and what care requirements are suitable is still your best defense.

Following are brief discussions on recommended care for some of the more sensitive gems. As mentioned before, virtually all gemstones will respond nicely to the careful application of warm water-detergent-soft brush. But here are some that take special attention:

Gemstone	Cleaning Technique	Comment
Amber	Damp cloth & dry. Warm water-detergent is also effective.	Amber is an organic gem, sort of a fossilized and hardened form of resin from ancient pine trees.
Amethyst	Warm water-detergent-soft brush	Most amethyst is heat-treated to bring out best color, but it can crack as well as fade if exposed to high temperatures.
Aquamarine	Warm water-detergent-soft brush	This blue beryl is also heat-treated to bring out its blue color. Heat can still cause color fading.
Carnelian	Moist cloth. Rub with dry cloth briskly.	It's a tough variety of the quartz group. Wax won't adhere to it, so it was famous as a seal material.
Citrine	Warm water-detergent-soft brush	A heat-treated quartz, it will fade when exposed to heat.
Coral	Damp cloth & dry.	Another organic gem which comes from the exudations of tiny marine

		animals. Extremely sensitive to flame, heat.
Diamond	Ammonia based cleaner. Warm water-(grease cutting) detergent-soft brush. Mechanical cleaning systems.	Diamonds can take heat well, but mechanical systems could pose a danger if stone is not examined well beforehand. Removing any grease is the key to diamond brilliance.
Emerald	Warm water-detergent-soft brush.	Most emeralds are routinely bathed in warm oil after fashioning to improve color . . . and sometimes a dye is added. Mechanical systems could boil out the oil. Inclusions in emerald often weaken the stone, and mechanical systems have potential to cause breakage.
Garnet	Warm water-detergent-soft brush.	Relatively hard and tough, garnets are heat sensitive.
Helidor	Warm water-detergent-soft brush.	These yellow beryl gems tend to be flawless, reasonably hardy and tough. Temperature extremes should be avoided, though.
Ivory	Wipe clean with damp cloth & dry. Also, warm water-detergent-soft brush.	Another organic gem consisting of calcium phosphate. It's sometimes dyed so harsh chemical cleaning could impair its appearance.
Jade	Warm water-detergent-soft brush. Dry rub briskly	Both jadeite and nephrite are tough with little to worry about. Takes a high lustrous polish which takes professional equipment if surface needs re-polishing.
Kunzite	Warm water-detergent-soft brush.	Has distinct cleavage plane which opens with little impact. Sunlight causes its lavender color to fade; this is definitely a "night stone."
Lapis	Warm water-detergent-soft brush.	Material is porous, varies greatly, is often dyed to improve color.
Malachite	Cool water-detergent-soft brush.	Polishes bright but wear can cause finish to dull; rub briskly with wood to help restore finish. Sensitive to acid, ammonia, heat and hot water.
Opal	Warm water-detergent-soft brush.	Very sensitive to pressure and thermal shock (hot or cold) which causes crazing (surface cracking). Soft and fragile.
Pearl	Wipe with damp, soft cloth. Stains should be removed with mild soapy solution on rag—don't dip it into liquid. Dry thoroughly. Blow out drill holes carefully; moisture there often causes discoloration.	Special care is required to keep pearls looking their best. (See more complete discussion later in this chapter.)
Peridot	Warm water-detergent-soft brush	One of the softer gem materials, it is attacked by acids (it etches) and heat may cause damage. Use carefully because peridot is soft and surface scratches diminish finish.

Gemstone	Cleaning Technique	Comment
Ruby	Warm water-detergent-soft brush	More and more rubies are being oiled and mechanical cleaning could remove this oil. High heat, though, could cause damage because of inclusions and other imbedded crystal materials.
Sapphire	Warm water-detergent-soft brush	It's the same material (corundum) as ruby so same treatment applies: oil may be added for color, and inclusions may weaken normally tough structure.
Spinel	Warm water-detergent-soft brush	Hard and durable, spinels tend to be flawless in gem grades. Should give little trouble, and hold its beauty.
Tanzanite	Warm water-detergent-soft brush	Blue color is created by heat treatment, but tanzanite is fragile, relatively soft, and sensitive to heat, vibrations.
Turquoise	Wipe with damp cloth; wipe dry immediately	Turquoise is a porous material so avoid soap, detergents, cleaning solutions. They tend to penetrate the material's pores, turning turquoise green and/or unattractive off-color blue.
Topaz	Warm water-detergent-soft brush	Easy cleavage makes mechanical cleaning relatively dangerous, both for vibrations or heating. Stone may have undue pressure points caused by setting prongs.
Tourmaline	Warm water-detergent-soft brush	Reasonable hard gem but tends to be brittle. Pink variety often flawed, could be structurally weak and thus vulnerable to vibration damage. Moderately sensitive to heat. Bi-colored crystals sometimes split at color junctures.
Zircon	Warm water-detergent-soft brush	Prone to impurities, it can be affected by heat extremes, although fine blue and white zircon is heat treated.

As you can see from the above list, most gemstones don't really require all that much gemological background. There are enough differences in individual characteristics to demonstrate, though, the possibilities for disaster should one go about the task of cleaning in a harsh manner.

Done carefully, and with a reasonable amount of attention, your gems should retain their beauty for years.

This is not to say that a few of them don't deserve the title of "beautiful problem children."

Pearls, Opals Take Special Care . . .

Because of their organic origin some non-mineral gems require more specialized attention.

No gem has a longer history of value and acceptance—and a greater need for delicate understanding and care—than the pearl. Close to this reputation, comes the Opal, steeped in tradition and superstition, and which has created more joy—and probably more tears—than most of the

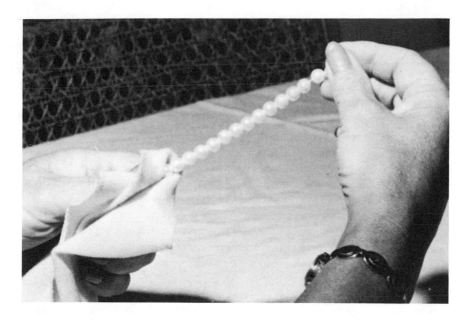

Fig. 2-4 After wearing, you should always wipe off pearls with a damp cloth (don't wet; water stains pearls), being careful not to wet the silk either. Then damp dry with a lint free cloth and wrap carefully for storage. Use same care with coral and ivory.

other gems.

Let's review the pearl. As you may or may not know, a pearl has a predictable life of some 150-200 years before age will probably destroy its beauty. That two-century lifespan is predicated, too, on proper care.

Proper care, naturally, begins with correct cleaning. Nothing harsh should ever be used on a pearl to remove stains. The best solution is a detergent in warm water.

Wet a thin-mesh rag with the solution—it's usually best not to immerse the strand in the liquid to avoid getting moisture into the drill holes. This moisture, if left in the drill hole unattended, can cause discoloration and accelerate the deterioration of the silk or nylon string.

Use a magnifying loupe to inspect each pearl. If there is a lump of dirt or grime, try to flick it off with your fingernail. Check carefully the string, especially if your strand has knots between each pearl (the better pearl strands have double knotting as protection against excessive losses should the string break and to cushion against knocking).

Dirt, grime from perspiration, etc. tends to build up in the knots themselves and at the juncture of knot and pearl. Using a very soft brush (not a toothbrush regardless of how soft it's SUPPOSED to be), remove as much residue as you can, from the pearls and from the knots.

Sometimes a sharpened toothpick can be used to pick gently at the knot grime build-up to dislodge it. Wet the knot if you must.

Dry with a lint-free cloth. Daub at the moisture buildup in the knots.

Blow briskly to get any excess moisture away from the knots and the drill holes.

Check the clasp. It generally has a dirt build-up, particularly if it's a delicately fashioned item. Lay the strand on a turkish towel, so the towel may absorb moisture and speed up the drying. If you wish to contribute to the drying process, blow on the pearl strand gently. Never use hair dryer or a heat producing appliance; pearls react very badly to heat.

They also react violently to ammonia based cleaning products which attack the pearl on contact. Pearls are actually a concretion consisting of calcium carbonate and an organic substance called "nacre" which the oyster mollusk secrets in such a manner that it builds up in concentric layers over a foreign substance which enters its body.

This carbonaceous material is somewhat gritty and allows you to make a quick test between genuine natural or cultured pearls versus imitations. A natural or cultured pearl when scraped or rubbed gently across the cutting edge of the upper teeth will produce a gritty or rough sensation.

Imitation pearls, consisting of smooth glass or plastic beads or even beads with a coating of *essence d'orient* (made from the scales of certain kinds of fish) feel smooth when rubbed across your teeth in the same manner.

Once the nacre has been destroyed or damaged, it is virtually impossible to repair a pearl. For the same reason that you should apply perfume BEFORE putting on your pearls or applying perfumes and colognes where they won't come in contact with pearls, you should likewise never be wearing pearl jewelry and immerse your hands (and the pearls) in commercial bleaches such as Clorox.

In some cases spotted or damaged pearls can be peeled by an expert. This consists of removing the outside concentric layer. Generally, though, the damage is much deeper than a single layer, running to the seed pearl itself. On an average cultured pearl, the outside nacre layer is only some 0.8-1.2mm thick (that's slightly less than the thickness of a toothpick).

If the damage is localized, an expert can cut away the defective portion and offer the remainder as half or three-quarter pearl for use in earrings or brooches. Despite claims to the contrary, it's almost impossible to restore the lost luster to a pearl, even with bleaching or dying.

Incidentally, while pearls of any color have the best general wearability of all gems, fair-skinned women in Europe and the U.S. tend to prefer rose color pearls. Dark-haired or brunette women with golden/copper complexions tend to prefer cream color pearls.

Whether buying a new strand of pearls or having an existing strand restrung, it's to your advantage to specify silk. If the pearls are valuable you might also order them strung with knots between each pearl—or between every so many pearls.

Silk does deteriorate more quickly when exposed to water and perspiration, but it more than compensates for this disadvantage. It doesn't attract dirt and grime as much, and it won't stretch.

Nylon, on the other hand, is elastic. Eventually the weight of the pearls or a stretching moment on the strand itself can cause the string to stretch, allowing room for the pearls to slide back and forth between the knots or simply to slam into each other if the strand is intermittently knotted. This can cause damage at the drill hole.

Then, too, nylon attracts more dust and dirt than silk. This attraction problem is aggravated by the fact that twisted nylon affords a capillary action for the dirt, grime, and grease to advance. Such a situation contributes to a build-up of dirt on the knots and in the drill holes. The cleaning task is much more difficult.

Turn now to the incredible gemstone of which the poets say,

> "When nature had finished coloring the flowers,
> dying the plummage of the birds,
> and painting the rainbow,
> She swept the colors from her palette
> And molded them into the Opal."

Nature may indeed have outdone herself in creating the beautiful Opal. But if beauty is delicate, then nature also outdid herself in making the Opal delicate.

A relatively soft gem, Opal is extremely sensitive to thermal shock whether the extreme runs to hot or to cold. A too rapid change in either direction is usually damaging. Because of its softness, it scratches easily. It can't take shock well. For no apparent reason, it might simply up and craze (develops tiny cracks in the surface). Acids and alkalis affect it.

For years it was believed that the rainbow-like opalescence which changes with the angle of observation was caused by the bending of light through a thin surface layer. The powerful electron microscope ended the mystery in the 1960s when it was discovered that the color patterns of opal were due to multitudes of tiny spheres layered in a siliceous jelly material (not unlike millions of marbles stacked tightly in a medium so that each marble is in contact with those surrounding it).

Furthermore, opals always contain water. The content varies up to as high as 30%. The loss of this water content, it is believed, leads to crazing and the opalescence disappears. Saturation with water or oil can help restore some of the lost grandeur.

Keeping an opal wrapped in soft moist cotton can prolong the gem's life. This simple step avoids the loss of the opal's natural water content, and perhaps replaces any lost by evaporation. With this observation it's not difficult to understand why opals and heat are not compatible.

Australian Opal is probably the best quality—and least resistant to crazing—of all opal found in the world. Opals found in Nevada, U.S., and in Mexico seem most susceptible to crazing.

To keep your opal looking bright, clean it with the usual warm water-mild detergent-soft brush approach. Store it in soft, moist cotton, and isolate from other jewelry so it won't get knocked. Wear it carefully so that you avoid shock or heat.

For years, gemologists have been emphasizing that opal is not truly a good ring gem because of opal's softness and inability to accept the shocks and hits that a ring involves. Fortunately, there are too many intelligent and discerning opal ring owners who have ignored this sound, logical nonsense. Opals are just too magnificent to keep off people's fingers.

A word of design advice may be helpful here, though. Try to avoid opals on a pinkie ring; they take the most hits of all. Also, consider designs that bring the metal up over the opal in such a manner as to provide protection.

You might also consider avoiding opals in gypsy or bezeled settings (where a continuous ribbon of metal is hammered down over the perimeter of the opal). These kinds of settings tend to exert tremendous pressure on the Opal—and an opal detests pressure. Consequently, your opal could be under severe strain and one slight bump or impact could cause it to shatter or break.

If an opal is prong set inspect the prongs themselves with a magnifying loupe. Look especially for any chipping of the opal under the prongs; that's where you'll find evidence that the setter may have exerted too much bending pressure while turning the prongs over—so much pressure that the opal split under the strain. Not only will a tiny chip indicate excessive setting pressure, but there is the additional danger that stress fractures of an even greater magnitude are immediately in that prong area . . . just waiting for the opportunity to bring grief.

Store Gems Individually, Carefully . . .

While cleaning and regular inspection of your gems and jewelry will prolong their life, value, and beauty, the care with which you store your gems when they're not in use is just as important.

For valuable jewelry, a good, serviceable jewelry box is a must. This will enable you to provide separate compartments for valuable pieces. When gems are permitted to bang against each other the risk of chipping and damage is high.

A good jewelry box will have cushioned inserts into which you may place your rings so they will not come in contact with each other. Metal jewelry items may strike each other without too great a risk of costly damage.

But gemstones are all subject to chipping. In too many cases, it seems, the harder the gem the greater are its chipping tendencies. Diamond may be the hardest of all—but it chips with surprising ease.

By taking a few moments to wrap your jewelry pieces separately in a cloth, a tissue, a pouch or some similar protective covering you will prolong and insure many years of enjoyment with your jewels.

Also, make advance plans for taking your jewelry when you travel. It may be an expensive trip for you if you merely "throw" a few favorite

Fig. 2-5 A pouche for carrying jewelry on trips is invaluable, with separate envelopes to provide maximum protection against collisions. Ring bands in such pouches leave something to be desired and you should insert a soft cushion material between rings.

jewelry pieces into a handbag and hope that not too many shocks will occur before returning home again.

Velvet wrap-around pouches made especially for carrying jewelry are available in most jewelry and department stores. You should obtain one or two of them, depending on the size of your jewelry collection and how many items you normally take with you when traveling.

Be certain to obtain a supply of the smaller, thick material envelopes for carrying individual items. These can be placed in the deep pockets of the pouch and they'll serve as reasonable protection.

Be cautious about the ring holders in some of these pouches. They consist primarily of a thick cloth strap with a snap at one end. The intent is to run the strap through a series of ring shanks and then secure them by closing the snap. Such an arrangement may be convenient for the pouch manufacturer, but it could be less than satisfactory when valuable rings are involved.

With a number of rings all snapped in a row, hitting against each other is a certainty. The ring shanks and metalwork may offer some protection —but it's not enough. Try separating the rings on the strap with a cut-out piece of sponge or heavy material which can absorb the impact and cushion the rings against too much battering.

The care and maintenance of fine jewelry isn't all that difficult. In most cases, it's just common sense—and an awareness of some of the unique nature of the precious materials involved.

For example, you now know many of the unique features of at least 26 different gems. Did you know, though, that going swimming in pool water which contains chlorine might be injurious to your gold rings?

Yes, chlorine and carat gold are antagonistic to each other, and the chlorine can dissolve enough gold over a single swimming season to loosen or destroy the tiny prongs holding your gems. That's why so many gems turn up in the bottom of a swimming pool or in the filtering system. You might remove your gold rings the next time you swim in a chlorinated pool—and be careful of chlorinated chemicals in daily use in your home.

Some self-admitted gem experts contend that you should keep your valuable pearls wrapped in moist cotton—the same care that's recommended for opals. You should already know the response to this advice: pearls can be discolored by moisture, and the water accelerates the deterioration of the silk string. Just wrap your pearls in dry cotton or cloth and keep them separated from other jewelry pieces, that's all that's needed.

When you clean your jewelry, do it over a single colored towel. Should you dislodge a gem it will be easier to find in the towel, and should you drop the piece, it will have a cushioned landing.

That's about as tender as you can get with your jewelry. It proves that tenderness does pay rich dividends.

CHAPTER THREE

GEM ENHANCEMENT: Where Good Gets Better

She had been the proud owner of a 37-carat sky blue Precious Topaz, set with small accent diamonds in a 14K yellow gold setting of her own choice. Now she was unhappy.

The unhappiness had developed quickly and sharply. She'd simply compared her round brilliant cut topaz with her friend's 41-carat blue topaz that had been cut in the traditional emerald cut.

"The color of her topaz is so much bluer looking than mine," she complained. "It couldn't possibly have come from the same rough material."

But both gems had been cut from the same rough. Furthermore, she was quite accurate in her complaint. The emerald cut topaz did look bluer because it was cut to show color before brilliance.

In this little story lies a gemological truth: cutting enhances a gem . . . and so do other forms of "treatment".

Treatment of gemstones is, at best, a highly controversial subject. In a world where mind-expanding drugs, additives, pollutants, and counterfeit techniques are making it increasingly difficult to distinguish the real from the unreal it becomes rather disappointing to learn that gemstones are routinely "treated" or "doctored."

That gems have been treated to improve their appearance for centuries doesn't reduce the shock.

Yet concern in the area of gem treatment should be kept within the realm of reason. Legitimate treatment to improve appearance is one thing. Chicanery is something else entirely.

After all, the mere faceting of a rough gem crystal or the cutting of a beautiful cabochon, together with careful polishing which coaxes interesting optical qualities from a mineral, are, in the final analysis, treatment techniques.

These human applications are directed toward improving a gem's appearance . . . and they represent a significant departure from the attitude of a mineral collector who appreciates a minerological specimen in its natural occurring state . . . or the attitude of many Japanese who, finding an oddly shaped stone, find full appreciation in the stone's original shape and would regard with horror the suggestion of altering the stone's naturalness in any way.

Cutting Has Its Purpose . . .

The cutting of a diamond or of a colored gemstone is an accepted form of treatment. Each style of cutting achieves a specific objective.

It was this fact that the blue topaz owner had forgotten.

A round brilliant cut—best seen in the well-known eight-fold 58-facet round brilliant—strives to show off the brilliance and fire in a gemstone. There is little doubt among gem fanciers that the round brilliant cut, followed by one of its close variations, will produce flashier appearing gems from most gem materials, especially those that are clear white or light in color but with good optical potential.

The step cut—best seen in the traditional octagon-shaped emerald cut—best dramatizes the color of a gem. It does reflect back a reasonable amount of light when cut to proper proportions, but generally it's not intended to produce a great deal of scintillation or fire.

The unhappy topaz owner had wanted a colored gem and she had wanted it enhanced with sparkling excitement, too. Her round, rigidly symmetrical fashioned gemstone gave her that. But the white reflected light of the brilliant cut tended to overwhelm the basic blue color.

Her friend's classically elegant emerald cut appeared a deeper, richer blue—because the blue did not need to compete with the multitude of light reflections that comes from the round brilliant cut.

When you select gems you should keep firmly in mind what your objectives are—color or brilliance—and then select accordingly. A round brilliant and an emerald cut will both provide an acceptable amount of brilliance and color.

But each kind of cut specializes. The round brillant is designed to show brilliance and fire; the step cut is intended primarily to showcase color.

It's not accidental that the most brilliant gem of all, the diamond, is overwhelmingly cut in the round brilliant form.

Haven't most of the diamonds you've seen been cut in the round brilliant? If not in the round, haven't most of the others been in a variation of the round—the oval, marquise, pear, heart, etc.?

The explanation is not difficult to locate. Only the round brilliant form satisfactorily highlights the unique qualities of the diamond.

Because it is the hardest of gems, it takes the best polish and therefore boasts the highest (adamantine) luster. It possesses, for all practical purposes, the highest refractive index (often abbreviated with the letters R.I.) which is a measure of its ability to bend light.

The higher is a gem material's R.I. the higher is its ability to return light to the eye. A properly cut diamond will return virtually all of the light that enters the stone—that's why the diamond is the most brilliant of all gems.

Treatment of a gemstone through cutting is an exacting process which involves a full understanding of the kind of gem material to be fashioned. Because gems have their own peculiar atomic structure their R.I.'s, or light bending character, are usually different. This obligates a cutter to change cutting angles to conform with each different R.I.

What is important to you is that the most important angles—those from which a competent cutter is most reluctant to deviate—involve the crown (the top of the cut gem) main facets and the pavilion (bottom of the cut gem) main facets. (Fig. 3-1).

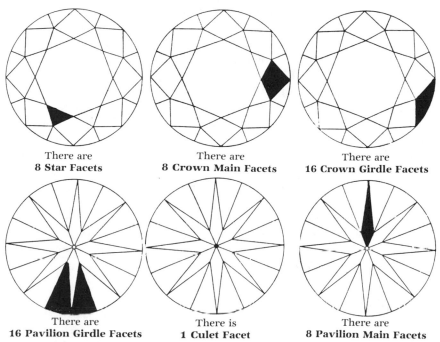

There are
8 Star Facets

There are
8 Crown Main Facets

There are
16 Crown Girdle Facets

There are
16 Pavilion Girdle Facets

There is
1 Culet Facet

There are
8 Pavilion Main Facets

Fig. 3-1/4 A standard round brilliant cut consists of the above facets plus the table facet for a total of 58 facets.

The bottom mains are sometimes referred to as the culet mains—not to be mistaken with the culet itself. The culet is the tiny facet at the extreme bottom of a faceted gem created by grinding away the sharp point or knife edge line where the pavilion (or culet) main facets meet. This is done to minimize the danger of chipping.

Why does the round brilliant cut showcase brilliance and fire so much better than an emerald cut?

The human eye appreciates uniformity and balance, i.e., good symmetry. The round brilliant cut consists of eight identically cut large facets on the pavilion, with an equal number of large kite-shaped main facets on the crown.

The purpose of these main facets is to contain and admit light into the gem and then reflect it back out of the gem in a controlled direction, i.e., give brilliance to the beholder.

Nothing in the diamond cutting or lapidary art is more vital than cutting these main facets at their appropriate angle, especially the pavilion facets.

Although the R.I. and therefore the critical light bending angle differs between gems, the importance of appropriately angled main facets in the crown and in the pavilion of all gems is equally great.

In addition to these 16 important main facets, three additional rows of facets are added to the round brilliant cut to provide sparkle and dispersion. One row consists of 16 pavilion girdle facets which start at the gem's girdle and extend about three-quarters of the way to the culet (Fig. 3-2).

Directly above this row—on the crown—are 16 girdle facets (also triangular shaped) which extend from the girdle to about two-thirds of the way up the crown (Fig. 3-3).

Eight additional facets are placed near the top of the crown to outline the table (Fig. 3-4). These "star facets" help break up white light by dispersing it into its component colors. All gems, especially clear ones, have a dispersion factor which is a measure of the gem materials' "fire" potential.

Add the facets described above, then add two more for the large flat table facet topping the gem and for the culet, and you have the 58-facet Standard Brilliant cut.

It achieves outstanding brilliance and fire because the rigid symmetry allows it to gather light equally from all sides. There are no variant facets to appear as dull spots or to distort light movement. No last minute decisions need to be made to fit in a facet at a different angle or at a unique position.

All is in pleasing, geometrical balance.

If unusual attention seems to be devoted here to the round brilliant cut, it is because it is so universally popular and recognized . . . and so desirable for use with clear and light colored gems. Even more deeply colored gem materials with relatively high RIs will respond well to this cut.

For persons wishing versatility in the faceted form, many variations of the round brilliant are available. The oval, marquise, pear, and heart shape cuts are all derivations of the round (Fig. 3-5).

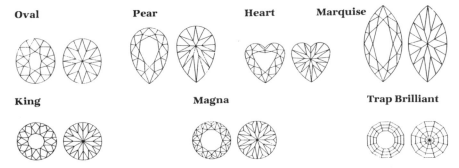

Fig. 3-5 Some Variations of the Round Brilliant Cut

To obtain these cuts, some small sacrifice in fire and brilliance must be made.

Why?

Turn one of these faceted gems upside down and check the pavilion main facets. On the variations you'll note that the main facets arrive at the culet with distorted angles and shapes. This can mean only one thing: some of these pavilion facets can't possibly be cut at the same critical angle so the pavilion can't possibly return the maximum amount of light.

The oval, of course, is the closest in brilliance and form to the round but even here because of its length-to-width distortion a cutter must deviate in the pavillion angles to reach a single culet point, or, if the same proper angles are maintained, the cutter will produce an oval with a culet as a line.

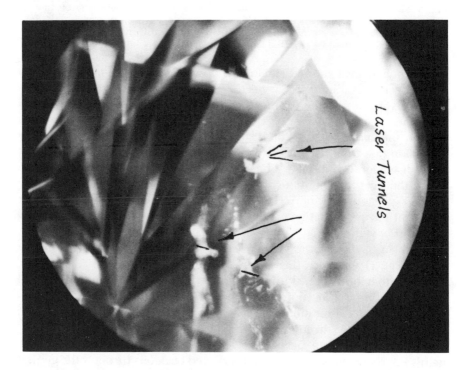

Fig. 3-6 The use of powerful laser beams to "tunnel" down through the table facet and turn carbon spots into less noticeable white flaws is standard technology. By viewing the diamond from the side with a loupe, you can usually detect the tell-tale tunnels that are left open. Jewelers aren't obligated to inform you if a diamond has been lasered (and thus improve the clarity grade, i.e., the price to you) so be on the lookout yourself.

When you inspect a round brilliant cut, or one of the variations, here are some of the elements in the cut treatment that you should look for:

The girdle facets on the crown and on the pavillion should be almost like mirror reflections of each other (Fig. 3-7). You'll seldom see a diamond mis-match as in Fig. 3-8, but it's sometimes seen in carelessly cut colored gems. There's a decided loss of sparkle in the latter case.

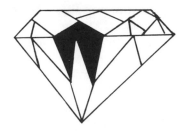

Aligned Properly   *Severely Misaligned*

Fig. 3-7/8 Watch carefully to make certain the crown and pavilion girdle facets line up directly over each other to form a kite shaped figure ("A"). When the top and the bottom of the gem have been misaligned (you'll seldom see this in a diamond but occasionally in colored stones) the girdle facets will appear in a straddled figure ("B").

When viewing a round brilliant cut down through the table facet you should get even mirror-like reflections from all facets. If one or more of the facets appears blacker or more glassy and doesn't seem as reflective as the others, you may have a cutting problem.

Rock the gem back and forth slowly, keeping a careful watch on the facet(s) in question. If the same facet(s) continues to respond differently, then distortion is indicated. The cutter may have cheated on an angle to bring the facet into position.

The rigid symmetry of the brilliant cut doesn't allow for even one facet to be cut incorrectly. If one is out of place, there will be at least another facet out of symmetry.

Check immediately the girdle facets over and adjacent to the faulty main facet; chances are this is where the cutter made the corrections. They'll either be wider, thinner, longer, shorter, or their junctions will occur at a different location than other girdle facets.

Watch for any indication of transparency or glassiness which enables you to see directly through a gem.

When pavilion main facets have been cut at an angle too low for the gem's R.I. requirement, light is not reflected back out through the gem, it simply dumps out of the bottom.

Such a gem is referred to as a "fish eye."

A "fish eye" is a serious cutting deficiency in any faceted gemstone. Unfortunately, many fish-eyed stones are offered for sale, and they are purchased by individuals who do not realize that the true beauty of the gem is often absent.

In defense of the jeweler, he sometimes has little choice in offering such merchandise. Many of the countries where gem rough is mined have adopted a policy, to provide employment to their own citizens, whereby all rough is faceted by native cutters.

Sophisticated equipment which can be calibrated to precisely controlled angles is not available to these native cutters whose primitive equipment and "eyeball engineering" too often leaves "facets, facets everywhere. and not a one too bright."

The result is many facets on a piece of precious gem material, but the pavilion main facets—the most critical facets of all—are cut at an inappropriate angle so the gem is either too dark (the lesser sometimes of two evils) or it "fish eyes."

It is not unusual for sophisticated lapidaries to buy poorly cut native gems and re-cut them to acceptable and commercial proportions.

Primitive cutting equipment isn't the only culprit, though. Many times a cutter seeks to retain as much carat weight as possible from a given piece of rough. Rather than sacrifice expensive rough material to cut a properly proportioned small stone the cutter will opt for a bigger if not so well proportioned gem.

Only when gem buyers insist on properly cut gems which display the maximum beauty of any given gem material rather than large pieces of gem material with "glassy bottoms" will the "go for size and proportions be hanged" philosophy diminish. So, too, will go the shallow argument that gems must be cut "fish eyed" so their shallow pavilions will fit into shallow commercial mountings.

Step Cuts Are For Color . . .

The emerald cut—a form of step cut—wasn't named after the deep green queen of gems by accident.

Where the round brilliant cut is tightly limited to a round shape by the demands of symmetry, a step cut can assume virtually any shape (Fig. 3-9), including a remarkably close approximation of a round cut.

It is this versatility in shape potential as much as the ability to show off color that makes step cutting so valuable.

Given two different pieces of rough, both of the same size, weight, and shape, a step cut will usually recover more weight than the round cut. A cutter, using small straight cuts, can fashion a gem into almost the same size as the original piece of rough (Fig. 3-10).

The high content of the brilliant cut's brilliance and sparkle may be absent, but enough light is returned in a step cut that the natural color of the gem material is enhanced significantly.

As a matter of fact, for some very deeply colored gems (such as certain garnets and the sapphire colored Iolite) it is sometimes necessary to cut a shallow pavilion and thus deliberately create a "fish eye." The color is so deep that were such a gem to be cut at proper angles the finished gem would be too dark.

A step cut is generally characterized by six rows of facets, three rows on the bottom and three rows on the top. Sometimes an emerald cut will have only two rows of facets, but three is preferred inasmuch as this gives the cut additional depth thereby intensifying color. (Fig. 3-11).

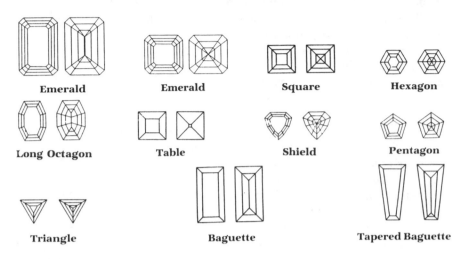

Emerald **Emerald** **Square** **Hexagon**

Long Octagon **Table** **Shield** **Pentagon**

Triangle **Baguette** **Tapered Baguette**

Fig. 3-9/10 The step or trap cut provides outstanding adaptation privileges, allowing a cutter more flexibility and original gem rough recovery by fashioning a gem closer to the original rough shape. Step or trap or emerald type cuts are usually preferred for enhancing gem color—especially for light to medium colored gem materials.

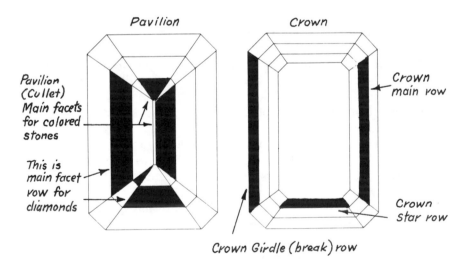

Pavilion Crown

Pavilion (Cullet) Main facets for colored stones

This is main facet row for diamonds

Crown main row

Crown star row

Crown Girdle (break) row

Fig. 3-11 Emerald and trap cuts generally consist of three facet rows above the girdle and three below the girdle. The pavilion main facets are on the extreme bottom, and the crown mains located in the middle top row.

Subject to the dictates of the cut itself and how the cutter treated the rough material, look for uniformity in the rectangular or square facets. Such a cut has a great many 4-corner facet intersections and these facet meets should be precise.

Sometimes, particularly with lighter colored gems, you will find small triangular facets on a top that is predominately characterized by the squared off facets of a step cut. If it is done in a manner that indicates a pattern—and not just an extra facet thrown in to cut out an inclusion or cover up a cutting error—chances are you'll be dealing with a *mixed cut* (Fig. 3-12).

This is done where the cutter wants to mix shape versatility offered by step cutting with the desired sparkle that extra, triangular facets provide. Mixed cuts are most often found as some modified form of a square or emerald-cut shape. The pavilions of mixed cuts, too, most often retain a step cut mode, i.e., the facets are generally square or rectangular.

Where you'll most often find a mixed cut is in the native cuts from the Far East. Sapphires that come from that part of the world are often referred to as "Ceylon cut" which means the top has been cut in a near-brilliant style, while the pavilion consists of a series of step-cut rows. Sometimes the culet mains are cut at the correct angle—and sometimes not, which seems the usual case.

Diamonds are seldom cut in the mixed style. A recent cutting breakthrough by South African diamond cutting expert Basil Watermeyer, though, is creating considerable excitement in the diamond cutting business—and in the colored stone cutting business, too.

Watermeyer in October, 1971, developed a unique cutting concept called the Barion. This concept, for which a patent has been granted, successfully combines the intricate craftsmanship of the emerald cut with the brilliance of the round cut (Fig. 3-13).

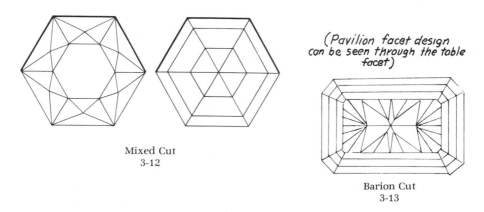

(Pavilion facet design can be seen through the table facet)

Mixed Cut
3-12

Barion Cut
3-13

Fig. 3-12/13 Mixed cuts—often seen in native-cut gems—use a step cut pavilion with a brilliant cut crown to achieve color enhancement and brilliance (left). Don't be misled by many rows of pavilion facets often seen in native cuts: the bottom row (culet mains) must still be cut at appropriate angle or gem's full beauty is sacrificed. New Barion cuts differ in that (right) they have step cut top with unique brilliant cut pavilions, providing special light fountain effect.

At last, a single cut exists that can provide color enhancement and brilliance in the same gem. This breakthrough could prove to be as important as the development of the Round Brilliant diamond cut by Italian diamond master *Vincenzia Peruzzi* in the 14th Century (Fig. 3-14).

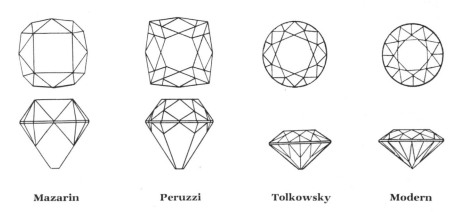

Mazarin   Peruzzi   Tolkowsky   Modern

Fig. 3-14 The standard round brilliant cut evolved from the near-square cutting style practiced under the aegis of Cardinal Mazarin in the 17th century, to Peruzzi's innovations of 32 crown facets and 24 pavilion facets, then to engineer Marcel Tolkowsky who established proportions that have since become known as the American or Ideal Cut. Modern brilliant cutting has a somewhat larger table and longer pavilion girdle facets (reaching about 75% down the pavilion) than Tolkowsky's original design.

As you may note from the illustration, the crown of the Barion cut is a traditional emerald or step cut. The pavilion utilizes a half-moon facet hanging from the girdle from which radiates a fully adapted brilliant base.

Tests indicate than when a Barion is cut to proper proportions and angles its scintillation, dispersion, and brilliance are equal to the standard brilliant. Further, while the Barion cut reflects slightly more white light than the round cut it produces somewhat of a different type of reflection.

This different type of reflection seems to come from the unique light fountain effect caused by lower-half reflections through the step cut crown.

Should a jeweler present a Barion cut for your consideration you might take the time to give it your full attention. Barions haven't yet penetrated fully the conservative diamond market, but they make for an extraordinary diamond—and extraordinary colored stones, too.

One of the principle advantages of Watermeyer's concept is its total versatility. No longer does a cutter need to sacrifice brilliance to achieve a unique color return. Any cut made in the brilliant mode can be successfully adapted to a Barion cut.

It's easy to keep from getting mixed up between a Barion and a mixed cut. The Barion has a step cut crown with a uniquely designed brilliant pavilion.

A mixed cut generally has a step cut pavillion with extra facets cut into the crown—and it's not nearly so brilliant or exciting with light treatment as the Barion.

Diamonds as Treats of Light . . .

The appearance of a diamond or a colored stone can be immeasurably improved by the addition of the brilliant white light flashes from small diamonds.

Throughout history, small diamonds (when a group of small diamonds are all of the same size, cut, quality grade, etc. it's called a "melee;" when the diamonds vary in size, color, clarity, etc., the group is called a "melange.") have been used to accent other gemstones, including other bigger diamonds.

A sudden, dazzling flash of white light in, say, a ruby ring lends a charming esthetic burst while, at the same time, dramatizing and attracting attention to the red of the ruby.

So popular is the use of accent diamonds that they are faceted down to less than a single point (there are 100 points in a carat).

Below, usually, a 3 point diamond, the cutting of full 58-facet cuts becomes uneconomical. Therefore, most smaller melee diamonds are fashioned as "single cuts" (Fig. 3-15), often referred to by the misnomer, "chip." Technically, the jewelry industry's definition of a chip is a diamond cleavage fragment of small size, usually under one carat . . . not a small faceted piece.

There are, as the illustration shows, at least 17 facets in a single cut, eight main facets in the crown and eight main facets in the pavilion, with a table facet. A culet at the bottom would run the count to 18 facets, but it's often not done because of the small size.

A lack of clear understanding between a single cut, a chip, and the decimal reference to carat weight contributed to the promotional success of a diamond mail order campaign in 1981.

The mail order program offered 9-facet diamond chip of .25 point size for a modest price of about $5. What the people got for their money was a diamond all right.

It's size wasn't .25 *carat* as they may have expected; it was .25 *point.* That's the difference between a quarter-carat diamond and 1/25 of 1/100 of a carat. The latter diamond was so tiny it might have been appropriate to send a magnifier along.

"En Cabochon" From the French . . .

While faceting is the principle fashioning approach for transparent gems, the opaque and translucent gem materials depend on their surface appearance and finish for beauty.

The cutting treatment in such a case must be different, so the final shape is usually done "en cabochon." It's a word that derives from the

French meaning slightly egg shaped.

In this style of cutting, the gem material (Fig. 3-16) is given a rounded, convex shape, usually with a flat bottom. For best effect, depending upon the characteristics of the material, the rounded dome is cut high or low.

Moonstones and opals generally are cut low; star rubies and star sapphires and cat's eye gems are cut high so that the needle-like, parallel inclusions in these gems will catch the light in such a manner as to form a star or eye pattern.

With no particular need for proper angles in the bottom of an opaque material—and certainly no requirement for containing and directing light internally—cabochon cuts feature flat bottoms (fig. 3-17). This is true even for star and cat's eye gems.

| Single | Cabochon | Phenomenal |

Fig. 3-15/16/17 The single cut, often called a "chip", usually has 17 facets. Opaque gem materials lend themselves to "en cabochon" cutting—egg shaped—to dramatize texture and color; shapes are virtually unlimited. Phenomenal stones such as stars and cat's eyes depend on proper surface light reflections so must be carefully oriented and then cut. Watch out for excess weight below the girdle: it doesn't help the optical effects at all and merely hikes up the price through extra weight.

Too many times, as a matter of fact, a cutter will seek to improve the carat value of an opaque gem by leaving unnecessary weight below the stone's girdle.

In buying a stone with this treatment, you are merely paying for additional material that contributes in no way to the beauty of the gem . . . and most of this additional material will be hidden by the setting anyway.

Prices on even average quality star sapphires and star rubies are sufficiently high that careful consideration should be given toward insisting on flat bottomed gems with most of the weight visible and polished.

Phenomenal Gems Popularity Growing . . .

A number of gemstones achieve value because of striated light effects or color effects which are not related to the gem material's basic color. Nor are they the result of the gem's chemical composition or of it's impurities.

These effects are created through a combination of interference and refraction of light plus reflection—with the cutting treatment carefully done in order to bring out the inherent phenomena.

For example, the star rubies and star sapphires discussed above produce the star effect—when properly cut—as a result of elongated silk-like crystals which orient themselves in a sort of criss-crossing pattern within the basic corundum mineral.

There are other star gems—quartz, tourmaline, diopside, enstatite. They even differ in the number of rays in their stars. If there are three sets of these miscroscopic needles, a 6-ray star is created; two sets will produce a 4-star ray. Should all the needle crystals run in one direction they create an "eye" as in cat's eye or tigereye.

You'll often hear a jeweler or gem cutter refer to the "silk" in a gem of this type. The specialist is really talking about the tiny crystals—which give the same visual effect you see when light strikes a spool of thread and causes a narrow illuminated band to appear.

The effect of light rays causing a star is called asterism. It occurs as star rubies and sapphires, star garnet, star quartz, star beryls (the mineral from which we get emeralds and aquamarines). Diopside and enstatite, which usually occur as quite dark minerals, are often cut and sold as inexpensive 4-ray asteriated gems.

What to look for in a star gem?

The most critical elements are color, the centering of the star, and the sharpness of the rays. The rays should be straight with no serious breaks or intermittent blank spots. Don't look for total perfection in the rays if the gem is genuine; a perfect ray is often a sign of a man-made gem whereas there are some minor defects (such as slight irregularity or hazy spots) in a natural gem's rays.

Also, star sapphires aren't necessarily blue. They occur in rather wide variety of colors, with so-called black sapphires from Australia enjoying a growing acceptance. As these gems approach transparency, the price per carat increases.

When the needle crystals or tubes run in one direction so that light resembles the slit eye of a cat the effect is called *chatoyancy* (cha-toy'-an-cee). The most precious cat's eye is chrysoberyl and this is the mineral when one refers simply to cat's eye. All other cat's eye needs an additional designation, i.e., quartz cat's eye, hawk's eye, tigereye, tourmaline cat's eye.

As the most valuable of the cat's eye gems, the chrysoberyl features the sharpest eye because the fibres are tightly packed and extremely fine. It is usually yellow or greenish in color, but the most desired color is a warm yellowish-brown "honey" hue.

Regardless of the gem's body color, the contrast with the slight bluish cast of the eye is spectacular and much stronger than in other "eye" gems.

Labradorescence is the designation for the play of color in metallic hues of green and blue which occur in labradorite, a form of feldspar. The origin of the names are quite apparent. As for the phenomena, it's caused by the interference of light which occurs at the plane where two crystals intergrow (called a twinning plane). The two examples of this effect are spectrolite and, of course, labradorite.

Opalization is well-known to most people. It is the play of color so characteristic of the opal. Small microscopic spheres of the mineral cristobalite in a silica gel cause the light reflection interference which provides the unique color patterns in the opal.

If you've ever looked at Moonstone and noticed the billowy blue-whitish wave which glides over the surface of the stone you are familiar with *adularescence.* The Moonstone, a variety of feldspar, must be cut en cabochon after being oriented in a specific direction that maximizes the reflections from the mineral's layered structure.

Other phenomena found in gemstones include: *aventurization,* a colorful play of glittering reflections of small, leaf-like flakes in a mineral of which sunstone is a good example *iridescence* a play of color caused by rainbow-like light dispersion as a result of cracks and flaws. It comes from the Greek word *iris* meaning "rainbow." This effect is often commercially realized by heating rock crystals and dousing them immediately in cold water which "crazes" the crystal surface.

Gem Cosmetics is Extensive . . .

That a natural effect like iridescence can so easily be produced by human endeavor brings up the always controversial subject of gemological cosmetics. In other words, is it done, how much, and in what manner are gemstones treated or altered as a technique to artificially improve the appearance of the gem?

The answer is: treatment or alteration of gems to improve their appearance artificially is extensive—and it has been a common practice for centuries.

Yes, you can craze rock crystals by a heat and cold water bath to create iridescence. There is nothing totally virtuous nor totally sinful about this. It's what you do afterward—the intent—that is the line of demarcation.

For example, you can take man-made ruby, facet it in small square cuts (called calibre cuts), then apply the same heat and cold water treatment.

Once these crazed rubies have been placed into an expensive bracelet or necklace even the most qualified gemologist is hard pressed to distinguish them from natural rubies.

It is done—and it is patently fraudulent.

Rubies have been synthesized in the laboratory since the latter part of the last century. These man-made rubies are identical in every optical, chemical and physical way with natural occurring rubies. The fakes are true rubies, please remember that.

Sold as synthetic rubies, they are most welcome to anyone who would like to own a beautiful gemstone at a bargain price.

But sold as *genuine* rubies, even at a bargain price, well—there are many, many individuals walking around with bargain rubies and sapphires which they, or a friend of theirs, purchased directly in the Far East—and that's all they are wearing: fake bargain rubies. You can even ask the people who made them.

Also, don't let the appearance of antiquity—or true antiquity itself—lead you into a miscalculation about the value of a ruby or sapphire. Age means nothing; they've been creating these synthetics for too long that a legitimate old piece of jewelry is just as likely to have a man-made ruby or sapphire as the "psst . . . wanna buy a real ruby cheap?" variety of today.

There are two ways of applying human skills—fairly or unfairly in the jewelry industry. First, the gem material itself is "doctored" as a technique to improve on its original appearance, that is the application of treatment that will convert dull, lifeless material into beautiful and valuable merchandise. Second, a manufacturing process is used to synthesize or imitate beautiful, valuable gem stone materials—and metals.

As for treating gems themselves, this is as old as the idea of gem value itself. From the time that Africans thought diamonds to be frozen chunks of lightning that had fallen to the earth, man has sought to improve what already exists.

In the first century, Pliney the Younger, one of history's earliest writers on gem lore, noted that, "such smaragdi (emeralds) as are not naturally green may be improved and reach their full beauty by being washed in wine and oil."

Today, emeralds are almost routinely given a bath in warm oils after cutting. The oil has a refractive index closer to the beryl mineral than to the air—and thus nicely camouflages by penetrating, the flaws and inclusions. In some cases, a drop of green dye is included in the oil bath and what was originally a rather nondescript piece of not-too-valuable green beryl leaps into technological life as the valuable, beautiful, emerald, the "queen of gems, and the gem of queens."

Detection? Sometimes the oil dries out or an owner or jeweler drops that expensive emerald into an ultrasonic cleaner or gives it a steam cleaning—and the green queen abruptly becomes a scrub woman. A drop of four or five color grades and the sudden appearance of flaws the owner never knew existed before can produce just that kind of effect on everyone concerned.

It's not only emeralds that are oil bathed today. Rubies and sapphires are increasingly being dumped into the warm oil pots, prior to and after fashioning.

With the availability of top grade rubies and sapphires apparently awaiting new finds, technology has moved in to improve the appearance

43

of these lower grade materials. Rubies and sapphires are also being "cooked" to improve body color. The Gemological Institute of America has reported that sapphires are even being cooked in an unidentified chemical which penetrates and hides inclusions.

Almost all aquamarine of good quality blue is heat treated, the heat improving a natural occurring light blue or effecting a color change from certain brown beryl crystals. Blue topaz occurs naturally but often in a blue tint that is too light to be commercially valuable. To get around this shortage selected topaz types are irradiated and then heated to obtain a deep, rich blue.

The popular sapphire-blue gem called Tanzanite is the heat treated consequence of dull brownish ziosite. And those beautiful blue and clear zircons? Heating is standard treatment to turn drab and unattractive brown and green zircon material into these crystal clear beauties.

Other gem materials for which "cooking" is an accepted treatment technique, of course, include smokey quartz and citrine quartz formed by heating amethyst. Even since Roman times, heat treating chalcedonies (a form of opaque quartz which includes jasper, onyx, sardonyx, etc.) to improve their appearance has been common practice.

Is this heating treating or cooking a matter of questionable ethics?

Not really.

For most of the gem materials involved, heat treating is merely the duplication of a natural process. Furthermore, in most cases it is permanent and undetectable.

When someone offers you an aquamarine or a blue topaz and assures you that the gems have not been heat treated, you might smile knowingly. Not even laboratory examinations can confirm whether they were heated by nature or man.

Some gemologists insist they can detect "cooked" rubies and sapphires because of whitish, glassy appearance on the lips of inclusions when viewed under high magnification. Perhaps they can.

Atomic Technology Arrives . . .

Today, there's a newer wrinkle in the world of gemstone treatment. It's atomic technology.

Many gem materials respond to irradiation treatments—*of the non radioactive type.*

It's been found that irradiating and then heating certain types of gems can produce magnificent gems. Certain colorless topaz, for instance, turns an extraordinary deep, rich blue when exposed to this new treatment. (Although this is currently the most expensive of blue Topaz, the irradiated blue does have an unnatural, artifical blue appearance, seemingly much too deep for some gem fanciers.)

Colored diamonds called "fancies" are among the most expensive of gems. Yet, irradiation treatment can turn colorless diamonds into a series of fancy colored gems.

Unfortunately, irradiation effects are not always permanent. Some stones that have been colored by irradiation may fade with time or exposure to light or heat. Just which materials will fade, when they will fade, and how much they will fade is, for the most part, unpredictable.

It's a situation that is similar to nature. Some gem minerals are exposed naturally to heat and radiation. Under molten conditions, some minerals are naturally "cooked" so that their color and chemical contents or crystal structures undergo change.

At the same time, many gem deposits are located near sources of natural radioactivity. Radioactivity is thought to be the difference between low-grade green zircon and high type.

Gem minerals thus can be unstable due to natural causes. Some forms of brown topaz found in Mexico will fade upon exposure to sunlight. Kunzite, the lavender colored variety of spodumene, fades to a colorless form quickly when exposed to sunlight.

The deep irradiated blue aquamarines (called Maxixe) as well as some irradiated blue topaz have been known to fade with time and exposure to heat and light.

Lasering Improves Clarity . . .

Another modern technological treatment involves the laser beam.

Using the powerfully controlled light beam of the laser, technologists are now able to "laser" out impurities in gems—including diamonds. The laser beam cuts a tiny, almost imperceptible "tunnel" through the gem material and then burns out black carbon spots or imbedded foreign crystals which appear as dark inclusions.

The tunnel remains after the treatment, of course, but in the absence of magnification which discloses the tell-tale "spider legs" of the laser tunnels, a gemstone's clarity grade can be lifted a step or two. In a clear, brilliant gem a white or empty inclusion "hole" is not nearly so noticeable as a black spot.

Depending on whether your jeweler even knows if a particular gem has been heat treated, irradiated, oiled, dyed, or lasered he may or may not say something to you. The Federal Trade Commission requires a jeweler to disclose to you any artificial treatment or enhancement but is understandably silent on how the jeweler himself is supposed to detect the often undetectable.

In too many cases, jewelers are left in an understandable quandary. They can't disclose something when they can't even prove—or know—if it was done or not done.

Your best defense is your own knowledge of gem treatment possibilities, and a realistic attitude towards the whole matter. It's perhaps good that you know how an inexpensive piece of white opal by soaking the white opal in a concentrated sugar solution for a few days

45

before giving it a quick dip in sulphuric acid which carbonizes the sugar, can turn the opal black.

It's of much greater advantage to know that only certain kinds of opal respond well to this treatment—and that you can see the carbonized sugar particles by looking carefully at the opal under strong magnification.

Below is a list of the better known gem materials with some helpful information on their treatment and how you can provide yourself with maximum protection short of a full-scale laboratory examination:

Gemstone	Treatment Technique	Effect of Treatment	How to Detect Treatment
Aquamarine	Heat	Enhances blue color, induces blue from certain green, brown beryls	None. The treatment duplicates a natural process.
	Unfiltered shortwave UV	Induces intense blue (Maxixe is name for it)	Color looks unnatural will fade if exposed to light
Calcite	Staining and Dyeing	Imitates Jadeite, Lapis Lazuli, other more expensive stones	Concentrations of dye often visible under magnification; touch of fingernail polish remover with cotton will blot up loose dye particles sometimes
Chalcedony: Agate	Staining or dyeing	Color contrasts become more vivid	Magnification often shows dye
Jasper		Jasper stained blue to imitate Lapis, called "Swiss Lapis"	"Swiss Lapis" has streaking & lacks pyrite inclusions of natural lapis
Black Onyx Blue Onyx Green Onyx Brown Onyx	Gray agate is often given sugar solution soak and sulphuric acid bath to produce black onyx	Dyes change agate color banding and body color to effect single hued impression	Cotton with fingernail polish remover often picks up dye stains
Coral	Staining or Dyeing	Light orange is dyed to "ox-blood"	Cotton with fingernail remover
	Bleaching	Hawaiian black coral to golden tones	Sometimes magnification will show dye, original color in pores
Diamond	Painting and sputtering	Metallic fluorides and coatings, usually on pavillion, to "hide" improperly cut bottoms lack of brilliance	Flouride gives slight purplish tint, similar to camera lens. Immersion in water often shows color difference in coated vs. non-coated part; new transistor

Gemstone	Treatment Technique	Effect of Treatment	How to Detect Treatment
			industry coatings are virtually indistinguishable
	Lasering	Tunneling (done perpendicular to table) to burn out dark inclusions	Magnification through side of gem: look for "spider legs" as giveaway

Note: Sputtering a faceted gem's pavillion with a fluoride or similar type coating is the imitator's favorite technique for giving any pavillion a near diamond-like mirror brilliance. Many of the cheaper "diamond counterfeits" such as man-made spinel, man-made white sapphire, clear topaz, clear quartz, etc. are often sputtered. Foil is the old technique—still used with rhinestones and, occasionally, with other inexpensive materials.

Gemstone	Treatment Technique	Effect of Treatment	How to Detect Treatment
Emerald	Oiling and dyeing	Hides inclusions and improves green color	Magnification discloses dye in cracks and fissures
Jadeite	Staining and dyeing	Provides green and mauve colors	Magnification shows dye concentrations
Lapis-Lazuli	Staining or dyeing	Evens out blue color	Cotton and fingernail polish remover picks up dye stains
Opal	Sugar/acid treated	Produce form of black opal from white opal	Magnification discloses sugar concentrations
	Smoke treated		Smoke treated appears brownish
	Plastic impregnated		Hot needle on back gives plastic "odor"
Pearl	Bleaching	Cleans off yellowish or brownish tinges	A bath in hydrogen peroxide is standard pre-market preparation of all pearls
	Staining and dyeing	Change pearl color; enhance rose tone	Cotton tip with fingernail polish remover (very carefully near drill hole —and then wash thoroughly)
Quartz Amethyst	Heated	Change violet to yellow and green color	Not a natural process duplication
Tigereye	Stained and dyed	Used to obtain various colors in tiger eye	Magnification discloses dye concentrations
Citrine	Heat	Amethyst, smoky quartz changes to brown-yellow, gold-yellow and orange red	None: duplicates natural process

Gemstone	Treatment Technique	Effect of Treatment	How to Detect Treatment
Ruby	Heated	Cooks out grey-brown colors, intensifies red	Not detectable
	Oiled	Diminishes notice-ability of flaws	Oil in fissures can be seen usually when magnified
Sapphire Blue	Heated	Cooks out secondary colors, intensifies blue	Not detectable
	Heated in chemical packing	Intensifies color by cooking or diffusing color into the surface of natural stones	Magnification sometimes discloses chemical used, but laboratory usually necessary
Spodumene	Heat and irradiation	Turns pink stone to intense greenish-blue	Not detectable, but color has no counterpart in nature. Fades quickly
Tanzanite	Heat	Turns brown zoisite into intense voilet-blue	All blue tanzanite is heat treated; its part of the process to make Tanzanite
Topaz Blue	Irradiation and heating	Changes colorless and pale blue to deeper blue gems; only some stones can be irradiated to the deepest blue	Virtually all deeper blue topaz is heat treated. It is undetectable because it duplicates a natural process.
Pink	Heat	Changes some brown topaz to pink	Not detectable. It duplicates a natural process.
Tourmaline	Heat	Lightens green stones. Intensifies red stones	Not detectable. It duplicates a natural process.
Turquoise	Plastic	Improves blue color	A hot needle applied to back will give off noticeable plastic "odor".
	Wax		Friction—such as quick, vigorous rubbing against cloth or shirt—followed by quick smell test often produces paraffin odor.
Zircon	Heat	Changes brown & green stones to clear and blue.	Not detectable. It duplicates a natural process.

As a final word, the discussion here about treatment and cosmetics in gemstones is reasonably complete. Reading this information may cause some people to gain the unwarranted and inappropriate idea that buying jewelry is fraught with danger or at least near fraud.

Such is not the case. Such an impression is not even close to the truth.

Treatment, in and of itself, is not inimical to an industry which thrives on the real and the beautiful. There is no more trickery involved in making a gemstone more attractive and valuable than there is in a woman applying lipstick or a man touching up his face with an aftershave lotion . . . or simply combing and grooming one's hair.

No one applies treatment to a gemstone with the idea of diminishing its good qualities. Of course, some treatment techniques may have a minor effect on a gem materials' inherent strength but many of the treatments given here are but part of the manufacturing process of bringing a beautiful gem to the market.

The soaking in hydrogen peroxide of pearls is but a single component of the long, traditional process of pearl from nacre-bearing mollusk to the neck. You can't have the beautiful gray and black pearl tones without the silver oxide treatment which reacts chemically with the pearl material itself.

And the diamond—king of all gems—is literally cooked and boiled clean in hot sulphuric acid as it makes it from the iron cutting wheel to the diamond setter.

Years of experience have proven that peroxide soak for a pearl or an acid bath for a diamond are all part of a necessary and beneficial process . . . just as other processes are quite legitimate as an accomodation for the requirements posed by other gemstones.

Rubies and sapphires, good ones that is, are increasingly scarce—so man's technology is coming to the fore to improve on the existing supply WHICH NEEDS SOME ASSISTANCE.

Most legitimate jewelers will be quick to disclose and explain. This chapter should give you the background to pose meaningful questions —and to understand for yourself on those occasions when any disclosure is not forthcoming.

CHAPTER FOUR

SYNTHETIC GEMS: An Improvement on Nature

Is there an accepted place for man's genius in the world of gemstones?

After all, over the centuries human endeavor has produced a wide range of treatments to alter the appearance or color of a natural gemstone. Stripped to essentials, these treatment techniques consist of three major approaches: 1) heating or annealing; 2) impregnation or surface modification; 3) irradiation.

Even with treatment, though, natural gemstone materials are limited in quality and quantity and this existing supply can't be expanded.

If success could be so easily attained in making low-grade undesirable natural materials into commercially acceptable gems think about the possibilities of human effort duplicating these miracles of nature. Would it not be a logical step to imitate nature?

History shows that man went to work on this problem earnestly and early. His efforts were not directed solely to imitating beautiful gems; green glass can be made to look remarkably like a fine emerald.

Rather, he also directed his energies—like the ancient Merlins who experimented for so long to turn lead into gold—toward producing true gemstone crystals, that is man-made materials that duplicated nature's efforts in every physical, chemical and optical way.

Today, human genius has succeeded in manufacturing nearly every important and valuable gem mineral in nature's inventory.

So successful has this duplicating process been that, in many cases, the demarcation line between nature and human is virtually indistinguishable . . . and growing more so every day.

Think of the difference between a cultured pearl and a natural pearl? It's but a matter of insemination, isn't it? A piece of sand accidentally enters the mollusk and this initiates the protective process of nacre deposit which produces a natural pearl. A cultured pearl process begins with the deliberate introduction of an irritant such as a small seed pearl, a piece of mother-of-pearl, or perhaps a section of mantle tissue. The moment this foreign object is inseminated into the mollusk the same layering process begins—and a cultured pearl is produced.

Rubies?

In 1980 a well-known and respected ruby dealer named Abe Nassi went into the mining areas in Thailand where native miners sold him a large rough ruby crystal of outstanding clarity and color—at a splendid price.

The happy dealer's suspicions were aroused, though, when the miners contacted him the next day in Bangkok with the information that they had found another equally excellent piece of ruby rough. Of course they would sell this new piece at another surprisingly low price.

Delaying his response, the dealer arranged to have the first ruby crystal flown for an emergency examination to the Santa Monica, Cal. laboratory of the Gemological Institute of America. Back came the answer: the marvelous piece of ruby rough was man-made Kashan ruby manufactured in Dallas, Texas.

Even a renowned ruby expert had been hoodwinked; a lab was needed to save him. This story is fully documented in the December, 1980, edition of *Fortune Magazine.*

For years, the presence of so-called fingerprint inclusions (this particular inclusion appears as a series of bubble-like white spots in a flowing near-fingerprint pattern) had been regarded as proof positive of a natural occurring gem (Fig. 4-7). Today, manufacturers can reproduce these inclusions in their synthetic creations.

In the far East, manufacturers for a long time have been quenching heated synthetic rubies and sapphires in cold water to form cracks. The newest wrinkle has chemicals introduced into these cracks and, yes, they produce fingerprint inclusions.

Natural alexandrite has a distinct color change from green (in daylight or flourescent lighting) to red (at night or by candle or tungsten lighting). This gem material is so rare and costly that few people have actually seen this chromium influenced chrysoberyl.

The *Alexandrite Effect* color change was long used to separate the real from the fake. Early imitation efforts involved synthetic corundum—and to a lesser extent synthetic spinel—but the corundum fake's color change from greyish green to an amethyst-like purple clearly unmasked its synthetic true origin.

Since 1973, though, with patented techniques used by a California company, Creative Crystals, Inc., synthetic chrysoberyl alexandrite gems with a natural-looking green-to-red color change have been available. They are apparently not produced in large quantities—but a careful laboratory examination is required to separate the natural from the synthetic.

Man-Made Gems Were Inevitable . . .

To be overly concerned with the technological developments in man-made or synthetic gemstones is probably unwarranted.

"Probably unwarranted" seems like a realistic warning. Man has been trying from the beginning to duplicate nature. That he would seek to reproduce nature's crystals is but a part of his effort to know and under-

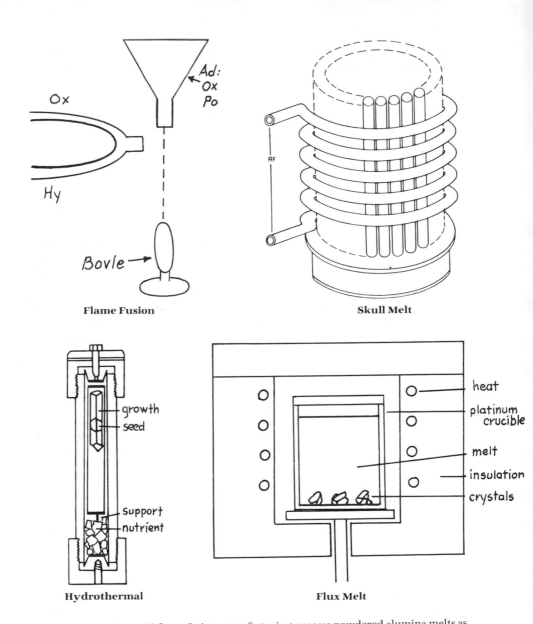

Flame Fusion

Skull Melt

Hydrothermal

Flux Melt

Fig. 4-1 In the Verneuil flame fusion manufacturing process powdered alumina melts as it passes through an oxy-hydrogen flame, crystallizing in a boule. The skull melt system consists of two skull halves joined in a round base and filled with zirconia powder so heat creating rf waves can pass through the water-cooled fingers and melt the interior powder while the cooled thin powder "skin" layer serves as a containing "skull." In the flux melt systems, powdered ingredients are mixed with a chemical flux and then heated so the mixture melts. Upon cooling and evaporation, the molten ingredients crystallize in place, or a seed crystal is touched to the molten mass and growth is initiated as the seed is pulled and rotated from the melt. The hydrothermal system most closely approximates nature in that a supersaturated ingredients/water mix is subjected to temperature and pressure in a closed autoclave. A slight temperature differential within allows the material to deposit on seed crystals until the growth process has been exhausted.

stand himself and his surroundings.

Therefore, when we speak of gems made or created by man we really mean crystal growth. With but a few exceptions—mainly opal and turquoise —all of the gemstones that man makes are single crystals. That is, man has been able to arrange the conditions—and the chemicals —conducive to orderly crystal growth for virtually all major gems.

The technology for this crystal synthesis isn't all that ancient either. As long as man still considered natural gems to possess mystical, theological, and magical powers, the very idea of reproduction by man was unthinkable.

Then, too, how could humans ever hope to duplicate the inspired process described by Sir John Manderville in 1360:

> "A diamond is synthesized when two larger ones, one male and one female, come together, in the hills where the gold is. And the diamond grows larger in the dew of the May morning."

Not all men believed that. Nor did all believe as did the Arabs, that a diamond was a piece of a star that had broken off and fallen to earth, or, as the Africans believed, that it was a particle of frozen lightning.

By 1830 man had brazened through the magical cult and learned enough of the composition and nature of complex crystals that he could proceed beyond the growth of simple crystals from water solution so familiar to every high school science student.

But most early efforts were strictly laboratory events or curiosities. By 1902 this continued effort in the laboratory paid dividends as French scientist Auguste V.L. Verneuil gave the world its first commercially successful synthesized gemstone—a synthetic ruby.

There had been previous synthetic rubies in the jewelry market prior to that. But they were small, of questionable quality, with limited production.

Verneuil scored his breakthrough to true production by dripping a feed powder (a mixture of aluminum oxide and, to provide red coloring, chromium) through an oxygen-coal gas flame so the molten drops would fall on a cradle where they crystallized into a pear-shaped "boule." (Fig. 4-1).

In a manufacturing process that has changed remarkably little over the years, the boule gets split along its long axis and the pieces are then cut or faceted into gems.

Continued research has produced other gem synthesizing systems. The major systems include what is called flux melt growth and hydrothermal growth.

In simple terms, a flux melt consists of combining the basic gem material from which the crystal will form with a chemical solvent and then heating and cooling.

The hydrothermal growth systems consists of supersaturating a water solution with the basic material from which the crystal will form and then heating and cooling inside a closed crucible.

No matter which growth systems are used today, they represent the culmination of thousands of years of man's progress which, one can guess, began with the Egyptians. It was they who probably produced the first gem imitation, a glazed-ceramic composition called *faience* as early as 5000 B.C.

Faience was the forerunner of transparent glass, and apparently was still in use in Egypt by 1000 B.C. Among its uses were the imitation of gem materials such as emerald, lapis lazuli, onyx, and turquoise.

Indeed, the Romans thought so highly of glass—which rapidly replaced gold and silver for drinking vessels—that they regarded it as more valuable than natural gems. Colourless glass was the most valuable of all.

These early efforts were imitations—not synthetics. It is important to distinguish carefully between what the jewelry industry defines as an imitation and what it defines as a synthetic.

An *imitation* is a material that can be manufactured or fabricated so as to *simulate* the wanted characteristics of natural gem materials. It may or may not have any of the same qualities as the natural.

A *synthetic* is a manufactured material which *possesses* the same physical, chemical, and optical properties as the natural gemstone. It is gem crystal—man-made, to be sure, but usually with outstanding color and clarity.

Man hadn't learned, in 5000 B.C., to create a material which *possessed* true gemstone characteristics. His early glass-making only allowed him to *simulate* these qualities. As a matter of fact, artisans did so well simulating natural gems that Roman Emperor Diocletian about 300 AD decreed that all books explaining the assembly of artificial gemstones be burned.

He, too, was no doubt aware of the same danger that a Hindu poet had penned:

> Silly glass in splendid settings, something of the gold may attain. And in company of wise ones, fools to wisdom may attain. Glass will glitter like the ruby, drilled with dust—are they the same?

A synthetic or imitation gemstone establishes its value from the cost of production, marketing costs—and to some extent the popularity and scarcity should there be some difficulty in the manufacturing process.

A natural diamond has all the requirements, obviously, which produce gem value. Yet the price of a diamond valued at, say, $30,000 per carat, is also part function of the comprehensive monopoly control over diamond supplies yielded by the De Beers syndicate of companies. These companies influence to a large degree the price of diamonds by control of these supplies.

The General Electric Company successfully synthesized diamonds in 1955, but manufacturing costs are still much greater than the cost of processing natural diamonds for the gem trades. So, few synthesized diamonds, if any, are seen in the jewelry market place.

The powerful attraction of diamonds has long supported an opening for an imitation. Currently, a man-made imitation material which has no counterpart in nature called Cubic Zirconium is most popular. C.Z. *simulates* closer than any other substance the fire and brilliance of the diamond—and it can be purchased for a fraction of the cost of a diamond.

What makes C.Z. so attractive is that even an experienced jeweler or gemologist can sometimes unduly stretch his gemological arrogance by trying to "eyeball" an evaluation. Thus, a wearer runs a minimum chance of the embarrassment of being "found out" because it's just too dangerous to attempt a casual eye inspection of this excellent imitation while it's being worn in a mounting.

A good grade commercial emerald can cost $3,000 per carat. At the same time, a top quality Chatham Emerald, the fine flux grown synthetic emerald, can be purchased for about $300 per carat—and in many instances can be purchased for much less.

For a jeweler to sell you the diamond imitation in the form of a C.Z., or an emerald synthetic such as the Chatham emerald is to provide an ethical and valuable service . . . as long as you KNOW what you are buying. Few are the number of jewelers who would knowingly sell you a synthetic or imitation gem and represent either as genuine.

But the sale of misrepresented bogus gems outside the normal jewelry trade occurs often enough and the scale of fraud is high enough that some alarm is justified. It was jewelers themselves and pawn shop operators who were the principle target in the nearly $2 billion in C.Z. frauds perpetrated by con artists in the 70s. If even these professionals can be "had" as it were, your concern is justified.

When C.Z. first hit the market and the jewelry trades hadn't yet learned how or had the instruments, to identify it, the frauds came right and left. With education and detection instruments, the chances now of a legitimate jeweler buying or selling—unknowingly—a counterfeit diamond like C.Z. is minimal.

You should always be alert that the ". . . psst . . . wanna buy a real gemstone cheap" streetcorner operator is still around—even if he's not operating on the street corner or in the classified advertisements. The business of cheating is still lucrative.

Your own reluctance to accept quickly from anyone what appears to be a "fantastic bargain" or a "steal" remains your best defense. It's highly unlikely that a naturally expensive gem of great scarcity will be sold to you cheaply; it's too easy to sell it legitimately for much, much more. The full-price demand for commercial grade natural gemstones is worldwide—and good grade crystals are in constant short supply.

Some people feel that the market for natural gemstones is a separate and distinct market from imitation, fabricated, and synthetic gems. Perhaps, but this may be making a distinction that isn't wholly justified.

Man-made gems have an important niche in the realm of jewelry, and they certainly will allow you to enjoy the beauty and the pleasure of wearing gems that might not have otherwise been available to you for a number of reasons.

You might expect difficulty in purchasing synthetics from the older, more traditional, self-professed higher quality jewelry store. Many jewelers look with distain on anything but natural gems—which could be the reason that more and more jewelry is being marketed outside the jewelry store complex.

For one stated reason or another, many jewelers feel that imitation or synthetic gems will impair their reputation for high quality. Perhaps so, but you can always find a nice selection of natural and man-made crystals in department stores.

The Eye is the Arbiter . . .

As stated earlier, your chances of encountering a questionable gem will be much greater outside the jewelry stores. It's in this larger arena where you'll meet the street corner operative, the classified ad "jeweler(?)", or a friend with a hand-me-down gem of unknown identity.

These are the individuals who can afford to be a bit more careless in their identification or representations.

Your own safety process begins with a realization of the skill levels of manufacturers. In dealing with any gem then, the primary guideline—if there is such a thing as a primary guideline—is: the duplicators are very, very good at what they do so only in a few rare instances can "eyeballed evaluations" authenticate a gem. In other words, what you see may not be what you think you are getting.

If a ruby dealer of long years experience can be "conned," so too, can you.

As you now know, nearly any gem crystal can be synthesized and then treated to appear even more natural. As you also know, colors can easily be duplicated both in imitations and in synthetics.

Also, some man-made crystals have no counterpart in nature and so are used only because of their unique optical qualities. To this group belongs Cubic Zirconia (introduced in 1976), strontium titanate (introduced in 1953), and yttrium aluminium garnet (YAG—introduced in 1966). Both C.Z. and YAG come in a wide variety of authentic-looking colors which makes these crystals available for imitating other gems.

As cautious as you should be about relying on the eye alone to give you information about gemstones, there are certain characteristics that you can "read" in natural vs. synthetics/imitations/constructed gems that, short of a full fledged examination by a professional gemologist or gem laboratory, can help "tilt" your opinion.

Take diamonds as the first case.

Scientific efforts to imitate the diamond date back to the Egyptians who initiated the ubiquitous diamond imitation—colorless glass. Glass is low in brilliance and hardness so it makes a poor substitute. Even the high lead content type glass (called "paste") with its higher refractive index and dispersion fails to satisfactorily measure up.

Over the years, the industry has utilized more than a dozen natural and man-made colorless gem crystals to imitate the diamond. Man has even combined one or more different kinds of crystals into a constructed gem with the same objective in mind.

Pending a significant technological breakthrough, nothing is in sight that matches the diamond. Only the synthesizing of a diamond by GE can be considered a true match-up. Yet this high-cost synthetic diamond is not likely to exert much impact on the gem diamond or diamond duplication business. At least for the near future, you will be faced only with the question of the real thing vs. one of its imitators. Making a diamond is much more expensive than finding one naturally; until that equation finds a closer balance the market will consist of the real.

Here is a listing of natural and man-made gems that are most used to imitate diamonds together with some specifications and comment:

NATURAL GEM MATERIALS

Material	Refractive Index (Measures Brilliance)	Dispersion (Measures Fire)	Comments
Beryl	1.58	0.014	Low brilliance, fire, appears watery
Garnet (grossular)	1.73	0.028	Some brilliance, fire-rounded facet joins
Quartz	1.55	0.013	Low brilliance, fire, appears watery
Topaz	1.62	0.014	Low brilliance, fire, appears watery
Tourmaline* (elbaite)	1.63	0.017	Low brilliance, fire, appears watery, doubling
Sapphire	1.77	0.018	Some brilliance, low fire
Zircon*	1.96	0.039	Good brilliance, fire, doubling

* Viewed straight down through the table facet, you'll notice that the facet meets/intersections appear almost fuzzy as the lines look doubled. Strong birefrigence causes this doubling which is always noticeable in Zircon and rutile, often noticeable in tourmaline.

MAN-MADE GEM MATERIALS

Material	Refractive Index	Dispersion	Comments
Cubic Zirconia	2.16	0.060	High brilliance and fire, facet joins sometimes rounded
GGG	1.97	0.045	Good brilliance and fire, sometimes slightly brownish
Sapphire	1.77	0.018	Low fire
Spinel	1.73	0.020	Low fire
Strontium Titanate	2.41	0.91	High brilliance, excessive fire
Rutile*	2.8	0.33	High brilliance, excessive fire, doubling
YAG	1.83	0.028	Good brilliance, low fire

DIAMOND

Material	Refractive Index	Dispersion	Comments
Diamond	2.42	0.044	High brilliance and fire, sharp facet joins, waxy girdle, variable polishing lines, "naturals," "bearded."

Fig. 4-2

There are certainly additional optical, chemical and physical properties useful for distinguishing a diamond from its imitators. They could be covered here were this a lengthy treatise or an explanation of laboratory and gemological gem testing techniques. It isn't, so—

A discussion of the diamond compared with the 14 different materials listed here—plus a few "indicator tests" that are quickly and easily done—should provide you with a sufficiently useful "read out" knowledge so as to raise the flag of warning when it's appropriate.

I'm fully aware of the old truism that ". . . a little bit of knowledge can be dangerous." I'm also aware of a larger truism that "no knowledge is even more dangerous." Or, as Mark Twain informed his wife after she chided him for giving her a diamond that he'd accepted in lieu of a cash settlement: ". . . even an old second hand diamond, my dear, is better than none."

Diamond simulants need not frighten you. In most cases you can spot them—although a few take a very careful inspection, preferably with some magnifying help.

Many of the simulants' clues can be picked up easily by a trained, practiced eye. Even the best fakes won't fool the person who knows what to look for in a genuine diamond versus what the counterfeits lack.

Of course, detection instruments allow the quickest and most reliable way. Diamonds are marvelous heat conductors and a probe pen will tell quickly if you're dealing with a diamond or not. But in many instances you may have need to make a reasoned judgement when no instrument is available—and a visual examination can be done anytime, anywhere, and under varying conditions . . . as long as you recognize and give credence to the limitations that are sometimes imposed on you.

The four simulants—as shown in the listing—which cause the most difficulty include 1) C.Z.; 2) strontium titanate; 3) gadolinium gallium garnet (GGG), and 4) yttrium aluminum garnet (YAG).

Each of these man-made materials feature two strong similarities to genuine diamond . . . which is why they make such commendable imitations. Each has a refractive index which exceeds the top limit of a refractometer (a lab instrument used to measure the light bending or light refracting character of a gem crystal).

Also, each is a singly refractive material (when light enters the crystal it remains as one ray and does not, as in most gems which are doubly refractive, split into two rays. If you'll check the chart listing you will note the specific mention made concerning Zircon's "doubling" which comes from double refraction.)

A visual examination of a diamond versus one of its simulants is not a single-step operation; the process generally consists of a series of tests gradually leading to a conclusion. You'd be better off to follow a four-step procedure . . . going through each step even when it is sometimes impractical.

The first step is:

Fig. 4-3

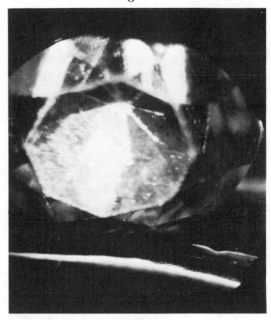

Notice the hazy or "doubled" appearance of facet edges, a characteristic of zircon. This effect is caused by light rays splitting as they pass through the gem material.

Visually appraise the gem in question by reflecting light off its surface while looking for the unique brilliance and, especially, fire (flashes of color) which a diamond displays.

If you own a diamond hold it up under an incandescent light. Do you notice how a diamond as you tilt and tip it fires back at you with little flashes of color? A diamond sparkles with subtle color flashes. It literally dances before your eyes.

Don't be too disappointed in the beginning if all diamond simulants appear as brilliant and fiery as a diamond. The better simulants do indeed *approach* the diamond. For the most part, it's a matter of training your eye to detect the differences. This ability will come quickly enough with a bit of practice.

Notice, too, that the first five natural gem materials used as simulants all appear "watery" or "glassy." Their optical qualities don't come near the diamond so detection is relatively easy.

The next time you visit a store with costume jewelry, look carefully at one of the so-called "diamond simulants." You won't see much dispersion of color. The reflections might appear bright—but not nearly as brilliant as a diamond. Hold your own diamond next to it; note the differences. One gem—the diamond—is alive and fiery. Against it as comparison, the other is dead, non-responsive . . . "watery."

You might use your diamond as a comparison stone anytime you make an identification. A comparison stone is a powerful aid, because you will be testing a known against an unknown. Differences are much more evident.

In many cases, this visual examination will produce your first clue. Some of the obvious simulants will fail the test flat. Others will get past this "indication" test—such as C.Z., GGG, strongium titanate, YAG, and Zircon.

YAG, when clean and viewed directly down through the table, gives an impression of brilliance. But its lack of dispersion produces a watery appearance for the most part, especially if you tilt the gem or if it's the least bit dirty. Doubling, or the fuzzy appearance at the facet edges marks the Zircon (if you'll take a careful look at the culet, too, you might notice an additional row of 16 pavilion facets adjacent to the culet, inasmuch as the zircon is often cut in the "zircon cut" which consists of this extra row of facets as added reflective "kickers;" diamonds don't need these extra facets because they can achieve powerful brilliance with the customary 8 pavilion main facets.)

Strontium titanate explodes with excessive dispersion, throwing far more color than a diamond. GGG has good dispersion but often has a slight brownish tint in body color because manufacturers have not yet been able to color stabilize the material which turns quickly from clear to brownish caste. Rutile, too, is excessively dispersive, so much so in fact that it is seldom used anymore to simulate diamonds. Rutile also displays excessive "doubling."

Cubic zirconia and GGG (which hasn't yet acquired the brownish tint) imitate much of the visual excitement of a diamond. They might need exposure to the second indication test.

The second test is:

Look straight down through the table facet and then slowly tip the gem, looking for the "spill of light" or "read through" effect.

At various angles, the "read-through" of each gem will differ. You can tilt a one-carat sized diamond almost vertically (Fig. 4-4) before it "spills light", i.e., the facets in your direct line of sight turn transparent, allowing you to "read through" the gem. A "fish-eye" diamond or one sputtered with a fluoride coating negates "read through" testing.

Only strontium titanate (with an R.I. of 2.41) and rutile (with an R.I. of 2.80) can match the diamond's ability to return light to the eye. But, as mentioned, their dispersion factors are so excessive compared to the diamond that little question should arise about these two colorful performers.

Because of lower R.I.'s the other simulants "spill light" readily. None can pass this test to a learned eye without arousing suspicion, although C.Z. comes uncomfortably close.

There is another reason for caution. Smaller stones with their smaller tables make it exceedingly difficult sometimes to recognize the "read

Fig. 4-4 Many gems provide "read through" even when the gem is placed table down over newsprint. This test, obviously, is most practical for unmounted stones.

through." This test admittedly works best on stones of one-quarter carat size and larger. Just remember that when properly cut in the round brilliant mode diamond and strontium titanate usually won't "spill light."

Keep in mind, too, that the "light spill" or "read through" effect occurs—even with diamonds—to a much greater degree in fancy cuts, i.e., pear, heart, marquise, oval. The variations in the pavilion main facet angles needed to achieve these modified shapes allows greater light "leakage" or transmission.

It's all relative, though, and you may expect that a fancy cut diamond will not "spill light" to the same degree as a fancy cut in one of the simulants.

To aid your eye examination in this step, you might take a piece of brightly colored paper, fold it in a "V" and place the suspect gem's pavilion into the "V". By tilting you can more easily detect the "light spill" when the color comes directly through the now transparent facets. The lower the R.I. of the crystal, naturally, the more quickly will the color become apparent. It won't come through a properly cut brilliant diamond.

"Read through" is also visible when a colorless stone is placed table down over a newspaper. With quartz, glass, etc. the print may be a bit distorted but it can be seen easily. As the R.I. of the material climbs, the difficulty in "read through" increases. Printed letters are almost indistinguishable when looking through C. Z., but there is *no* "read through" with diamond or the same high R.I. crystals.

The stone doesn't need to be unmounted—although the test is easier to conduct on a "loose" gem—to conduct a "light spill" examination. That's the beauty of this "indication test." You can quickly and conveniently check out a diamond (?) ring; just tilt the gem and watch carefully for the tell-tale clues.

The "light spilling" or "read through" effect should be recognized as no more than merely another indication. It doesn't necessarily "prove" if you're dealing with a diamond or not—but it is another step down the path of identity.

In any event, you should be reasonably certain of one thing at this juncture: if the gem shows high brilliance and good dispersion (fire) with no appreciable "light spill" or "read through" you're probably dealing with a diamond or a C.Z. or GGG. Dispersion would eliminate a strontium titanate, and the GGG would still be possible only if the clear body color still prevailed.

As an added tip: a comparison stone is extremely useful with this test, too. The spill differences literally jump at you when you can compare with a known diamond.

The answer to identity may be found in the third test which is:

Using at least a 10x magnifier, inspect the gem for tell-tale signs of the diamond—waxy girdle, "naturals," facet functions which are sharply defined, inclusions, polishing marks running in different directions.

The diamond is truly unique. It contains qualities unmatched by any other gem crystal. The presence of one or more of its unique features will have you well on the way to a near-positive identification.

Look for inclusions or flaws. Unless you are dealing with diamonds of investment grades, a diamond will contain inclusions (interior flaws are called inclusions) or blemishes (exterior flaws are called blemishes) which are characteristic only of the diamond.

As a matter of fact, the absence of inclusions or blemishes should start you worrying a bit. Man can get near perfection; but nature is a bit more casual. The absence of any crystal defect hints strongly of synthetic or imitation, especially in counterfeit diamonds.

Nature provides most diamonds with such typical inclusions as cleavages, fractures, knots (sometimes called by the Dutch name "naat" and which means another tiny particle of diamond imbedded into the crystal) as well as other included or imbedded foreign crystals.

Although the presence of these inclusions may dampen a diamond's value usually, they are as trustworthy as human fingerprints when it comes to identifying a particular diamond. The expression, "by its inclusions will you know it," is quite valid.

A diamond's great hardness allows for two feature characteristics, one you always see and the other sometimes. The facet edges of the cut diamond invariably appear sharper and more defined than its imitators —provided, of course, it's been cut with at least reasonable skill.

Only diamond will cut and polish diamond so this great hardness allows the facets to be cut with much greater sharpness.

Over time, diamond facet junctions will become abraded or chipped. But they will seldom be rounded off because of wear. The simulants, all being much softer, usually can't be cut with such sharpness in the first place. Consequently, their facet joins are noticeably less sharp, appearing rounded which time aggravates even more.

Again, be a bit careful. C.Z. and YAG are relatively hard crystals. If a cutter uses an extremely fine mesh diamond powder for final polishing, both of these man-made materials can be fashioned so as to nearly duplicate the sharp facet joins of a diamond. Only a truly experienced eye can detect this—and then not all the time.

The second visible clue derived from the diamond's hardness deals with polishing marks. Since diamond cutting will only occur when the soft grain of one diamond is matched up against the hard gain of another diamond, each facet on a cut diamond will be cut from a different direction on the cutting wheel.

This means that under magnification you can often detect these polishing marks traveling in different directions on each adjoining facet. Generally, only the diamond will have this visible clue.

ALL other gem crystals may be cut by a diamond without regard to hard or soft grain. Thus, the simulants will show polishing marks (if they're visible) usually running in the same direction on the same row of facets. Lapidaries (cutters of gems other than diamonds) generally set a piece of rough into their faceting machines and proceed to lay in an entire row of facets based on the first key setting, changing only the indexing or facet number. Directional hardness is a non-consideration to the lapidary although almost all gem materials vary a little bit in directional hardness, too.

The girdle area holds a host of clues to the trained eye. Again, the hardness of a diamond and the method of bruting (shaping up the perimeter of the intended cut) with another diamond leaves a mat or waxy appearance on a diamond's girdle. Sometimes, of course, the girdle is polished.

But mostly a diamond is simply bruted, leaving the girdle with the shiny appearance of wax. Girdles of most simulants are polished. If not, simulants have a somewhat duller look, approximately a frosted appearance. Certainly, simulants do not display the diamond's unique waxy look. With a 10x loupe study some diamond girdles; get accustomed to their special appearance.

Compare them with known simulants and, gradually, you'll notice your eye able to detect the subtle difference.

Look, too, at the girdle for two more potential clues. One is the

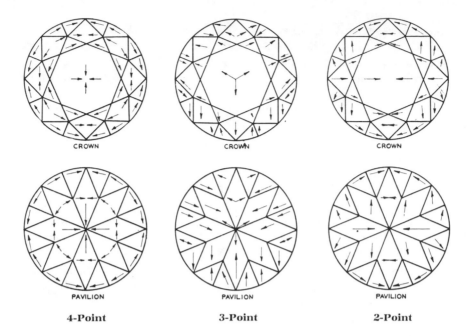

CROWN	CROWN	CROWN
PAVILION	PAVILION	PAVILION
4-Point	**3-Point**	**2-Point**

Fig. 4-5 Hardness in a diamond varies with the grain direction, and magnification sometimes reveals the appearance of varying polishing line directions (right). In 4-point cutting, a diamond's facets are cut in the directions shown by the arrows . . . when the table is parallel to a cube face; the 3-point cut has the table parallel to an octahedral face, while the 2-point cut has a table parallel to a dodecahedral face.

presence of "naturals" and the other is the presence of "bearding"—both evidence of a diamond. (Fig. 4-6).

A "natural" is but part of the original crystal surface that was allowed to remain on the diamond through its manufacturing process. In a manner of speaking it's evidence of the bruter's skills because he was able to round up or shape the diamond on his lathe-like machine with such precision that some of the original surface was left. Unless it disfigures the diamond outline, a "natural" is not considered a deduct in the diamond's value.

The natural will have a special luster which distinguishes it from the rest of an unpolished girdle. It'll even appear a bit wrinkly. If you can't find one on your own diamond, the next time you're in a jewelry store ask the jeweler to point out a natural.

Chances are, if not busy, a jeweler will be delighted to find a diamond with a natural and show it to you (not all diamonds, remember have a natural). You'll really need to see a natural or two to train your eyes accurately.

"Bearding"—if present—is relatively easy to see with a 10x loupe. It appears as hairline feathers which start at the girdle and extend into the

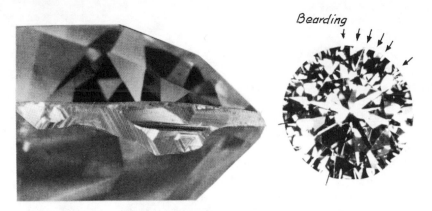

Fig. 4-6 Only diamonds—and not all of them—sometimes have the wrinkly appearing original crystal "skin" remaining on the girdle. Unless it disfigures, a natural is not considered an imperfection. If the stone is bruted or rounded up carelessly, minute fractures—called bearding—extend into the gem itself.

crown or pavillion a short ways. These features are actually tiny fractures which were caused by too rapid bruting or rounding up.

You'll generally not see "bearding" in the simulants'. It's primarily a unique indication of diamond. A diamond chips away at another diamond causing bearding: A diamond scratches through all other gem materials like a hot knife through butter leaving little chance of bearding except for very careless *pre-forming* (cutting a piece of rough into an approximate gem form so the cutting or faceting can proceed faster due to less waste material).

One final non-laboratory type clue involves the culet. If you'll recall, this is the tiny, flat facet on the extreme bottom of the gem. It's placed there to avoid possible chipping or breaking of the sharp, pointed, weakened tip. The inherent brittleness of diamond makes it susceptible to chipping. Thus, a culet is almost always present in a diamond; not always in the simulants.

The counterfeits are not as brittle—or as valuable—as a diamond. A culet is not solid proof, just one more piece of evidence.

By this time, your visual examination should have provided sufficient clues to distinguish between a diamond and one of its imitators. Still, before you make your final decision you might want to consider the fourth test, which is:

Examine the gemstone for any sign of "cosmetic treatment" or "doctoring" or "construction."

Because they appear watery and lack brilliance, many diamond simulants—both natural occurring and man-made crystals—are subjected to various forms of treatment.

Truth is, some diamonds are treated, too.

A white sapphire is hard but it doesn't provide much dispersion. Strontium titanate is soft and has lots of fire. Why not arrange a marriage of convenience? So you have a doublet, i.e., a "constructed" gem with a hard sapphire top which can take the abuses of time and hard knocks attached to a strontium titanate bottom which provides fire, brilliance—and whose softness is protected by the setting cage.

Such a "constructed" gem makes a very effective diamond counterfeit.

Why would the diamond itself require cosmetics? If the cutter misses the proper pavilion angle either through carelessness or lack of sufficient depth in the original piece of diamond rough, the diamond will "fish eye" i.e., leak light through the bottom. You can easily "read through" such a diamond.

To help hide this error, the pavilion may be painted with the same metallic fluoride used to coat camera lenses, or it may be "painted" with one of the more esoteric coatings developed in the electronic industry. The latter treatment virtually defies detection ... and improves color, too.

Sputtering a fluoride solution on the pavilion of man-made spinels is a favorite among manufacturers of cheap low-cost "diamond engagement rings" usually found in the Five 'n Dime stores. It improves color.

Detection of these coatings can sometimes be flushed out with special heavy or high refractive liquids used in the laboratory. Because water has a higher refractive index than the air, you can use ordinary tap water the same way . . . with slightly less visible accuracy.

To test for a two-part constructed stone or for fluoride treatment, drop the stone into some water so you can view the top and bottom of the gem at the same time. If two different crystal materials have been used, one will appear more transparent than the other. The connection junction will be quite noticeable.

Likewise, the fluoride treatment. The top of the gem will react normally to the higher refractive quality of the water, while the fluoride will interfere with light flow just enough that you can see the difference.

This interference usually creates a brownish or purplish tint, clearly visible in comparison to the river clear appearance of the top. Again, this isn't an acid test because some of the new coatings are so resistant to detection.

The more visible coatings are used mostly in relatively low-cost diamond simulants.

Is there a double check if you suspect diamond coating? Yes. First, of course, reputable jewelers are required to inform you of any treatment. Second, to be on the safe side you might measure the depth of the diamond (more on "reading" diamonds will be found in Chapter 6). Divide this measurement by the diamond's diameter.

Your ratio figure should be between .59% to .61% indicating that the diamond was probably cut properly on the pavilion angles and doesn't need a coating. In those cases where this depth ratio might go up to, say, .62% or .63%, it might be that the alteration was due to some other adjustment in the cutting proportions—and thus not hint that coating is involved. A proportion falling below 59% suggests a shallow gem—which should be having "fish eye" problems, ordinarily.

In summary, when confronted with a clear stone represented as a diamond you should 1) visually examine it; 2) check it for "read through:" 3) identify unique characteristics, and 4) evaluate for "doctoring."

A professional gemological examination or laboratory test will identify with absolute certainty. When doubt still persists about "is it really a diamond?" your jeweler can usually tell you by using a diamond pen (a device which tests surface tension with a liquid—a damp finger will usually pick up a diamond but hardly any simulant—or a diamond probe, the devise which measures thermal conductivity).

Colored Gems Are Man-Made, Too . . .

The true synthesization of gem crystals occurred first among colored stones. It's here where human effort has reached such wide ranging commercial success. Today, you may purchase virtually any synthetic gem crystal—and usually with a better color and finer clarity than nature provides.

Ruby, of course, was the first true synthetic, and most of the man-made rubies sold and used today are still made in the Verneuil flame fusion process.

But continued research and progress particularly in the semi-conductor and laser industry, has spawned new processes of crystal growth and new crystals, many of which have the optical qualities found useful in jewelry.

It's one thing to distinguish between a natural gem and one that imitates it. It's something else entirely to differentiate between a natural and synthetic gem. "Eyeballing" just isn't adequate anymore.

Few people holding a jeweler's loupe can safely declare "authenticity" of a gemstone after a quick peek through the magic magnifier. You should be wary of anyone who claims such mystical powers.

The art of synthesizing gems is just that: an art. Manufacturers are very competent. They create synthetic gems as close to the natural as possible . . gems than can hold their own even in the laboratory.

So, realizing full well you cannot—nor can anyone else—eyeball through the maze of synthetic gems with supreme accuracy and confidence, why not turn to the realm of the possible? While care is necessary when dealing with colored gem synthetics, a trained eye can still tell much and avoid the more obvious traps. In many cases you can "see" a warning signal, or detect perhaps a minor item slightly out of focus, a break, as it were, in the steady line of evidence.

Age is no protection against a synthetic ruby. They've been making them since the late 1800s. But the early synthetic rubies—and some made today—often contain tell-tale clues.

The first clue is the description. When you see the name of the gem in quotation marks such as "Ruby" it is often a signal that an imitation or synthetic is involved. Fakes, too, as mentioned elsewhere, often have a geographical or limiting qualifier attached to the gem type, such as "German Lapis," "Herkimer Diamond."

Because so many synthetics are still made by flame fusion, you should be familiar with their physical clues. Remember, though, that modern Verneuil corundum synthetics have been refined greatly and you probably will not be able to see the clues that were so predominant in earlier products.

As the molten drops fall to the "boule" they crystallize in a specific growth pattern. This leaves growth signs which are visible as *curved* striae and color bandings. Also, because the flame sometimes got too close to the boule itself, the excess heat caused gas bubbles to form.

curved striae   Gas Bubbles

Fig. 4-7 You won't see it too much in today's products because of improved manufacturing processes, but flame fusion synthetic materials are often identified by the presence of curved striae (caused by the rounded shape of the growing boule) and by gas bubbles (caused by temperature unevenness and proximity of flame and boule). Color banding—similiar to striae—is characteristically *straight* in natural rubies and sapphires.

In transmitted light—and with magnification—these bubbles show up with high relief, taking the shape or form of spheres, tadpoles, and even doughnuts.

The striae and color banding of a natural corundum ruby or sapphire are *straight,* not curved. Natural corundum crystals have *no* bubbles, they contain imbedded crystals and "normal" appearing inclusions.

Synthetics tend to be flawless—a characteristic not shared by all or most natural corundum.

You will undoubtedly hear self-appointed "experts" tell you that curved striae and color banding and gas bubbles are the sine qua non of synthetics, that you can *always* tell a synthetic by these signs.

No! You can not!

In early flame fusion synthetics these _were_ the clues. The Verneuil process today has been so improved that you usually can't see these clues.

Furthermore, new flux growth processes for rubies are so extraordinarily refined that they are creating a major problem in the jewelry industry. Characteristic inclusions of genuine rubies can be manufactured right into the final synthetic product.

With Kashan rubies, for instance, many laboratories simply refuse to authenticate a Kashan so long as it's in the mounting. On top of this, Kashan itself claims that the labs may expect to miss on at least 5% of the rubies that they do authenticate.

New Chatham rubies—also apparently flux grown—are reportedly just as difficult to authenticate.

Therefore, when buying a ruby inspect it, certainly, but don't rely on its age as a protection; be slightly suspicious if its a flawless gem; remember that bubbles and curved striae usually indicate only older flame fusion synthetics and that the new flux grown ones give even the labs fits.

A known, trusted jeweler is your best defense. Even then, if a goodly amount of money is involved, a gemological inspection and an enforceable warranty from the one selling you the gem are not at all unreasonable.

How About Spinel Synthetics . . .

There really is no such thing as a true synthetic spinel. It's called synthetic spinel all right, but the chemistry of the man-made spinel differs markedly from the natural spinel. Commercially produced synthetic spinel contains a much lower magnesium-oxide content than does natural . . . so it's really only an imitation.

Regardless, man-made spinel is used extensively. Discovered accidentally when scientists were experimenting to try and produce a flame-fusion blue synthetic sapphire, spinel's great advantage is that it can be made to reproduce almost all colors except purple. The blue synthetic spinel sapphire imitant is much more genuine looking than a synthetic blue flame-fusion sapphire—and many of the synthetic sapphires being worn today are not man-made sapphires at all; they are imitation blue spinels imitating synthetic sapphires.

Although synthetic spinel is also produced by flame-fusion, any resemblance between man-made spinel versus Verneuil rubies and sapphires or other colored corundums ends at the torch. You'll seldom see bubbles or curved striae in man-made spinel regardless of age.

Some of the imitations using man-made spinel do contain clues, though. An imitation Lapis Lazuli is made by sintering finely ground synthetic spinel and then recompacting it under pressure. Sometimes, real gold is included in the product to simulate the pyrite (fool's gold) so characteristic of natural Lapis. You can generally spot this imitation because of the intensity of the color, and because this *color contains an inappropriate reddish influence.*

Compare the imitation, too, with natural Lapis and you'll see that the luster of the imitation is much too high.

A very authentic looking moonstone imitation is also possible with man-made spinel. Colorless material is reheated long enough for some of the chemical—alumina—to separate out into small corundum crystals. This creates a cloudiness which provides the unique adularescent (the wispy, billowy light wave) effect of the moonstone.

If the inclusions line up properly a star effect can also be produced. The star effect is often aided by thin metallic coatings on the base of the cabochon. Since it is usually a rather thin cab, there is a noticeable transparency—a good hint that man-made spinel is involved.

The star effect is easily produced in man-made spinel and man-made corundum. A good indication of imitation or synthetic is the sharp rays of the man-mades; they're just too perfect and straight. Other imitations are achieved by ruled metallic foils underneath and scribing. You can see the coatings (unless it's hidden by the mounting) or foil backs. Also, a sideview while the stone is immersed in water reveals the tell-tale transparency.

Even though man-made spinel is a popular material because of its accommodating nature in manufacture, color, and cut, it still has its shortcomings. Throughout the range of colored gems that it seeks to imitate, a practiced eye can determine that the colors are "off" just a bit from the naturally colored gems. This can be of great help in tipping you off to a man-made.

That Amethyst Can be Man-Made . . .

Amethyst is a purple colored quartz and, as the birthstone for February, is a lush, beautiful gem. Because quartz is common and easy to extract, quartz gems tend to be among the most economical . . . including the amethyst.

Still, using a hydrothermal synthesizing process quartz can be made in such quantities and so inexpensively that synthetic gem production of an inexpensive gem material is still profitable.

This means that a manufacturer can cheaply produce colorless iron-containing synthetic quartz. Then this manufacturer can subject the crystals to non-radioactive gamma ray irradiation.

The result: a carefully colored controlled purple amethyst of the finest color which is competitive in price with natural amethyst.

The process duplicates nature's techniques in almost every way. There is therefore no provable difference between a natural amethyst and a synthetic one.

As Dr. Kurt Nassau, world-famous crystallographer and scientist has stated as late as 1980 in his book, *Gems Made by Man*, there are no consistent identifying features known that provide for a reliable differentiation between synthetic and natural quartz . . . so the two are indistinguishable.

If you ask the question, "You mean that the amethyst that I just bought could be a synthetic, a man-made? . . . and this could be true of Citrine,

Smokey Topaz Quartz and some of the other quartz gems."

The answer is "Yes."

Before you get too concerned, though, try to see that there is a powerful analogy in the quartz and in the pearl situation. The difference between a natural and cultured pearl is merely a matter of inserting the irritant.

The difference between a natural and a synthetic quartz is who turned up the heat. After all, the synthesizing material is crushed and refined natural quartz and the process in both cases is hydrothermal.

The great advantage of man-made amethyst, for instance, is in the accurate color control that the manufacturing process provides. For all other gemological, economical, and crystallographic purposes there simply is no difference—and no one can prove otherwise.

Knowing Man-Made Emeralds . . .

Emerald has shared the throne of high value for thousands of years. It was therefore a natural and early candidate for imitation and synthesis. The unique color of this green beryl had long eluded the imitators and it was not until man had learned to synthesize the gem itself that a true look-alike was possible.

Today, most synthetic emerald is grown—it is believed—by a flux growth process. Some of the other beryl colors have been grown in the laboratory—aquamarine, helidor, morganite—but given their average quality and cost of commercial production it seems unlikely that you'll see them in the jewelry store in the immediate future. Only the synthetic emerald seems cost effective at this time.

The same chromium oxide which causes red in rubies causes the green in emerald, a finding suggested by J.J. Ebelmen as early as 1848, and demonstrated in 1888. The German firm, IG-Farbenindustrien, produced gem emeralds in the 1930s. These early efforts all produced small gems.

The breakthrough came in 1947 when American scientist Carroll Chatham, culminating his own research which had begun in the 1930s, announced emeralds of improved quality and greater size, capable of commercial production. Since then other companies have developed processes to synthesize emerald. Gilson and Linde are the better known names.

As you know, most natural emeralds are heavily flawed. These flaws are generally so profuse that they take on an acceptance of their own. It's not unusual to refer to an included area as a "garden" (from the French *jardin*) of included "flowers."

Like their natural counterparts, synthetics also are included. Therein lies an opportunity to distinguish the man-made from the genuine.

The flux-grown Chatham and Gilson emeralds contain characteristic flux inclusions. These consist of veils (Fig. 4-8) which under 10x magnification, appear somehwat like waving nylon or silk curtains. These veillike curtains are actually solid flux from the growing mixture.

71

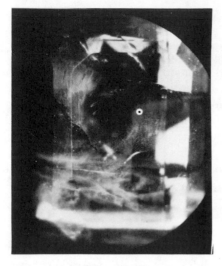 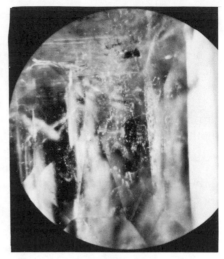

Synthetic Veils   **Natural Emerald**

Fig. 4-8 The inclusions in natural emeralds and man-made emeralds may appear similar but the differences are invaluable in distinguishing one from the other. Most synthetics inclusions appear as waving nylon or silk curtains—resulting from solid flux in the growing mixture.

Another visual clue indicating a synthetic emerald consists often of a series of parallel bands of zonal lines—sometimes referred to as the "venetian blind effect"—which can be observed running straight across a facet.

Again, a gemologist or lab expert with the necessary instrumentation is really necessary when it comes to authenticating most emeralds. The above discussion on inclusions is helpful, but they are only indications and the ability to recognize two-phase and three-phase inclusions is a necessity in the authenticating process. For this, a powerful microscope is almost a necessity.

Other Man-Made Gems . . .

Although you're probably less likely to come across them, a number of other gem materials have been successfully synthesized.

These include, of course, the flux-grown synthetic alexandrite, as well as synthetic turquoise, opal and Lapis.

The Gilson turquoise resembles the finest Persian turquoise, known for its light blue color uniformity, and good density. A microscope is required to see the tell-tale tiny dark blue microspheres which are visible in the light colored background mass.

For the most part, natural turquoise is "color stabilized" though impregnation with wax, sodium silicate (water glass) and/or plastics. Frankly, it's near impossible to obtain today natural turquoise which has not been treated.

To check a piece of suspect turquoise, heating (this can also be done by briskly rubbing the cabochon on your sleeve or shirt front) which will often cause the wax to sweat or release a slight paraffin odor, while a hot needle applied to the back of the plastic impregnated turquoise will produce a camphor, carbolic acid or fruitlike odor indicative of plastic types.

Opal is produced by Gilson in both white and black varieties with such skill that a gemological examination will be necessary to determine anything with certainty. The same Gilson has also suceeded in synthesizing Lapis Lazuli. The same must be said of this synthetic as was just mentioned of the opal . . . get it to a qualified lab.

Doublets, Triplets Declining . . .

Once upon an imitation past, doublets and triplets were the favorite device of the gem imitators. Their assembly techniques were marvelous examples of trickery and fraud . . . and expertise.

Basically, they fabricated gems using and mixing the various qualities of different crystals to achieve their own ends. With the advent of better imitations and synthesis, use of the doublet and triplet has declined noticeably. Still, you might run into one occassionally and it would be helpful to be able to detect them.

One of the favorite doublets for imitating various colored gems was the garnet and glass type. (Fig. 4-9). As you can see this consisted of attaching a hard garnet top to a softer glass bottom—or some other gem material for a bottom depending on what effect was desired.

It may seem strange that a piece of wine colored garnet could be used so effectively to imitate other gem colors. But the color coming from the colored glass or gem pavilion simply dominated the gem.

An effective way to detect such an assembled stone, as well as other doublet fabrications, is to immerse the suspect gem in water, so you can take a sideways look. Because the garnet's R.I. will differ from the material used in pavilion by a considerable margin, the two parts should show up clearly.

Triplets, understandably enough, consist of three parts. One famous triplet used widely to imitate emeralds earned the name *Soude Emerald*. This "gem" consisted of two pieces of clear quartz or clear spinel held together at the girdle (Fig. 4-9) with green cement. Viewed from the side, Soude Emerald gives up its chicanery quickly.

As you can well imagine, the material selection available for constructing doublets and triplets is limited only by the fabricator's imagination. Water immersion will reveal almost every one of them. Often too, magnification will show bubbles from the cement or adhesive used.

Where you will continue to see doublets and triplets is in opal jewelry. Opal often occurs naturally in thin veins. As a result lapidarists cement these thin pieces to a piece of backing material for strength. The dark backing material also provides some optical assistance, such as making the thin white opal look more like an expensive black opal.

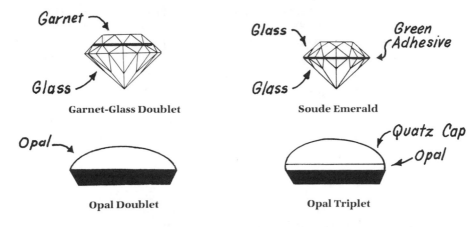

Garnet-Glass Doublet

Soude Emerald

Opal Doublet

Opal Triplet

Fig. 4-9 The use of doublets and triplets to simulate valuable gems has declined as synthetic production has improved; such assembled or fabricated stones are more often seen in older jewelry. The manufacture of opal doublets and triplets, though, continues as a means of using valuable, colorful opal which often occurs in pieces too thin for fashioning.

With a backing—either opal, onyx, plastic, glass, etc.—there can be somewhat of a pricing problem. The top of an opal doublet is true opal, but the doublet construction does not justify a carat price. The fashioned gem always should be sold as a unit.

This is true, too, of an opal triplet. Here you have a doublet with a quartz or glass cap applied over the soft opal to protect and to provide a magnifying optical contribution to the play of color.

You should be careful when buying opal jewelry. For the most part the motive for making doublets and triplets is more efficient recovery of existing natural material as well as protection and strengthening. Consequently, there's usually no great effort to conceal the fact that the gem is assembled.

Sometimes, though, doublets are made with high grade opal on top and low grade opal as the bottom piece with the sides of the stone covered over with the mounting metal.

Under these circumstances, it becomes easy to pass the stone off as solid opal. If you suspect—and you should always approach a closed mounting with some cynicism—a strong light and magnification often shows bubbles from the cement.

Lacking a definitive answer with this test, the stone may need to be unmounted so a visual inspection of the joining plane may reveal the answer. It's often unlikely that the top of an opal will display a brilliant play of colors and the bottom will be dull and colorless. If the bottom is colorless, wet it. Moisture sometimes makes the colors more pronounced—and you can make a judgement if the lack of color is due solely to the absence of polishing . . . or if it's a separate piece of opal.

With regard to any piece of jewelry where the mounting conceals the gem you should practice caution. Your first question should always be, "Why was this done? Was it to conceal something?"

Pale emeralds can be coated on the back to improve color; a doublet joining plane may be hidden; foil might be giving a brilliant boost in a colorless quartz called rhinestone: the foil backed bottom of a star gem may be scribed with 60° crossing star producing lines; dyes, paints may be in use as color improvement aids.

If a jewelry piece is slightly fraudulent, the mounting is useful to throw off the unwary—and the fact that karat gold is being used doesn't change much of anything . . . except, perhaps, the asking price.

As one final warning: in most cases you will be evaluating gemstones under the most severe conditions—mounted in some kind of setting and without gemological instruments to assist you. The visual clues given in this chapter are, at the best, helpful—but not conclusive.

"Eyeballing" is dangerous. But it's better than going in totally blind as is the case with most gem purchases.

In the absence of a gemological examination, you are taking a risk. But you take a risk buying a car, too.

Regardless of the circumstances, be most conservative in your estimation of a gem's authenticity. The whole idea of imitation and synthesis is, remember, to simulate . . . to look like the real. By knowing the clues and observing carefully the limitations of a non-instrument supported inspection, you'll at least come closer to the point where you recognize danger.

CHAPTER FIVE

PRECIOUS METALS: More So Than Gems

From the dawn of recorded history, the bright yellow glitter of gold has fascinated men and women.

Just why gold has ascended to the king's value throne and remained there in such undisputed glory is questionable.

Gold, of course, has many excellent qualities that give it a higher value rating than other metals.

It is *malleable.* Gold can be worked easily by hammering or pressure without crumbling. Only silver comes close.

It is *ductile.* An ounce of gold can be drawn into a fine wire fifty miles long.

It is *fusible.* Gold can be combined with other metals to produce alloys.

It has *tensile strength.* Gold has tenacity which enables it to be worked to withstand longitudinal stress without cracking.

True, no other metal has these same qualities to the same extent that gold possesses them. But these qualities alone don't answer the real question: why is gold the king . . . the only king?

Early craftsmen used gold to fashion decorative pieces of all kinds. The ruins of every civilization on earth have disclosed how their citizens regarded gold. Their attitudes were no different than today's.

While no definitive answer appears acceptable, perhaps there are some indications that help to explain the puzzle. For one thing, gold is the only true yellow metal found free and almost pure in nature.

To cave people this could have proved to be a valuable asset. No smelting was necessary and the softness of the metal lended itself to intricate fashioning. That little buffing or polishing was necessary to bring up a brilliant finish must have added the speed with which gold climbed the scale of preciousness.

Also, that gold has lost none of its desirability is a self-evident truth. Open today's newspaper and you will see half a dozen advertisements offering to buy old gold and silver.

Franchise operations to buy and sell gold sprung up quickly—particularly when gold prices hit a record high of $825 an ounce late in 1980. Gold fever ended somewhat abruptly when the price went into a slide for 1981, but the gold bugs never lost their sense of confidence in the yellow metal.

For 3,000 years it's been on a price climb and a temporary setback, to gold lovers, is nothing to worry about. After all, gold is the only truly universally accepted form of money. Someone might refuse payment in some coins or paper, but generally will accept with alacrity the payment in gold. Don't some nations base the value of their currency even today on the amount of gold in their treasuries?

As important as gold is in the economies of the world and in the jewelry industry, it isn't the only metal by far that finds its way into a piece of fine jewelry.

Metallurgists make a sharp distinction between the ferrous and the non-ferrous metals. Before proceeding into the complexities of precious metals it would do well to first have some understanding of such distinctions.

Simply put, a ferrous metal contains iron. Nonferrous metals don't contain iron and are classified as precious metals, base metals, and alloy metals.

Precious Metals in Jewelry . . .

The precious metals are gold, silver and platinum. Base metals include copper, nickel, zinc, aluminum and lead.

Alloy metals are karat gold, sterling silver, gold solder and silver solder, brass, bronze, pewter, nickel silver, and duraluminum.

About the only metal used in its pure state is silver. Pure 24 karat gold is seldom used because it is much too soft; it would wear, scratch, and bend easily, and lack holding security for gems. To the North American eye, too, it appears excessively yellow—like cheap gold plated costume jewelry.

All metals are referred to as elements. The pure metal elements can be combined with almost any other metal and the combination is referred to as an alloy.

You should know that almost all of the gold you see in fine jewelry is an alloy.

24 karat gold has 1,000 in fineness and is at least 99.9% pure gold. The amount of gold therefore in 18K gold is only about 75% with the remaining 25% represented by such alloys as copper and silver. The gold content in 14K gold is 60% and the balance consists roughly of 6% zinc, 20% nickel, and 15% silver.

Under federal law, the word gold cannot be used for any alloy less than 10K gold, which represents approximately 40% gold content and 60% alloys.

There is little change in the consideration of white gold. The only major difference is in the use of other metal elements to obtain the white color.

For example, 18K white gold has a gold content of some 75% while the alloy mix runs 10% nickel, 5% zinc, and 10% palladium.

In recent years—especially after Queen Elizabeth of England introduced to the world the concept of two-tone gold (use of both yellow and white gold in the same piece of jewelry)—colored gold has increased in popularity.

Today, you can buy gold in such colors as red, pink, light and dark yellows, and green. These colors are achieved merely by the shift in percentage content of essentially the same alloys as are used in white and yellow gold.

Below, for your information, is a listing of the alloy and gold contents in various gold colors:

18K GOLD	Red	Pink	Yellow	Green
Gold	75	75	75	75
Copper	20	17	12½	5
Silver	5	8	12½	20

14K GOLD	White	Red	Dk Yel	Lt Yel	Green
Gold	58½	58½	58½	58½	58½
Silver	15	7	15	21½	24½
Copper	—	34½	26½	20	17
Nickel	6½	—	—	—	—
Zinc					

You'll notice that in the above paragraphs there were some approximations regarding the gold content. For years manufacturers had been allowed some leeway in the gold content of any particular gold indication. In other words, for years a manufacturer could stamp a ring, for example, as 14K knowing that the gold content was actually closer to 13K perhaps because of gold solder content used in sizing the ring and maybe the alloy mix wasn't as careful as it could have been.

The jewelry industry itself was never especially happy with the looseness of this requirement. At the industry's insistence and encouragement, Congress in 1976 amended the National Gold and Silver Stamping Act, making jewelry manufacturers responsible for the metals content in their products.

This amendment went into effect October 1, 1981, culminating a long internal jewelry industry fight to be more precise in stamping gold karatage and to establish closer tolerances.

Manufacturers were given five years to prepare for the change. Until the effective date manufacturers could legally make and sell a soldered piece of gold jewelry marked 14K but containing only 13K, and for an unsoldered piece of jewelry the tolerance could legally be off by half a karat.

After the effective date, jewelry manufacturers must come within 7 parts per thousand (for soldered items) and 3 ppt (for unsoldered items). As a result of this amendment, you may expect to hear jewelers occassionally mention to you, "this item is 14K *plumb* gold."

Translated, that remark means that the item has been manufactured in accordance with the new, closer alloy tolerances—and what he says is what you really get.

IMPORTANT: These new, better, stricter rules on gold content apply to United States commerce. You can still get ripped off in overseas gold purchases where industry is much more lax about their stamping and selling requirements. The law does, though, apply to American firms who import gold jewelry from foreign manufacturers. Once gold hits the U.S. market, it must comply with the law.

These new tolerances will undoubtedly have a beneficial effect on the market. But remember, too, that the new amendment *applies only to manufacturers.* Retailers have forever to sell the merchandise now in the marketing stream and which was manufactured prior to Oct. 1, 1981. You will be seeing items marked under the old tolerances for a long time.

The difference isn't something to be overly concerned about. American gold jewelry manufacturers for decades have set the world's pace for integrity and quality consistency—and the gold content value between an item made under the old tolerances and the new, at best, would be slight.

The Price of Gold . . .

The price relationship between a fine piece of gold jewelry and the gold content generally isn't all that predictably strict anyway. It's true that as the ounce price of gold rises or falls there is somewhat of a price shift—admittedly, this occurs most readily when *your price* is going up in response to a change.

Gold jewelry, for the most part, is priced for the creativity, workmanship, and exclusivity of an item. Stock items such as engagement rings, earring mountings, etc. reflect gold ounce prices most.

Please remember that gold is primarily a commodity. There is an international market for the metal with publicly published prices. Because this price changes daily—and in quick response to every crises, minor or major, in the world—its gyrations are, to be sure, volatile.

The jewelry industry operates essentially on "gold price on date of delivery." That means that manufacturers, wholesalers, and retailers, don't know one day to the next what their gold purchases—or unfilled orders—are going to cost. When the order is filled from a supplier, the daily gold price is consulted and the metal is priced accordingly.

Retailers do their best at adjusting store prices to accomodate the rise and fall in their inventory values, but they are restricted somewhat by customer resistance to higher prices and to much price changing. As a result, many jewelers tend to price their merchandise at a level that will protect them up to a certain gold price threshold.

So long as international gold prices remain below a jeweler's own threshold number the retail prices in that store will tend to remain constant. But they're understandably sticky about cutting prices. (After all, prices might go right back up tomorrow and then a jeweler must change again—much to the consternation of customers who hold back when prices are unpredictable. After all, customers justifiably reason, why not hold off and see if the price drops again tomorrow? If it does, why not wait another day, etc. etc. ? Such much-to-be-avoided "Games That People Play" between a jeweler and potential customers may allow the customer the luxury of a long wait; it'll send the jeweler spinning into bankruptcy.)

As you perhaps already know, the price of gold is set daily in the London gold market where huge transactions between corporations, institutions, governments, and individuals occur. Buyers and sellers actually establish the price according to supply and demand.

The different amounts and prices are all transactions which cause the price fluctuations. At the end of the day the day's prices are averaged and published. And that's how we get the announcement, "Today, gold closed on the London exchange at—"

A daily price quote is easily obtained from banks, commodity brokers, coin and precious metal dealers—and from the financial page of the daily newspaper. It's based on the sale of the large 400 ounce (27.4 pounds) bars, known affectionately as "Good Delivery" bar. These bars represent the universally recognized medium of exchange between large banks and nations.

They are the biggest bars made for monetary purposes with a purity of .995. For these bars there is essentially little or no premium charged in their sale. Any amount of gold sold or purchased which is smaller than a "Good Delivery Bar" involves some kind of premium, commission, or brokerage fee added to the basic gold price.

Smaller bars come in 100 ounce size (6.85 pounds average) although the most popular seems to be the one kilo bar of 32.15 troy ounces (2.2 pounds average). Like the 100-ounce bar, the one kilo bars are produced in several grades of fineness, .995 and up.

There are also a variety of bars that refiners produce ranging in size from a single ounce up to 10 ounces.

All bars, you should know, are stamped with the fineness, weight and registration number. Some refiners also add their name as do some banks when issuing a bar.

It is generally regarded as prudent for an investor to ask for an assay of a bar which has been removed from the bank storage vault and later sold.

Because many investors wish to get into the gold market less expensively many small gold bars, wafers, coins, etc. are available and are sold by banks, coin shops, department stores, mail order houses, and jewelers.

Here's something that isn't generally recognized about these so-called small 24K "investment" items. When they're less than ½ ounce they are usually marked 24 karats—without the percentage of fineness. Without a fineness stamp, this places the item out of the money and into the jewelry category. If a bail or ring has been soldered on, then they can legally be as low as 23 karat. And you can bet that many such so called 24K investment pieces (?) will still be around until they are all sold.

If you're buying it for investment, be prepared to accept the lower tolerance possibility—or buy something with a fineness stamp. Also, the mark-up is quite stiff, usually two to three times the price of gold . . . even without a fineness stamp. Most financial advisors agree that the most economic purchase for gold investors (vs. jewelry) is a legitimate coin purchased from a reputable gold dealer where the commission usually runs 15% to 75% depending on the size coin.

Selling gold?

Small amounts of gold can be sold directly for immediate payment to a number of buyers . . . and their identity and availability can be easily located in the daily newspaper or in the Yellow Pages. Your best outlet here would be a jewelry store, jewelry supply house, coin dealer, precious metal buyers or, if you can locate a willing one, a small refiner.

Refineries generally aren't too interested in buying a quantity smaller than 100 ounces. That seems to be their profit break.

It goes without saying that your best price will come from a reputable and, probably, local dealer.

Your best protection against an inappropriate buying or selling price is still your own knowledge.

You should know how to weigh gold, recognize the vocabulary of gold dealing, and be capable of testing gold for its content. This way, you'll know going into a bargaining transaction when a reasonable offer to buy or sell has been proffered.

First though, you should approach gold with a reasonable attitude. At less weight than a Good Delivery Bar there is no realistic way for you to buy gold at the London price; you must and will pay a premium.

The middleman with whom you're involved must be reimbursed for his time, talent, risk, and investment. Whether that's a precious metal dealer or a jeweler they are entitled to a fair profit. If gold must be refined or worked in any way, there is a refiner and craft charge for that work—and this will be an add-on to the commodity price.

So be prepared to pay more than the daily quote.

The Specs on Gold . . .

Knowing that gold is valuable and that there is a daily gold price is fine, but it's not enough. There are a few other elements that need to fall within your familiarity.

Consider weight. Gold and the metals used for alloying with gold are weighed in troy ounces. It is important to know and understand the words or references used because references to weight vary, depending on the circumstances (sometimes this is done so that the average person won't be able to calculate quickly or accurately, I am sorry to say):

> 1 troy pound = 12 troy ounces
> 1 troy ounce = 20 pennyweights (dwt.)
> 1 pennyweight (dwt.) = 24 grains (gr.)
> 15.43 grains (gr.) = 1 gram (gm)
> 31.10 grams (gm) ≠ 1 troy ounce

Note carefully these equations—and, especially, the abbreviations for pennyweight (dwt), grain (gr) and gram (gm). These are the three weight references you'll be dealing with mostly, on a "price per _____" basis. When a seller tells you he or she isn't selling on the basis of weight, then the pricing is being done according to what the traffic will bear—arbitrary mark-up.

If you know the weight and karat of the gold item you can calculate the gold value yourself—and have a good idea of the seller's mark-up.

Here are three examples, using $400/ounce as the daily gold price:

YOUR PRICE QUOTED IN:

#1 Pennyweights (dwt.) 20 dwt = $400 (1 oz.)	#2 Grains (gr.) 480 gr = $400 (1 oz.)	#3 Grams (gm.) 31.1 gm = $400 (1 oz.)
Dealer sell price is $90 for 3 dwt item of 14K gold	Dealer sell price is $5 for 3 gr item of 14K gold	Dealer buy price is $15 for 3 gm item of 14K gold

How much of a mark-up is involved in the pricing of these three examples?

Take Example No. 1 where the dealer wants to sell a 14K gold item weighing 3 pennyweights for $90.00

To get the *pennyweight price* you divide $400 by 20 = $20/dwt.

To get the *pure gold price* for the item multiply 3 dwt. x $20 = $60

To get the *14K gold price* of the item multiply $60 x .60 = $36

So the 3 dwt item contains **$36** worth of gold when gold sells at $400 per ounce. A 14K gold item contains 60% gold and 40% alloy—so we can see that the mark-up for the alloys and anything else is about 2½ times the value of the gold.

Take Example No. 2 where the dealer wants to sell a 3 grain (gr) item made in 14K gold for $5.

To get the *grain price* you divide $400 by 480 = approx. 83¢/gr.

To get the *pure* gold price for the item multiply 3 gr x 83¢ = $2.49

To get the *14K gold price* of the item multiply .60% x $2.49 = $1.49

So the 3 gr item containing about $1.49 worth of gold at a gold price of $400/oz. had been marked up to $5 slightly more than triple.

Take Example No. 3 where a dealer offers to buy a 3 gram (gm) item of 14K gold for $15.

To get the *gram price* divide $400 by 31 = approx. $13/gm.

To get the *pure gold price* of the item multiply $13 x 3/gm = $39

To get the *14K gold price* of the item multiply $39 x .60 = $23.40

In this case, the 3 gm. item contains $23 worth of gold. The dealer has offered to buy for $15 a price less than the gold value.

In summary, finding the gold value content of an article is a simple 3-step process once you know the weight, gold karat alloy, and the daily gold price.

You know there are 20 pennyweights to an ounce, 31 grams to an ounce, and 480 grains to an ounce. Whichever of these weight references is used, you merely divide it into the daily gold price and use that figure to calculate the item price by the weight reference and the gold karat content.

Figuring the Karat Content . . .

Fine, you say, but how do you figure the karat content of the item? You need an accurate scale to determine how much a piece of gold or gold jewelry item weights. But it's the amount of gold that presents a problem . . . 10K gold or 14K gold or 18K gold or 24K gold—or gold plated or gold filled.

Because real gold is involved, let's first examine what is meant by gold filled and gold plated—and then proceed to the relatively easy technique for testing scrap gold karatage.

"Gold filled" is a term which indicates a manufacturing process whereby two thin gold sheets with a supporting piece of core metal forms a sort of metal sandwich construction which is then laminated with a brazing alloy into one inseparable sheet.

After this so-called fused ingot is made it is placed in a rolling mill and rolled out to the desired thickness. This filling process must be accomplished *mechanically* in order for the process to be identified as gold filled.

Stamping—under the new amended federal act—indicates the gold content of the sandwich by weight and the karatage. Thus, a GF article stamped "1/20-14K" means that at least 1/20 of the total metal content is comprised of gold and that the gold sheet used was 14K.

Gold plating is an *electrolytic* process is which direct current is used to deposit gold on a host metal. As with gold filled items, the stamping usually indicates the quality by weight in proportion to the weight of the article and the karat of the plate.

Many gold plated articles are not marked with the percentage of the weight of the gold plate. They are marked only with the karat, for example: "14K G.P." or "10K Gold Plate."

Various markings are found in the Gold Filled and Gold Plated area. Many items contain marks such as R.G.P. for "rolled gold plate" or HGP for "Heavy Gold Plate."

Old gold watches with gold plating rarely are marked with the weight or the karat value. The watches were so heavy that they could not be covered economically with gold so as to constitute 1/10 or 1/20 of the weight by gold.

These old watches are valuable, though. You can often find markings that indicate the probable number of years of expected wear . . . 10 year, 20 year and 25 year cases.

Lately, the jewelry industry has been utilizing gold and silver epoxies for low cost jewelry items. The technology here is so advanced that these epoxies need a careful look—and they often wear better than gold plating.

How do you know, then, if that old ring with no markings is gold? And if it is gold, how do you know if it's the minimum of 10K in order to be called gold—or if it's 14K, 18K or 24K? And is there a way to determine if that expensive looking gold piece is gold filled, gold plated, or epoxied. Yes.

There is a refined laboratory technique using a series of chemicals.

There is also a much simpler, less expensive way that was developed and announced by Harry Landis, Inc., a New York refiner.

Let's consider the Landis procedure.

The necessary equipment involves nitric acid. Before going any further, let there be a firm warning at this point: *nitric acid is a must to test gold, but nitric acid when used carelessly is very dangerous. If handled with care, nitric acid will cause no problems.*

Jewelers and precious metal specialists have used nitric acid for centuries with very few incidents, accidents or casualties. But this powerful acid can result in serious pain and injury, and will damage almost anything with which it comes in contact.

It is poisonous and deadly if ingested, even in trivial amounts. You should use it only in a well ventilated area, and wear rubber gloves. Water—for a quick emergency rinse—should be kept readily available. The author and publisher take no responsibility whatsoever for any consequences if or when you use nitric acid, and you take full responsibility for damages to yourself or to others.

To achieve maximum safety in any metal testing, you will need two acid testing bottles with dip sticks, two flat pieces of unglazed porcelain (one will be for 10K and 14K, and the other will be for 18K), pure-grade nitric acid, a pumice stone, a sample each of 10K, 14K and 18K gold, and a small metal file. (Fig. 5-1).

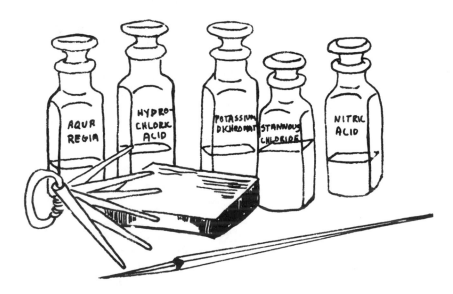

Fig. 5-1 Testing gold for karatage content requires only a few tools. You'll need two bottles to hold the nitric acid and the Aqua Regia, two pieces of unglazed porcelain, a pumice stone, a small metal file and gold samples consisting of 10K, 14K, 18K, and 24K. All of these items are available at a hardware store or chemical supply house.

The porcelain testing stones can be obtained by using an emery cloth to remove the glaze from a procelain dish or saucer. A pumice stone can be obtained at a drug store, and hardware stores—or a chemical supply house—generally can supply some nitric acid.

The gold pieces of various karatage are used as comparison pieces to check against unknown metals.

To test for yellow gold, rub the metal in question on the 14K gold testing stone so that it leaves a mark or streak on the touchstone. Then using the acid bottle dip stick, touch some nitric acid on the streak. Base metal (non gold) will appear green or gray, but 14K gold or better will remain unaffected.

Before proceeding to the next karatage test step, take the file and select an inconspicuous spot that will not mar the item's appearance and file a tiny slot through the surface and into the base metal itself. Apply a light touch of nitric acid to the filed slot and watch carefully.

If you see no change at all, the item is 14K gold or better. If a green color appears in the notch it is a base metal or brass: if the color is a silver alloy the notch will show a dark gray color. If the base metal is white and doesn't react with the acid it could be iron or steel.

For further, higher karatage testing the professional approach is to use *a chemical called aqua regia.* This can be prepared or purchased separately. You can make it yourself with the second bottle of nitric acid by adding a pinch of salt. This converts the acid to aqua regia. Aqua regia is used only on the 18 karat stone.

On the stone with the salt acid, scratch or streak marks made by 10K gold will disappear, a 14K mark will turn dark, and an 18K mark will remain unaffected.

You can clean the testing stones easily by rubbing them with pumice under running water. The stones can be wiped dry with any tissue.

Just be careful not to use the same area of pumice or the same tissue on both stones. If you wipe off the 18K stone and then use the same tissue on the 10K-14K stone the latter stone will be useless for any further testing.

That essentially comprises the technique announced by Landis. It is useful not only with yellow gold. It can be used for testing white gold, using white gold items as comparisons for applying streaks. Most white gold jewelry items are stamped with the karatage.

Silver, the Second Metal . . .

Silver has always played somewhat of a second fiddle to gold as a precious metal. Still, the bright, white metal has had its moments, from William Jennings Bryan's "Cross of Gold" peroration to the Hunt brothers effort to corner the silver market in 1980.

As gold advanced in price at the end of 1979 and into 1980, a greater interest in silver as a jewelry metal developed, not only as the primary metal but as a component of vermeil, a term for a gold plated or gold filled silver.

Like gold, it is a malleable metal, capable of hammering without crumbling, and its softness—a disadvantage for the most part in securing gems—makes it convenient to fashion.

That silver would increase in value along with gold is not too surprising. It is the most attractive of white metals and has enjoyed its role as a precious favorite almost as long as its yellow companion.

Because silver is too soft for general use, it is often alloyed with other metals which can contribute their own unique qualities.

Here is a list of the various compositions of silver alloys and their marks:

Mark	Alloy %	Fine Silver %
.999	Fine or pure	99.9
Hallmark	4.16	95.8
Sterling	7.5% copper	92.5
Coin	10% copper	90.0

Anything with a lower content than 90% fine silver is regarded as low quality silver. Much of this low quality silver is produced for the tourist traffic in Europe, India, Mexico, and the Orient. The fine silver content runs anywhere from 50% up to 80%.

Testing silver is not much more difficult than testing for gold.

Generally, if an item is marked "Sterling" you can trust it. Most silver metal buyers do—unless something is obviously amiss.

Nitric acid reacts very quickly with silver. To determine if the item is silver plated of solid silver, file an inconspicuous slot and apply a drop of nitric acid.

If base metal is underneath the slot will show a green color while the silver plating around the file mark will be gray. Should the item be solid, both the notch and the area around it will be gray.

Only silver does this. No other white metal reacts to nitric acid in this manner. Nickel-silver or the presence of zinc in German silver—both will turn green.

Should the white metal be stainless steel or platinum or white gold there will be no reaction to the acid.

Where you'll generally find silver plated items is in silverware. Inexpensive jewelry items usually are either silver plated or rhodium colored epoxy dip applied over base metal.

The silver plated dinner ware made in the United States is customarily marked "plate" or "plated," together with the maker's brand name and a signature indication. These days, if silverware does not contain a "Sterling" stamping you may be virtually certain that the merchandise is plated.

These Other Precious Metals . . .

The other metals used in jewelry include, of course, platinum, palladium, stainless steel and white gold.

You can spot stainless steel by its light weight and the fact that a drop of hydrochloric acid on the metal will cause tiny bubbles to form.

Both platinum and white gold will be dissolved by aqua regia on the testing stones. The alloys react with the salt acid with the white gold mark dissolving quickly and the platinum streak dissolving not quite so fast. These tests aren't conclusive.

If you wish to test for platinum you'll need another chemical called stannous chloride. Rub the suspected metal on an unglazed porcelain test stone and then dissolve it with a drop of aqua regia.

Once this is done, add a drop of two of stannous chloride solution—and then watch carefully.

Platinum will cause a deep yellow or brown color to form, and if the streak was very rich in platinum the color will be almost black. If palladium is present with the platinum the color will be blue green.

If the streak, though, contains gold the stannous chloride will cause it to first turn an intense purple and then black. If the content of gold is less, the color of the solution will be purple. The greater is the gold amount the more it will turn the solution black.

For the most part palladium, a silvery white metal, is alloyed with rhodium and iridium for a harder metal and is combined with gold and platinum for jewelry use.

Rhodium is a marvelous element which is resistant to oxidation and also impervious to any acid or other solution. Manufacturers of high quality white gold jewelry often electroplate the white gold items with rhodium and this incredible white bright finish—the finish that many people believe to be the look of high karat white gold—is really the rhodium.

Because it contributes to a permanent brilliance and long wearing capability, rhodium is used almost exclusively for electroplating of both gold and silver jewelry.

In the last few years there has been a pleasant revival of popular interest in pewter, a two metal alloy consisting of 65-80% tin and 20-35% lead.

In early New England most of the pewter used was shipped from England, the chief pewter center. It came here either already fabricated or as stock metal which the gifted colony craftsmen such as the renowned silversmith and pewter designer Paul Revere worked.

The one kind of pewter most used is called Brittania metal. It consists of 92% tin, 5% antimony, 3% copper—with no lead. You should consider making pewter purchases from a reliable jeweler or merchant if the items are to be used for food or drink.

A high tin content is necessary when making food vessels formed of pewter. If this isn't done the alloy will produce lead crystals as the molten metal cools—and these crystals can mix with food acids to corrode the metal, contaminate food, and cause lead poisoning.

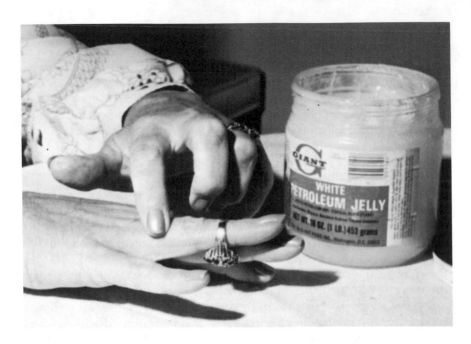

If you're one of the unfortunate few who develop the unsightly metal smudge even when wearing high karat gold and other precious metal, dabbing a little petroleum jelly on your skin just before putting on metal jewelry will inhibit the condition.

Skin Discoloration by Metal . . .

High karat won't discolor your skin like cheap metals will. Have you heard this?

No chapter on metal in jewelry would be complete without some discussion on this age-old problem.

And the answer is, "Oh, yes, even 24K gold can cause skin discolorations for some people." That's no test of the quality of a precious metal.

Is there anything that can be done about this problem? Perhaps.

A couple of manufacturers over the years have announced special salves or chemicals, usually with a petroleum base. I've tested them; gave them to people with a skin-gold problem and they were ineffective. Within a short time, the products had disappeared.

It is believed that individuals who are plagued by this problem—even with precious metals—have a high salt or chloride content in their perspiration with a possibility of some other triggering chemical.

Metals discolor the skin through a combination of secretions or perspiration containing these chlorides and, it is thought, sulfides, which interact with the copper and silver molecules in the gold alloy.

It isn't so much the gold that does it as it is the alloy. These baser metals and the chlorides and sulfides form dark-colored salts of either copper sulfate or silver chloride.

The chloride problem is particularly noticeable in seacoast and semitropical areas. The rubbing of these salts—both from the climate and the perspiration—is what causes the unsightly smudge.

There is the additional problem of smog. Fumes which are filled with particles of silver dioxide and phosphate will gradually attack jewelry and this assault is seen as a tarnish which rubs off on the skin.

If you have a skin discoloring problem, try moving up the karatage of your gold jewelry. Because of the lower copper content 18K gold doesn't smudge as quickly as 14K. You might also consider switching to white gold (which contains no copper) or palladium.

Some petroleum jelly applied to the skin area that will come in contact with metal has also been demonstrated to retard the smudge. Try painting clear fingernail polish on the metal where it contacts the skin.

CHAPTER SIX

DIAMONDS: The Greeks Called Them Unconquerable

Diamond!

The mere mention of the king of gems conjures thoughts of beauty, value . . . even intrigue.

Blessed with every desirable virtue of a gemstone, the diamond has conquered attention throughout recorded history. Is it any wonder the name derives from the Greek "adamas" meaning unconquerable? After all, no other mineral or element on the face of the earth comes close to matching the diamond's hardness.

One of the earliest scales designed to compare the relative hardness of minerals is called the Mohs scale. This scale assigns numbers of 1 through 10 to all minerals, with each number on the scale designating a hardness level capable of scratching minerals with a lower number (Fig. 6-1). On this scale, your fingernail rates 2½ in hardness and a steel file rates 6½—which is why a file scratches away at your nails so effectively. The diamond—alone on the scale at 10—would scratch away at the file at a prodigious rate.

This is partially why diamond setters, in touching up the metal prongs around a diamond, are so careful not to scrape their hard steel files against the diamond. Catching a facet edge with the file might cause a chip but the diamond can severely damage the file.

What's often not understood about a Mohs scale is that the scale is geometric rather than arithmetic. The diamond's 10 rating is many times harder than the second hardest mineral, corundum (the mineral, remember, of rubies and sapphires) which occupies a 9. Various tests have indicated that diamond is at least 140 times as hard as corundum, and some scientists have concluded that the difference is as high as 1,000 times or more.

It's this hardness which allows one to polish a diamond to such a fine adamantine (a gemological term signifying the highest possible polish) finish. The same hardness makes diamond invaluable as an industrial abrasive.

From the beginning, diamonds have followed a double path to value. On the one hand, they were treasured as valued ornaments and objects of awe. At the same time, cave dwellers saw in the diamond's hardness a benefit useful for engraving and drilling.

Mohs' Scale of Hardness

Talc 1
Gypsum 2
Calcite 3
Fluorite 4
Opal 5
Orthoclase 6
Quartz 7
Topaz 8
Corundum 9
Diamond 10

The following objects can be utilized to compare relative hardness.

	Mohs' Hardness Value
Fingernail	2-½
Copper penny	2-¾
Fine Steel Knife	6
Window Glass	5-½

Fig. 6-1 The scale of relative hardness is named after the German mineralogist Friedrich Mohs who proposed it in 1822. Numbers do not indicate equal divisions of hardness. Diamond is many times as hard as corundum, which is only slightly harder than topaz. Stones of higher numbers will scratch those of lower numbers although virtually all gems vary somewhat in hardness in different crystal directions. Please note why glass scratching is hardly a test for diamond authenticity (almost *all* gems are harder than glass.)

Thousands of years have seen little fundamental change. Today, computers drive diamond tipped cutting tools for the most intricate and complex purposes; the modern oil industry thrives on the famous diamond tipped drilling bit.

Until sufficient technology and crystallographic understanding came into the picture, diamonds were worn in their natural state as talismans in the belief that they imbued the wearer with courage and invincibility. By the Middle Ages the wealthy had attached themselves to the gems as adornments to reflect power and wealth.

In response to its spectacular qualities, early civilizations invested the diamond with supernatural powers. For example, a diamond is unwettable; you can test this because it is one of the only gems that you can pick up merely by touch with a damp finger.

Consequently, a drop of water placed on the surface of a diamond will "ball up." That unusual phenomenen did not long go unnoticed and it was a reasonable shift in thinking to believe that poison—often being a liquid—would "ball up" also. So, the belief developed that diamonds had the power to resist all poisons, that they became dark in the presence of poison because the particles of poison "balled up"on the diamond surface and couldn't penetrate.

But, if the diamond was taken internally, it was further believed, it was an exceedingly powerful poison. As a matter of fact, when Catherine de Medici's ring tipped and powder was spilled into a drink—the infamous *poudre de sucession*—it was thought to be powdered diamond. Historians

91

go along with this—plus the presence of a goodly amount of arsenic.

Diamonds also had an important role as medicine. When Pope Clement VII turned suddenly ill in 1532 he was prescribed the usual powdered precious stones as medicine. Powdered diamond was, of course, included in the concoction. Its effect was problematic because the Pope succumbed after the fourteenth spoonful, complaining of a certain sore heaviness in his tummy.

Magical powders? The diamond offered a splendid spectrum of benefits. It was greatly helpful in winning lawsuits in favor of the wearer (with no mention of the outcome should both sides wear one); it repelled demons and kept one free from nightmares, and it would protect a house from lightning and winds if all of the outside walls were touched by a diamond.

Curiously enough, the belief persisted for years that a diamond held between the teeth would cause the teeth to fall out. Today, a jeweler will recommend to you to hold your diamond ring in your teeth when you wash your hands in a sink.

The jeweler's advice, really, is directed at avoiding the experience of watching your diamond disappear down the drain hole after slipping from a well lubricated finger. Secondly, he wants you to avoid any contact between your diamond and any grease that may be in the water.

Diamonds may be unwettable but they have an enormous liking for grease. In the mining of diamonds, the diamonds are extracted from the blue ground by washing the diamond-containing mud over a belt smeared with a thick grease coating.

The dirt washes over the belt easily, but the diamonds stick to the grease as if magnetized. Plunge a diamond-ringed hand into sink water which contains grease—and you can't get your hand out fast enough to avoid having your diamond coated with grease. Needless to say, the brilliance and fire of the diamond is thus reduced as the grease increases the critical angle of the stone's light reflecting ability.

The disturbing element about the sink-grease thing is that grease coats the hardest-to-clean-part of the diamond—the pavilion—and it is here where the "soul" of a beautiful well cut diamond dwells. The top or crown can be a bit dirty and you can still have an exciting gem. When the bottom or pavilion is dirty the diamond has lost its awesome power—the ability to reflect so much light back into the eye of the viewer.

There is an additional danger in keeping a diamond ring on your finger in the sink. A filled sink contains an abundance of hard items—plates, metal frying pans, silverware. In working in the sink it is not unusual to bang your diamond hard against these utensils and possibly break or chip it. Diamonds aren't tough; they are brittle and break or chip surprisingly easy.

While a diamond is the hardest element in the universe its hardness varies with direction. Only a diamond can scratch a diamond and then only when the hard grain of one diamond is oriented against the softer grain direction of the second diamond.

In contast with the diamond's great hardness and low toughness, jade ranks only 6½-7 on the Mohs scale—but its fibrous structure makes it so tough that the Chinese—and modern goldsmiths have learned of this virtue—have been using it as anvil material for thousands of years.

Perhaps the confusion between hardness and toughness will never be cleared up completely. That diamond was also tough was even contained in the ancient writings of the Roman philosopher, Pliny the Elder:

> *"These stones (diamonds) are tested upon the anvil, and will resist the blow to such an extent as to make the iron rebound and the very anvil split asunder."*

Only a wisdom far, far greater than ours will ever know how many fine diamond crystals were destroyed in this belief . . . that a hammer test was the conclusive proof needed to authenticate a diamond. Indeed, there is evidence that early merchants in India often encouraged the ignorant miners to apply this test—and then scooped up the diamond fragments after the disappointed miners had departed.

A Touch of Diamond History . . .

So long as diamonds were used as medicines, magical amulets and talismans in their natural state—and while the knowledge and equipment was still absent—there was little need or desire to cut, shape, and polish the crystals.

As man became more familiar with the physical and optical characteristics of this hard crystal, he began the evolutionary process of fashioning. First, he probably learned how to polish natural diamond faces with diamond dust. Next, he may have learned that a diamond's hardness varies with direction . . . the key to cutting and polishing.

Then he perhaps found a way to cleave or split a diamond. A diamond can be cleaved easily—but only in a certain direction. Diamonds mostly occur in the octahedral shape (Fig. 6-2) which resembles two pyramids attached at their bases.

The cleaving direction runs *only* parallel to each of these pyramid faces. So any cleaving necessarily produces an increasingly smaller octahedral form . . . sort of like shedding or flaking off layer after layer of small triangular pyramid face shapes so the original octahedral shape merely grows smaller with each shedding.

Old records are convincing that the original faces of diamond crystals found in their natural state were somehow polished. Just how this was done is still not known because the natural pyramid faces (called octahedral faces) of a diamond crystal represents the hardest grain direction—and so the natural faces can not be cut or polished. The plane or angle of each octahedral face must be tilted slightly to obtain a softer grain direction.

With dust, the polishing could be done because it assures the hard grain-against-soft grain contact. Here, the random orientation of the small

Fig. 6-2 Diamonds are most often found in the rough octahedral shape. The cleaving plane of a diamond is parallel to the octahedral face, i.e., each of the triangular faces.

diamond dust particles assures that some of the particles will be scratching at all times with the hard grain up. The diamond being polished must be properly oriented to display its soft grain to this dust cutting action.

Refinement in the understanding of the hard-soft grain scratching aspect no doubt led to the technique of *bruting* which involves setting a whole diamond crystal into a stick. The tipped stick is held against a rotating diamond crystal so as to round up or scratch off the square corners. This allowed cutters to create the shapes they wanted.

Diamond cutting probably originated in Venice about 1330. By the 14th and 15th Century the mechanically turned iron cutting wheel had been introduced, and cutters were freed from the limitations of hand bruting or rubbing crystals against a flat powdered surface.

By the end of the 15th Century the art had spread to other cities. By this time, too, the secret of sawing diamond crystals was spreading. Small circular phosphor-bronze blades coated with diamond powder and turning at more than 3,000 rpm are used now, but in earlier times the task was performed with a kind of bow string which consisted of diamond powder smeared on a fine brass or iron wire attached to a piece of cane or whalebone.

Occasionally, diamond—whose carbon atoms form in the cubic habit—is actually found in the rough in a cube or square shape. The sawing direction of a diamond runs *only* parallel to one of the six cube or squared faces.

Inasmuch as pieces of diamond rough are found in many odd, complex shapes, it requires professional expertise—long kept secret by industry craftsmen who for decades have been close-mouthed about their art—to "read" the rough and determine in which directions the cubic faces run (which reveals the saw plane) and in which directions the octahedral faces run (which reveals the cleaving and cutting planes).

"Reading" the Diamond . . .

You'll probably never encounter the need to determine sawyering or cleaving planes through "reading" diamond rough. That's a job for diamond cutters (in 1907, world famous diamond cutter Joseph Asscher was entrusted with the task of "reading" the grain of the 3,106-carat Cullinan diamond—the biggest diamond ever found—and then cleaving it. On Feb. 10, before De Beers executives and photographers Asscher applied the multi-million dollar blow for his first, vital cleave. The crystal did not fall apart as expected—Asscher did, in a dead faint. He'd really "read" correctly, though, and the second, stronger blow did the job . . . when struck some time later. Asscher's son denies this fainting story.)

For buying or selling finished diamonds you should know how to "read" the quality of the crystal itself as well as to evaluate the level of workmanship going into the final product. Good workmanship can't make a fine diamond out of poor quality rough—but it can bring out as much potential beauty as the raw crystal has to offer.

The two elements must be in harmony . . . material and craft skill. When they are balanced the evidence is there for anyone to see . . . to "read." The clues are not secrets to be kept hidden from ultimate owners or to feed the "I know something you don't" ego of certain sales people.

The techniques given in this chapter are intended for your use under everyday conditions . . . less than ideal or laboratory conditions. It's been done this way for the simple reason that you will seldom inspect a diamond or gemstone under the best of cirucimstances. For properly evaluating diamond color, the professional recommends that viewing be done under special filtered, cool, low intensity flourescent lighting.

This isn't always possible or convenient.

Nor will you probably encounter a room whose walls, ceiling and floor feature the flat dead-white coloring of many gem labs.

What you will be dealing with are the interiors of modern jewelry stores—often majestic examples of the interior designer's skills . . . decorated in a manner to dramatize and enhance the merchandise offered for sale through a judicious combination of lighting, soft colors, and textures, showcases, trays, etc.

The jeweler isn't seeking to camouflage anything. He's merely a retailer who realizes that a pleasant, attractive, inviting store atmosphere is conducive to customer pleasure and sales. Often as not, the better jewelers prominently display instruments intended for your use.

Luxurious surroundings—rather than northern light, special light boxes, and dead-white rooms—aren't insurmountable obstacles to making accurate and intelligent evaluations. You can make a surprisingly precise judgement—and any additional appraisal or representation can be covered by the jeweler's warranty.

The Power of Magnification . . .

A knowledgeable eye is the most valuable asset you can bring to a diamond evaluation. Sometimes, though, it isn't enough and to aid you when the going gets tough you really should own your own magnifying loupe.

To the Federal Trade Commission and the jewelry industry a flaw doesn't—by definition—exist so long as a trained observer can not detect it even with the aid of 10x magnification corrected for any spherical or chromatic aberration.

Corrected 10 power. That's the industry standard magnifying help. Even with this you—and people in the jewelry industry itself—will be hard pressed to remain a "trained observer" without extensive daily exposure to diamond grading. In other words, you need constant practice to keep your eye in tip-top shape.

For the average individual this pretty much becomes an impossibility. To help equalize the situation between you and someone trained at viewing diamonds, buy yourself a 15x or 20x magnifying loupe. The greater magnification will assist your not tip-top grading eye to see things you might otherwise overlook, what a trained observer would see with a lower 10x magnifier.

By upping your magnifying assistance it tilts things a bit in your favor. Some industry people may wrinkle their nose a bit at this . . . but if there's any doubt you can always go back to a 10x loupe and, knowing where to look after the 15x inspection, check the matter out. Besides, diamond grading is best done with unmounted stones and you will be dealing mostly with set or mounted ones.

More and more jewelry stores are providing stereoscopic microscopes for their customers' use when making a gem purchase. *All* of these instruments have more than just the 10x setting and you should feel no compunction whatsoever about having the salesman "kick up the magnifying power so I can have a good look."

The response sometimes will be less than enthusiastic, even to the point of telling you it isn't or can't be done. You can decide on your own reaction to this putoff—but it is and can be done ALL THE TIME . . . even in laboratories (they say they never "kick up" for a good look but only the technician knows).

What looks like a magnificent diamond to the naked eye or even under 10x may, when viewed under 45x, abruptly resemble a white piece of material that has been riddled with a machine gun after being chopped with a woodman's axe. Most of what you'll see at the higher magnification just doesn't matter, but be prepared for a real shock on that first view. Water in a drinking glass looks fine but all those little bugs swimming around that are disclosed by a microscope view are anything but reassuring—and a highly magnified view of a fine diamond is disturbingly similar.

Just be prepared for it.

Take Your Initial Look . . .

Whether the diamond you intend to "read" is in a mounting or not, whether you are in a retail jewelry store or not, your first step in the evaluation process is to gain a general impression of the famous "Four Cs"—cut, clarity, color, and carat.

As the first step, make a mental note of the kind of lighting you're in so you can discount its influence accordingly. Intense white light might make a diamond sparkle but such light masks yellow as well as blue tints.

Cool, fluorescent lighting is best.

Make a tentative decision about the stone's color. Is it a clear transparent white, a tinted white (yellow, green or brown tint visible?), or a brightly colored fancy?

Turn the diamond so that you may look straight down through the table, peering toward the bottom where the culet is located (Fig. 6-3). Do the bottom facets present the usual mirror-like brilliance which comes only from light being reflected . . . or is the bottom "fish eyed" or "blackened."

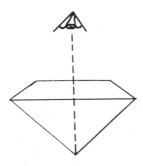

Fig. 6-3 Your first look at a diamond should be straight down through the table to make a tentative appraisal of color, shape, brilliance and fire.

Rock the diamond back and forth a few times?

Does this action cause it to sparkle, show fire, disperse colors with bright little flashes?

Now note the general shape of the diamond. Is it symetrical? If the diamond is obviously cut in the round brilliant mode is the round shape truly round? Are there any cutting distortions to the round shape making it

97

appear less round . . . or less than a true marquise shape . . . or less than true oval shape . . . or less than a true pear or heart shape?

If there are any distortions or flat sections in the girdle outline you may be assured that other cutting problems exist in domino fashion.

Check the outline of the table facet? It should be a true octagon in the round brilliant cut and possess a particular configuration for the round cut's variations (Fig. 6-4). For round cuts particularly, is the table symetrical? Check the border slant outline with the star facets (Fig. 6-5) as the first clue to table size.

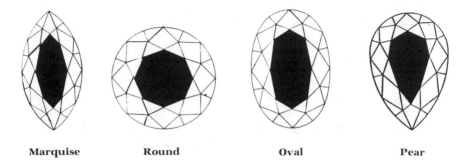

| Marquise | Round | Oval | Pear |

Fig. 6-4 If the diamond has been cut to normal proportions, the table facet will appear in the configurations shown above.

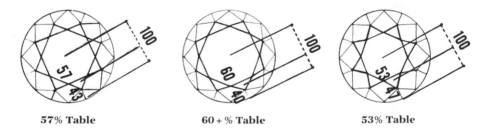

| 57% Table | 60 + % Table | 53% Table |

Fig. 6-5 The edges of the table facet and the star facets will provide a reference line for estimating the approximate character of table width.

If the line tends to bend in you have a table size close to the Tolkowsky proportions (long regarded in the United States as the *ideal* brilliant cut proportions capable of returning the maximum combination of brilliance and fire). If the line is relatively straight, you have the modern brilliant cut which has a "slightly spread" table (this cut, long popular in Europe as the Scandanavian cut has essentially replaced the Tolkowsky cut in the U.S. because it allows better recovery rates from rough to finished cut—and because it makes the final diamond look bigger).

Should the line curve in a sort of circular pattern, you'll undoubtedly note that it takes up much of the crown while making the stone appear larger. Such a table is "swindled" and gains the bigger appearance at considerable sacrifice to the crown facets which naturally must be smaller, and consequently show less fire.

Now look at the diamond from a sideview (Fig. 6-6). From table to culet, the pavilion normally should represent about two-thirds of the depth. The crown should be about one-third.

When using a loupe keep both eyes open, and brace the hand holding the gem against the other hand to steady the gem.

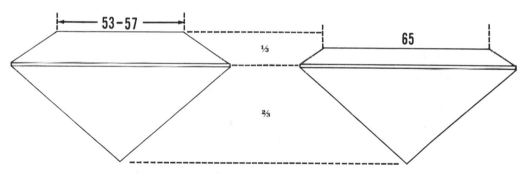

Fig. 6-6 A normally proportioned gem will have about one-third of its height above the girdle with the other two-thirds below the girdle. When a table is spread or "swindled", the distortion often produces a variation in this ratio.

If the diamond has a spread or swindled table it's unlikely that the crown will come anywhere near being one-third of the depth. It's thickness will be much less which makes it appear a bit out of proportion to the pavilion which now appears deeper.

Do you now have a general impression of the overall diamond? You should have some mental or, preferably, written notes of any peculiarity that you noted.

Following the general impressions, it's time to put your magnifying loupe to your eye and begin a more precise inspection.

If there is anything that reveals the amateur in a jewelry store, it is the unnecessary habit of squinting one eye while looking through a magnifying loupe. Those who work all day with a loupe do not squint because to do so would fatigue the eye muscles very quickly.

When you begin using a loupe, force yourself to keep both eyes open. This will seem awkward and confusing at first because most people are under the mistaken impression that they can see better if one eye is shut. Actually, the opposite is true; you can see much better when both eyes are open—and you concentrate on careful observation with the loupe eye. Try it; you'll soon see that closing or squinting one eye is but a habit and that by keeping both eyes open you have much less eye strain and difficulty seeing.

Hold the loupe firmly to the eye and the gem or jewelry piece slightly to one side. In order to keep the stone steady and in focus, try resting a finger of the hand holding the loupe on the hand holding the tweezer. This way, you can extend or contract your finger to achieve a fine focus.

As for holding the stone, you'll find that picking an unmounted stone up by tweezers or tongs is easiest if the stone has been placed table down on a flat surface. The tips of the tweezers should pass the center line of the stone. With unmounted stones, many people prefer locking type tweezers although they do tend to be a bit of a nuisance when you are switching position on a stone or viewing a number of stones at a time. If the stone is in a mounting, the shank of a ring or the metal is usually held easily by hand.

Let's begin with "CUT."

With the loupe to your eye turn the diamond so that you are peering directly through the table toward the culet.

First, check the culet size, shape and position. Is the culet small (it should be), octagonal shaped (it should be unless its been chipped or abraded or one of the main facets has been cut improperly) and is it directly below the middle of the table with the right facet join lines from the main pavilion facets arriving at the culet in rigid symetrical discipline? This is important because any off-center deviation of the culet suggests a cutting problem somewhere.

Where would you search for a reason if the culet appears off center? Cutting one or more main pavilion facets at more or less than 41° would shift the culet. The same would hold true if the cutter laid in some crown main facets at more or less than the angles at which the other crown mains were cut. All other cuts being equal, this would shift the table facet sidewise, making the culet appear off center. (Fig. 6-7).

If you had observed—or made a note of—any anomaly in your "once over lightly" perusal you'd find that one clue would re-inforce another until the domino effect became apparent and the cutting error was fully revealed to you. Now would be a good time to inspect with a magnifier any apparent defects the earlier look disclosed.

100

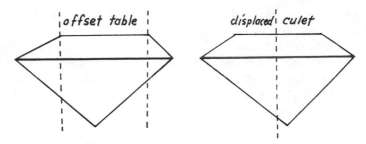

Fig. 6-7 The culet should appear off center because the pavilion main facets—in a round cut—or the crown main facets were not all cut at the same angle, thus causing the culet to actually be off center (in the case of pavilion shifting) or appear off center because crown angles have shifted the entire table out of center.

Be sure to check the size and uniformity of the row of eight star facets bordering the table, next the row of eight kite shaped main facets, and finally the row of 16 triangular shaped girdle crown facets. The facets in each row series should be the same size and shape?

With the diamond still perpendicular to your eye, double check the table width proportion. Current cutting practices provide for a table width —usually—of between 55% and 60% of the diameter of the stone.

Your initial overview probably gave you a strong indication of the approximate width. You can narrow the percentage estimate down now with the help of the loupe. Just estimate from the centered culet to the edge of the diamond what percentage of that distance the table represents (Fig. 6-8).

Does the table reach precisely half way? If so, you'd have a 50% table. You won't often find a table that small in a jewelry store. More likely

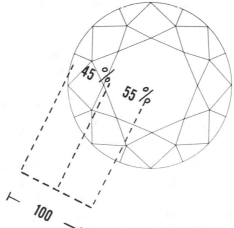

Fig. 6-8 The percentage of table width to the gem's diameter can be calculated rather closely by estimating the distance from the culet to the edge of the table and to the edge of the gem. Note that the line runs through the flat edge of the table.

101

you'll see one in estate jewelry sales or in a family heirloom because it's an old fashioned proportion.

Such small tables are often indicative of an old squarish looking cut, called a "miner cut," and they are sometimes responsible for amazing frog-to-prince success stories after a relatively inexpensive re-cutting (which is why estate jewelry buyers are so anxious to get ahold of them).

Old Miner   **Old European**

Some confusion exists between older cuts known as "Old Miners" and "Old European" cuts. The former is squarish in shape while the "Old European" is rounder looking; both have noticeably small table facets.

In a jewelry store you are more apt to encounter diamonds whose tables vary in width from 55% of the diameter to as high as 70%.

Now use a technique pioneered by the GIA for "eye balling" the correct pavilion cutting angles on reasonably well proportioned round brilliant cuts.

Without changing the gem's position relative to your loupe look for an umbrella-like gray reflection which begins at the culet and extends equilaterally about ⅓ to ½ of the way toward the table's edge.

The pattern—actually a reflection of the table—appears as a more reflective or brighter area (Fig. 6-9). Initially, you may have some minor difficulty perceiving it, but in a well-proportioned round cut it's there. Only poorly proportioned and non-round diamonds fail to produce this pattern.

To gain maximum advantage of the diamond's high 2.42 Refractive Index as well as its other high optical properties, the main pavilion facets of a diamond—regardless of the type of cut—must be 41° If these bottom main facets are cut at a lesser angle, the diamond will "fish eye" or turn transparent. As the facets are cut at a higher angle the bottom of the diamond will turn progressively blacker.

Cutting the main pavilion facets at 41° produces a pavilion with a depth 43% of the diameter of a round cut diamond. This depth proportion holds true only for the standard round brilliant cut; it does not hold for the variations of the round cut.

But the pavilion main facets of *ALL diamond cuts must still be 41°*. Diamond's optical character demands such a main pavilion angle, and it requires a 34° angle on the crown mains. Unlike the pavilions, deviations in crown angles don't carry such an extreme optical penalty.

A bit more of explanation may be in order at this point. The umbrella on a properly proportioned pavilion will be about ⅓—but it can go up to ½ and still reflect 43% if the crown is a bit thick. As it is but a reflection of the table the longer distance this reflection must travel through the gem depth the more the umbrella will tend to expand . . . yet the proper angle of 41⁰ is still being observed.

So, "eyeball" the depth of the diamond. Or take a careful measurement. Determine the depth of the top or crown part. It should be about ⅓ of the gem's heighth or, more precisely and ideally in the case of a diamond, 14.5% of the diamond's diameter for a 57% table or 16.2% of the diamond's diameter for a 53% table.

When the table is swindled beyond 60% of the diameter, it involves a thinner crown so the umbrella will be a bit smaller than ⅓—but not too much. When the umbrella starts shrinking below the ⅓ mark it's generally a sign that the pavilion is shallow.

In the round cut or one of its pear, marquise or oval variations, either all or at least two opposite bottom-most facets—the culet facets—must indeed be at 41⁰ (or at least very near 41⁰). Regardless, the pavilion must contain main facets which address themselves to this optical requirement.

About Other Umbrellas . . .

That's why, if you were to ask if there is an umbrella effect visible in the pear, marquise, or oval, the answer would be, "yes, but—"

A reflection of the table can be seen at the culet on these fancy cuts—*but* the reflection pattern is not an umbrella. Table reflections will only be visible on the two opposing facets that are cut close to 41⁰—in other words, only two facets will show the slight gray reflection. These two facets are the curve-edge facets, and the reflection will extend about halfway up because these facets, remember, were cut above 41⁰. Consequently, the depth of the pavilion is generally a bit deeper than a round cut's 43% ratio.

Summarizing, look for the umbrella effect in round cut diamonds; look for two reflections in the brilliant fancy cuts and these reflections will occur only on the two opposing curve-edge base facets. These latter reflections are often extremely difficult to see in modern point culet fashioning. They are somewhat easier to see on knife-edge culets because of the wider area taken up by the curve-edge base facets.

Emerald and step cuts? What about eyeballing them?

There's a bit of a different cutting approach—and optical challenge —with these cuts . . . particularly diamonds.

With virtually every gem material except diamond, the principle pavilion facets—those addressing the critical angle requirement for a particular material—are the ones forming the culet. These are the facets containing the angle from which any deviation will impair the stone's beauty.

When a cutter determines the required angle for a gem's main pavilion facets these individually angled facets are placed at the bottom of—usually—the three rows of pavilion facets. In the case of diamond, though, the critical or main 41º facets are in the *second* or *middle* row.

Cutters generally place an angle of 52º-54º on the row next to the girdle, then a main facet row at 41º-(max) 42º—with the bottom culet row at 37º. Prior to 1950, this bottom row was usually at 38º. With refinements in sawing diamonds, cutters thickened the middle portions of emerald cuts (to make them heavier and thus obtain a higher carat price) after 1950—at the expense of brilliance.

There was a short period of over-compensation when customers balked at the appearance and the bottom row was cut at 36º to pull "life" back to the center of the stone. This caused an optical problem—and one for which you should be on the alert.

When a diamond has been cut in the emerald or step cut with three pavilion rows and the bottom culet row has been cut at 36º you can detect this over-compensated cut by holding the diamond with tweezers so that the tweezer prongs grip the long side of the gem.

If the bottom row has been cut at 36º the tweezer ends will be reflected across the bottom-most culet facets. The same characteristic will be visible if the diamond is in a mounting and the claws or setting prongs are on the long side. If you must, hold a small object next to the girdle on the long side and check the culet facets. The reflection will be quickly and easily seen if the culet facets are at 36º.

This phenomenon disappears when the bottom culet facets are cut at 37º. That's why, today, the bottom row of diamond emerald cuts are at 37º—unless the cutter is doing a little "swindling" i.e., jacking up one or more rows of facet angles to get more weight into the finished gem.

The round brilliant with its near-perfect symmetry is the most brilliant performer of all diamond cuts. Other brilliant cuts are but variations of the round and they achieve their distinct configurations at the expense of brilliance.

To produce the oval, heart, pear, or marquise shapes the angles as well as facet shapes and sizes must be modified to produce a point at the culet (especially to meet the requirement that some main pavilion facets must be laid at 41°). The width to length distortions in these cuts produces a unique optical pattern called the "bow tie effect." (Fig. 6-10). When the pavilions of these variant cuts are properly angled you'll notice this specific effect, looking down through the table.

This is especially true for pear, marquise and oval cuts made prior to 1950. Up to that time, these cuts were fashioned with a knife edge culet and the base curve edge facets (curve edge facets are those bottom or top facets that are placed at the curving portion of these cuts) were laid in at angles of 41½ to 42¾. Other facets in the pavilion, obviously, were cut at shallower angles—and these opposing curve edge facets at the more precise reflecting angle give off the "bow tie" effect.

After 1950, cutters developed the technique for bringing all the base facets to a point culet. This tended to eliminate the "bow tie." Still, some cutters when faced with varying width-to-length problems continue to play with the angles on the curve edge facets, i.e., exceeding the maximum 42¾°—or they simply don't bring the base facets to a point—and the "bow tie" is visible even on post-1950 cuts.

Sometimes, too, you'll see a "bow tie" effect even with a point culet cut with proper angles. This can be caused because the brillianteerer did not bring the triangular shaped pavilion girdle facets the required 9/10ths of the way down from the girdle to the culet on the curve-edge facets. Unless the girdles are brought down this close to the culet, a "bow tie" can occur.

Because there is a great deal of optical excitement around the small facets in the sharp, pointed ends of marquise, pear, and heart shaped cuts you should remain on the lookout for "color draw" at these points.

The point facets should only be about 3° shallower than the adjacent facets (often called wing facets) on a diamond. When they are not, the points tend to draw color. If there is any residual yellow, green, or brown in the diamond's color it will be more readily detectable at the points.

Now, turn the diamond so that you may view it from the side or in silhouette.

| A | B | C |

Fig. 6-9 The gray appearing "umbrella" reflection which appears around the culet provides an accurate read-out on pavilion depth on well proportioned round cuts. An umbrella which takes up ⅓ to slightly under ½ of the table area indicates a diamond whose pavilion main facets have been cut at 41° which provides a depth of 43% of the gem's diameter. "A" shows the umbrella for a 43% pavilion; "B" displays the umbrella for a pavilion whose depth runs 45%; "C" shows no umbrella for a pavilion where the cutting angle is less than 41°.

Check to see that the table and the girdle are parallel (Fig. 6-11). This requires a bit of eyeball engineering, but any deviation can usually be seen.

Some observers lay the diamond table down on a flat surface—such as glass table top—and guesstimate parallelism by comparison with the girdle line to the table and if the culet position is perpendicular.

On mounted pieces—if the gemstone has a sufficiently large table—the same approach may be followed, watching the ring shank to see if it sticks straight up. You'll need to be certain that ring design or crooked stone settings aren't responsible for any leaning.

Shift your magnified attention to the girdle line, turning the diamond through a full 360° to ascertain if the girdle is the same width all the way around. Any change in the thickness indicates a facet—or more— is also

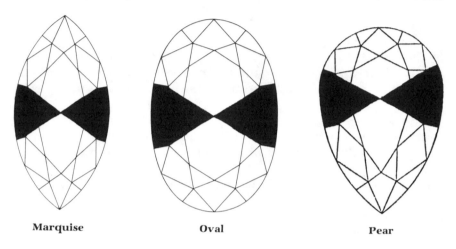

Marquise   Oval   Pear

Fig. 6-10 Only some of the pavilion main facets can be cut at 41° when variations of the round cut are cut to a point culet. This provides greater reflection from these facets, creating the unique "bow tie" effect seen in well-cut ovals, marquises, pears, etc.

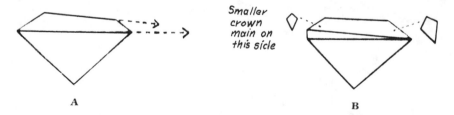

Smaller crown main on this side

A   B

Fig. 6-11 Parallelism between the plane of the table facet and the gem's girdle can be checked visually. In "A" the gem's table has been tilted, usually to remove an inclusion or simply poor cutting. A difference in size of the crown main facets often will reveal a tilted table—and a wavy girdle line "B" will also disclose that some adjusting took place.

off and you'll probably find the culprits immediately adjacent to the defective girdle section (Fig. 6-12)

Check also to determine if the crown facets lie directly over their pavilion counterparts in strict alignment. Misalignment is almost unheard of in diamond cutting—but it is sometimes encountered with colored stones. Also, the pavilions girdle facets should extend about 75% of the way from the girdle toward the culet.

"Flawless" is a Definition . . .

No diamond is truly "flawless" in the sense that it is devoid of any imperfection. Nature just wasn't that perfect when it made the diamond.

As you already know, when you view a clear white, brilliant gem purported to be a diamond and you see no inclusions or blemishes of any kind even with the aid of a magnifier—it's time to start worrying. Such

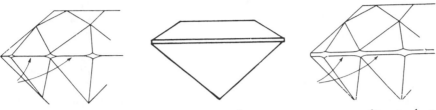

Too thin
Easily chipped in setting

Too thick
Exceeds 3% Maximum

About right
Runs 1-3% of
gem height even
when polished

Fig. 6-12 Normally, the girdle should be only about 2% of the total gem heighth. A thicker girdle comes from faceting the girdle, thickening to mute brown tints, touching up to correct other cutting errors, or defective cutting.

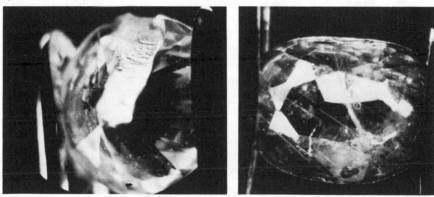

Fig. 6-13 Proof that diamonds are only hard—not tough. This diamond was fractured along the pavilion when its owner pounded it on a dining room table top to demonstrate to a friend that diamonds can take hard knocks (they can't). Diamond's hardness enables it to scratch anything, but a diamond is brittle . . . easily broken or chipped.

Fig. 6-14 Virtually all natural gemstones can be identified by their distinctive imperfections. Natural ruby, for instance, can often be identified because it contains long, slim needle inclusions which cross each other at 140°—and when enough of these inclusions occur they provide the necessary ingredient for a star.

perfection hints strongly that you aren't dealing with a diamond but rather a man-made synthetic of some kind.

Maturity is coming into the diamond marketplace. Once upon a hopefully forgotten time, the closing sales argument of every diamond sales person was something to the effect that it's " . . . a perfect blue white . . ." Perhaps you have heard this old bromide.

The Federal Trade Commission and the American Gem Society have both issued strict limitations on use of "perfect" including the use of "blue white" which is prohibited unless the diamond truly shows a blue color—and no other.

Today, most people know that a diamond contains imperfections that there are few if any "perfect blue-white". It's a beneficial realization. The inclusions and blemishes of a diamond are as distinctive as fingerprints and are invaluable in identifying one diamond from another.

With the recognition then that each diamond should have distinctive imperfections, let's turn to CLARITY.

In your first over-all impression you may or may not have noticed some inclusions or blemishes. It's a surprising fact that you will often overlook inclusions if you do not *deliberately* look for them.

Remember, too, that looking straight down through the table is the hardest way to go because that's smack into the maximum display of brilliance which succeeds in masking many inclusions. The earlier naked eye inspection could have separated the diamond between top end investment grade and lower commercial merchandise. When you can see inclusions with the naked eye—particularly when they also occur within the table—the diamond occupies the low end of the commercial scale and should be priced accordingly.

Inclusions can be tiny—so clarity grading should be performed while you're comfortable, preferably seated, under transmitted light (Fig. 6-15) which provides near dark field illumination so inclusions can more easily be seen, and in a manner which allows you to hold the diamond steady. A jeweler's stereoscopic microscope provides this kind of illumination and convenience of holding. In any event, you'll need magnification to check clarity.

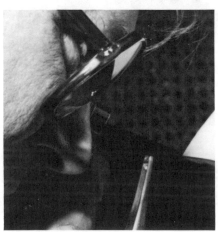

Fig. 6-15 When inspecting a diamond for imperfections, keep the gem out of the direct light. By viewing in transmitted light, the effect is to create a dark field background which makes inclusions stand out better. Keep the diamond behind the light or hold up a card or deflector as you inspect with your loupe.

If the diamond is in a ring or other mounting you obviously will have something to hold onto. For loose or unmounted stones you'll need a pair of tweezers, preferably the locking type so the stone won't fall if you perchance release pressure on the tweezer arms. Needless to say, have something under the diamond should you accidentally drop it. (Loose diamonds are like high-powered fleas; they jump and bounce with awesome zest, landing predictably in the one spot you overlook.)

You'll first want to examine the gem internally. The best method for this is to peer through the crown and pavilion facets (Fig. 6-16). Rather than fight the brilliance coming out of the table, the side view offers the assistance of the facets which can reflect an inclusion many times, increasing your chances of seeing it. Once you spot an inclusion and have a reasonably accurate idea of where it is, you can then look through the table. Turn the diamond a full 360° to make certain you miss no area of the gem.

Fig. 6-16 View a diamond directly through the table and you expose your vision to its full brilliance and fire—fine for appreciation but poor for locating imperfections. View perpendicular to the crown facet planes or, preferably, perpendicular to the pavilion facets. This minimizes the brilliance problem and cuts down on reflections, allowing you a better view. Turn the diamond upside down when you view it with a loupe.

For the surface or external examination adjust your diamond and your light source position so light will reflect off the surface of the diamond and again rotate the diamond a full 360°, examining both the top and bottom. The light hitting the surface greatly increases the visibility factor in locating surface imperfection such as naturals on the girdle, knots, open fizzures, extra facets (sometimes a cutter will polish in a tiny extra facet to remove an inclusion or clean up two facet joins, etc.), polishing lines, or burn spots (sometimes the cutter carelessly allows the diamond to drift off the polishing ring into a boundary rim of piled-up polishing powder which can cause a cloudy whitened burn spot on the facet surface).

Make certain, too, that you rotate the tweezers once or twice for unmounted stones to assure a good look in the areas where the tweezers had been gripping. With rings or mountings, take a long, extra careful look at the condition of the diamond crystal immediately under the prongs. Sometimes diamond setters will hide an imperfection under the metal prong—and sometimes they'll simply apply too much pressure on the metal against the diamond and cause a chip.

In Clarity It's Visibility, Position . . .

In general the severity of a diamond inclusion—that is the downgrading impact—revolves primarily around visibility, size, and position. A dark-colored, noticeable inclusion is obviously more serious than a white inclusion which could be hidden in the gem's brilliance.

Also, a noticeable inclusion in the middle of the table is quite serious and—if eye visible—pushes the rating toward an I grade. If the inclusion is very tiny and/or off toward the edge of the table, it's less serious.

An inclusion located in the bottom half of the stone affects a gem more than the same inclusion in the top half. That's because the pavilion imperfection will be reflected several times in a stone.

Not all inclusions, therefore, carry the same downgrading weight, and in clarity grading these differences must be taken into consideration before assigning a clarity value.

Inasmuch as it is unlikely that your clarity evaluations will be for gemstone certificates with their attendant liability—and since all clarity grading involves a relatively high level of subjective judgement anyway—this chapter will contain a numerical technique for you to postulate a reasonable clarity rating with acceptable accuracy. With the system given in this chapter you will at least be able to defend your rating—the same as pros must sometimes do.

Scandinavia	G.I.A.	A.G.S.*	
flawless	fl	0	No inclusions 10x loupe Clean
internally flawless	I.F.	0 +	
VVSI 1	VVS 1	1	Very tiny Inclusions Difficult to see with 10x loupe
VVSI 2	VVS 2	2	
VSI 1	VS 1	3	
VSI 2	VS 2	4	
SI 1	SI 1	5	Small inclusions easily seen w/10x loupe.
SI 2	SI 2	6	
Pique 1	I 1	7	Large, numerous inclusions visible to naked eye
Pique 2			
Pique 3		8	
Pique 4	I 2	9	
Pique 5	I 3	10	
Reject	Reject	11	*American Gem Society

Fig. 6-17 Diamond Clarity Grading Systems

The Gemological Institute of America has been largely responsible for efforts to establish a commonly accepted clarity grading language and basis, and others have either adopted the GIA approach or adapted a system similar to it. (Fig. 6-17)

Recognizing that some inclusions are not as serious as others, here is a method for developing a number value which corresponds to accepted clarity grades:

Tiny Inclusions barely visible with 10x	Tiny pin points, tiny white spots, naturals which do not influence shape or symmetry, a tiny surface scratch, a tiny extra facet—score any one of these with a ½-point value.
Noticeable Inclusions visible with 10x with some difficulty	Bubbles, imbedded crystals, feather, cleavage, visible cloud, series of white dots, black carbon spot, abraded spots, noticeable scratch, burn spot, flat on girdle, larger extra facet—count any one of these with a 1-point value.
Quite noticeable, often eye visible	Long cleavage, noticeable inclusion in center table, fair sized group of spots under table, large indented girdle flats, deep table scratch, noticeable bearding*, broken culet, large extra facets—count any one of these with a 2-point value.

*In bruting or rounding up a diamond shape the cutter sometimes works too fast or applies too much cutting force causing tiny feather-like fractures to extend visibly from the girdle into the crown or the pavilion

Keep in mind that the main criteria for evaluating any inclusion are noticeability, size, and position. Of necessity, these are often subjective decisions so there is no need to be overly exorcised in your number value selection. Chances are, most commercial gems will be in the SI and I categories anyway—and just being aware of an evaluating technique will quickly tip you off when you get into the top investment ranges.

Here are the ratings together with illustrations and example explanation of the values:

Grading Scale	Value Number	Description
F (Flawless)	0	No visible inclusions at 10x . . . OK on tiny natural . . . but nothing visible internally or externally.
IF (Internally Flawless)	½ (surface only)	Very minor surface blemish removable with re-cut or polishing . . . value usually at weight of re-cut gem.
VVS₁ (Very, Very Slightly Included)	½	No table involvement . . . very tiny pit, spot, scratch, imbedded crystal (must be under crown facets) . . .
VVSₛ (Very, Very Slightly Included)	1	One tiny inclusion . . . pit, spot, cleave, feather, abrasion, small extra facet . . . ½-point item in table . . .
VS₁ (Very Slightly Included)	2	Combination totalling 2—two tiny spots in table . . . crystal, bearding, fracture, cleavage, bigger natural, scratch group

VS$_s$ (Very Slightly Included)	3	Combination totalling 3—table inclusion if not in the center . . . cluster, bigger crystal, feather bearding more prominent . . . large extra facets.
SI$_1$ (Slightly Included)	4	Combination totalling 4—series of nicks, scratch group, inclusion cluster, small spot group in center of table . . .
SI$_2$ (Slightly Included)	5	Combination totalling 5—inclusion in table center . . . major flaws . . . cloudy area . . . inclusion cluster . . . large crystal imbedded . . . cleavage visible . . .
I$_1$ (Included)	6	Combination totalling 6—dead spot in stone . . . cleavages . . . feathers . . . imbedded crystals . . . carbon spots . . . cloudy sections . . .
I$_2$ & I$_3$ (Included)	7 +	Lowest GIA clarity grades. Any combination of inclusions totalling 7 or more.

In 1980 a full-fledged controversy embroiled the jewelry industry when it appeared that the Federal Trade Commission might allow jewelers to sell diamonds which had been lasered to remove inclusions—and not disclose this lasering to the buyer.

The industry split on this issue with some aghast that admission of such treatment should not be obligatory while others felt that jewelers should not accept the responsibility for disclosure because they couldn't control the situation adequately, i.e., they often didn't know themselves that a manufacturer had doctored a diamond.

Under present federal rules, this information *should be* disclosed to you. As you know, the lasering can conveniently give a diamond a better clarity grade appearance. If not detected a SI grade diamond could easily be represented as a VS.

Lasering leaves tell-tale marks. To eliminate the possibility of the tunnels being reflected, virtually all lasering is accomplished by directing the powerful beam perpendicular to the table. So, if you turn the gem so you can look at it from the side with a 10x or more magnifier you should be able to see what appears to be tiny spider webs running from the table down into the gem.

Take another look at the diagrams given later to demonstrate the different clarity marks. When a gemologist makes a clarity examination of a diamond he similarly marks up a diagram like this, showing the unique fingerprints of the gem.

To distinguish between internal imperfections (inclusions) and external imperfections (blemishes), the gemologist uses a red pen to mark inclusions, and a green pen to mark blemishes. There may be other ways of stamping the personality of a diamond so that you can never be fooled, but it's doubtful if any other system is as good as this one.

Every diamond, as you know, has its own distinctive all-inclusionary personality—and a drawn diagram of each inclusion, its type, and where it is, represents the best possible protection. If you don't already have such diagrams for your gems, sit down right now and make one up for each gem. Then put the diagrams into a safety deposit box.

In drawing a clarity diagram, be very careful to make your line thicknesses and sizes correspond as precisely as possible with the actual character of the inclusions. Gemologists are very careful about this. They know that a too thick line, for example might make the drawing appear that of a SI diamond when in reality the stone is a grade or two higher, VVS. For more on "mapping" a gem, refer to Chapter 10.

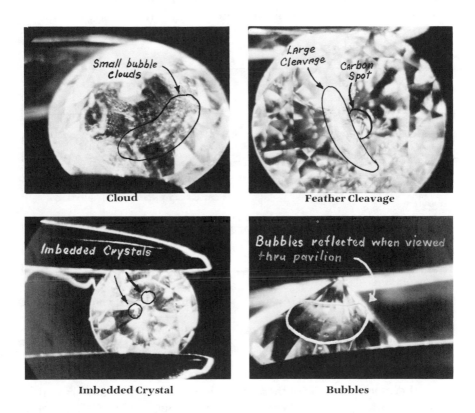

Cloud

Feather Cleavage

Imbedded Crystal

Bubbles

Fig. 6-18 Some Typical Diamond Imperfections

Colors, Colors and More Colors . . .

Color grading diamonds involves a determination of the amount of the deviation from the truly white colorless (the clear river color), in other words just how much "off-white" is involved. You may expect that the preponderance of diamonds you will inspect will fall into the white-to-yellow category.

If clarity grading is somewhat of a subjective decision process, color grading is even more so. Training the eye to distinguish the subtle color tints and differences requires extensive training, practice, and continued exposure.

Most professional graders work only for a few hours per day and then stop; they know their judgement grows faulty with eye fatigue.

They know, too, that even with their experience and professionalism some of their color judgements are arguable.

Yellow isn't the only color influence affecting diamond value. Diamonds occur along three major secondary color darkening lines: from white to yellow, from white to brown, and from white to green. Industrial diamonds also occur from white to gray. There is no clear line of demarcation between the three major gem diamond lines or groups. Separation depends on a grader's eye.

	COLLECTOR QUALITY				BETTER GEMS		FINE JEWELRY		TYPICAL JEWELRY GRADE				
G.I.A. SCALE	D E F G H				I J	K	L M	N	O P Q	R	S	T	U
AGS System	0	1	2	3	4	5	6	7	8		9			
APPEARANCE OF UNMOUNTED STONES	COLORLESS				NEAR COLORLESS		FAINT YELLOW		VERY LIGHT YELLOW				
APPEARANCE OF LARGE MOUNTED STONES	COLORLESS					INCREASINGLY TINTED				YELLOW			
APPEARANCE OF SMALL MOUNTED STONES	COLORLESS					INCREASINGLY TINTED							

Fig. 6-19 Diamond Color Grading Scales

The I-J intersection is generally regarded as the dividing line (to the untrained eye) for distinguishing colorless from tinted.

Note: Ability to detect a stone "drawing" color in the I-J-K grades represents a fine achievement for someone who is not constantly, daily exposed to color grading diamonds; top proficiency thus remains within the province of the diamond professional. Also, remember, top grade diamonds that are mounted cannot be accurately color graded even by the most skilled graders.

Furthermore, each one of these groups may be divided into as many as fifty different tint classifications . . . or only a few. The number depends on how narrow one wants the judging to be. Of the three groups, the white-to-yellow is by far the largest—and the one that most often serves as the basis for color grading systems (Fig. 6-19).

As the accompanying chart shows, the more narrow is each color grade the more it requires expertise to distinguish adjacent grades. Most people can be taught rather quickly and easily to distinguish three or four color categories. In most instances, this is adequate. It takes a full time professional working with diamonds every day to maintain the skill necessary to distinguish a D color from an E color. In those instances when a grader must decide whether a diamond falls into the white-to-yellow group or into the white-to-brown group even the professional has serious difficulty.

Unless you intend to become a fulltime diamond professional there seems little need for you to invest the time needed to become that professionally proficient, a level of grading skill that very few jewelers, despite their boasts to the contrary, possess. For your purposes, the ability to distinguish between colorless river clear diamonds, slightly tinted diamonds, and progressively color tinted diamonds is sufficient.

Should there be a need to assign a more specific color grade, you may ask the jeweler for a warranty on the color he represents, or have the gem graded by a professional laboratory such as the facilities maintained by the Gemological Institute of America

The Color Effect of Surroundings . . .

Some mention has already been made about the effect of certain kinds of lighting on a diamond's color. In the jewelry trade, professionals traditionally have sought to use daylight, facing north in the northern latitudes, toward dusk—so as to minimize the ultra violet content.

Incandescent lamps need to be filtered to remove their ultra violet influence, and fluorescent lamps need modifying to remove long waves. As you know, intense lighting masks yellow and blue tints and thus should be avoided.

Watch out, too, for blue walls and surroundings. It's not so much the immediate impact of blue on your color grading but the afterimage as blue walls reflect blue light. This color effect makes yellow diamonds appear less yellow and colorless diamonds appear blue.

Mountings? Diamonds should be color graded when unmounted, but usually you'll have no choice. Yellow or red gold obviously will affect the diamond's color giving a clear diamond perhaps a suspicion of color tint—and making an already yellow diamond appear less so in contrast to the metal coloring.

Platinum—a silvery-gray metal—won't affect diamond color all that much, although gray adjacent to any hue intensifies the hue so a yellow diamond may appear more yellow. As for white gold, the influence here depends on the alloy color and the yellowish-white metal is often more intense than a yellow diamond making the latter appear less yellow. That's why so many people prefer white mountings for their diamonds.

Professional diamond grader or not, you should have a comparison stone because it is the most reliable aid. If the jeweler has available a Diamondlite—a light box instrument made by GIA for color grading diamonds—it will be most helpful.

With a mounting, your best strategy is to try and determine if the diamond—regardless of the metal coloring—is truly colorless, beginning to "draw color" or has a noticeable tint. That's about the best you can hope for. Not even professionals can grade mounted diamonds accurately because the setting and surrounding stones affect the color and because one also is often forced to look into the table where the spectrum can confuse the eye.

As for a comparison stone, you might obtain a Cubic Zirconim of about 6.5mm size, which compares with the diameter of a one-carat weight diamond. Most commercial C.Z.'s have a color grade of G-H when cut—and are much less expensive than a graded diamond.

A G-H color will provide you with a basis for judging colorless transparent gems, and is just slightly above the J color where a diamond begins to 'draw color'.

To minimize any surrounding color influence, take a 3x5 flat white index card—or a piece of white blotting paper—and fold it accordian style. Place the unmounted diamond table down—so you can look into the stone perpendicular to the pavillion—with the comparison stone directly onto the side (Fig. 6-20). Only the most skilled grader can detect a trace of color when viewing table up.

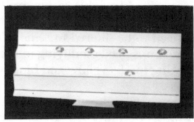

Fig. 6-20 To color grade an unmounted diamond, a folded 3x5 card or piece of white blotting paper serves quite well. Place the comparison stone on one accordian fold and the unknown on a level above or below—and then compare . . . *table down.*

Filter any artificial lighting by hanging a thin piece of paper in front of the bulb. You can even hold your hand up between an incandescent light bulb and the diamond so that direct rays don't fall on the stone. If the surroundings are generally illuminated with fluorescent lighting, turn away from the counter, with its brighter lighting, and view the diamond under the cooler lights. Indeed, you would be slightly better off going near the window and viewing the diamond in the folded concertina under daylight conditions, north or not, ultra-violet or not.

In case of a single diamond, you can also fold the white card into a single "V" for viewing. Place your comparison stone about one inch away and then study the two gems—preferably with magnification—through their respective pavillions. If the stone you are studying appears whiter, cleaner, more transparent than the C.Z. (which is rather unlikely if the diamond is being used for jewelry rather than investment) you would be dealing in the highest color grades.

Without practice, don't expect to see color tints right away. The untrained eye has difficulty detecting tints in the first 10-11 color grades. To improve your eye, make it a habit to look at diamonds which are displayed in store windows. They are mounted, yes, but soon you will find that you can discern the slight "off color" or tint. Furthermore,

116

many of the diamonds in the window are in the slightly tinted commercial range anyway.

The discount jewelry store window makes an excellent training location because the price of the item is prominent. When two one-carat diamonds whose settings are nearly equal are shown at dramatically different prices you may be certain that the merchant has priced for gem quality and the lower priced diamond will have either a lower clarity or color rating—or both—than the more expensive one.

Most diamond color grading in the United States and Canada is done according to the alphabetical system devised by the GIA. In many cases you may be confronted with other clarity and color coding systems, often the merchant's own invention. Inasmuch as interesting sounding color terminology can be interpreted many ways by different people, you would be better served by insisting on knowing the GIA equivalent for any questionable color or quality term; GIA's system is the closest thing to a universally accepted standard that exists. If the sales person can't—or worse, won't—provide specific GIA descriptions so *both of you are communicating on the same wave length*, well—caveat emptor (let the buyer beware). That may sound like harsh advice, but would you buy a used car from a salesperson who wouldn't provide you with the make, year, physical condition, or mileage of the vehicle?

Carat is a Weight, Not a Size . . .

"What a beautiful diamond," exclaimed the friend. "How big is it?"

"It's one carat," replied the owner of the diamond.

And therein lay the problem. The weight of a diamond is expressed in carats. The size of a diamond is expressed in millimeters. If a standard round brilliant diamond is cut to proper proportions one carat weight of diamond will finish off about 6.5 millimeters in diameter (about the diameter of an ordinary pea) and its depth will run about 3.9mm —providing no minor adjustments in cutting were involved.

No one really knows what the friend meant by "big." It could have been a referral to size or weight or both. In that case a proper answer—and probably one with the potential for concluding the conversation and, maybe, the friendship—should have been: "As for size, it's 6.5 millimeters in diameter, and 3.9 millimeters in depth, and it's weight is precisely one carat, that is 100 points."

Only a diamond jeweler would have appreciated such a complete and responsive reply.

This understandable, but sometimes serious, confusion over size and weight leads to problems for many buyers. They have seen round diamonds cut to one carat weight for so long that the diameter of 6.5 mm has become an "eyeball standard." Whenever a diamond fails to match this memorized standard, the size (?) of the diamond is immediately suspect.

A diamond of precisely one carat weight could, indeed, have a diameter greater than 6.5mm. That's what swindled tables with their thin crowns are all about: they weigh no more but their diameters are often larger because of the depth distortion in cutting.

A diamond with an extra large pavilion, crown, or girdle could weigh a carat or more and still have a diameter less than 6.5mm. The extra weight is in the thickness. For example, a diamond cutter knowing that a piece of rough has a brown tint will often cut a thicker girdle so the light admitted through the girdle will help mask the tint, making the stone appear clearer.

The problem of size measurements and weight becomes even more critical when diamond is fashioned in one of the round cut's variations, or in step cuts. In these cases no so-called eyeball standard exists, as step cuts often consist of multiple rows of facets on the crown and the pavillion. Such cutting makes standard proportions inoperative; the depth percentage can vary considerably—and so can the carat weight.

To know the weight of a diamond, it must be weighed on a scale. To know the weight by measuring the diamond one must know one of the various formulas and then be satisfied with an approximation however close the answer.

Calculating the weight of a diamond in a mounting invariably involves a formula (unless the weight of the setting is known precisely). Here are two formulas which are used to calculate diamond weight when the diamond can only be measured not weighed:

P. Grodzinski's formula provides 5% accuracy estimation for a round brilliant cut diamond in relation to its diameter (d) in millimeters:

$$\frac{d^3}{6.42} = \text{weight in carats}$$

For those with a millimeter gauge, B.W. Anderson's formula is even more accurate and involves the diameter (d) and the height (h) in centimeters:

$$6hd^2 = \text{weight in carats}$$

The word carat comes from the greek *keration* (meaning *tree*). As a weight it traces its history to the seed of a tree common in the Middle East called the locust or Carob tree. Small black beans growing on the tree contained a syrup and tiny seeds which, when dried, were extremely consistent in weight. From these came the carat weight.

Eric Bruton in his outstanding book *Diamonds,* suggests that it was the syrup from these locust beans that John the Baptist probably ate in the wilderness—and not the flying grasshoppers called locusts.

Over the years, most countries accepted the standardized carat weight but expressed it in terms of their own weight measures. It wasn't until the 20th Century that countries agreed on the international standard metric carat. Today, the metric carat expressed as 0.2 or one-fifth of a gram is used with gem weights shown in decimals instead of fractions.

There are 100 points to a carat. Thus a diamond of one and one-half carats could be described as 1.50 ct., or as 150 points. Notice that the decimal system lists a quarter-carat as 0.25 ct.—placing a zero before the point and two digits after the point. Note, too, that the abbreviation of "ct." appears after the numbers.

Remember the 1980 consumers who were delighted to learn that they could purchase a *0.25 pt. diamond for only $5* No one knows how many people interpreted this to mean a quarter-carat diamond, failing to note that the trick was in the description 0.25 *pt.* and not 0.25 ct. The decimal expression 0.25 pt. represents 1/25 of 1/100 of a carat—not 0.25ct. or a quarter of a carat. What the careless consumers received for their $5 was a tiny, dust particle of diamond which could be purchased at that time, for about 35¢.

You should insist, too, when buying a one-carat diamond the weight be a full 100 points. A 0.99 ct. diamond is *not* a full carat and 0.49 ct. is *not* a half carat. They are *nearly* a full (1.00 ct) and half carat (0.50 ct.) respectively, but they are not truly at these popular weight levels and the one point differential often means a price break.

In summary, there are no incontrovertible ratings in diamond. Professionals can grade the four Cs with greater skill and precision than can non-professionals. But all evaluations are a matter of subjective decision making.

A combination of your own knowledge and ability to "see" and "read" a diamond with the representations and warranties offered by a legitimate jeweler will provide you with a fine diamond at the most competitive price. In diamonds—given the different cuts, color and clarity grades, and weight—you pretty much get what you pay for . . . and if you know what you're paying for you minimize the chance of unhappiness.

When a potential diamond buyer can walk into a jewelry store and tell the salesperson, "I'm interested in possibly buying a 100 to 125 point diamond, of G to I color, with SI1 or SI2 clarity, standard brilliant proportions with no more than a 58% table, " well, when you feel comfortable about conducting your diamond buying with that kind of language—you have arrived.

Of course, you'll probably scare a good proportion of salespeople half out of their wits—and absolutely delight the knowledgeable and legitimate ones.

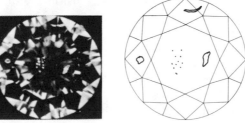

Fig. 6-19 Here is a "mapping" for an I2 diamond with a 6-count in inclusions.

119

CHAPTER SEVEN

COLORED STONES: The Emerging Phenomenon

A short time ago the jewelry industry concentrated its efforts primarily on four colors—clear, red, blue, and green—and on the gemstones, called the Big Four, that represented these colors.

The gemstones were diamond, ruby, sapphire and emerald.

For the most part, they were the only gems that the buying public knew about and were interested in owning. Jewelers seldom carried a varied or valuable inventory in other colored gems because of the understandable difficulty in selling them.

A small market of gem knowledgeable individuals existed. Generally speaking, though, this segment was never big enough or influential enough to provide the broad based support which would justify a viable retail market in colored stones.

All that has changed.

In the last 10 years particularly, the public has found out about colored gemstones and has responded with unusual enthusiasm. People increasingly are seeking out these gems and their knowledge, interest, and financial commitments are keeping pace.

Because the potential has improved for turning over inventory in a reasonably acceptable time period, retail jewelers are now stocking a wider variety of colored gems—and they're also offering in many cases, a selection of variously priced selections of each gem type.

A "pigeon blood" ruby may sell for a five or six-figure price per carat in top gem quality, but quite attractive lower quality natural rubies are also available for a fraction of the top-end prices. Furthermore, you can improve on the pricing of lower-end rubies if you know about and elect to purchase an alternate genuine red gemstone with a color which challenges even the finest rubies.

The big advantage in colored gems is their flexibility.

Colored gems aren't in abundance either, but nature has provided enough of a variety that you can pick almost any color or choose from a number of alternatives . . . each of which possesses its own unique blend of sparkle, brightness, liveliness, color, and excitement. Some are extraordinarily expensive (these usually are the well-known ones) while others, with a remarkable similarity to the hue, tone, and intensity of their more familiar brethren, are surprisingly inexpensive.

Money often isn't the principle key to owning a splendid collection of natural gems. Your own knowledge of colored gems—especially a knowledge of what nature has to offer in color groupings alone—can provide you and your perseverence with a fine collection of gems at a price significantly less than another person can obtain when armed only with a checkbook.

An aquamarine is a beautiful sky blue gemstone which in its finer clarity, color, and transparency grades is becoming increasingly rare and expensive, sometimes approaching four figures per carat. A Precious Blue Topaz matches the aquamarine in color, clarity—and beauty—and can be purchased for a fraction of the aquamarine's cost.

In 1980, Paul Desautels, curator for the Smithsonian Institution, declared on the Today television show that the Blue Topaz, when purchased for under $75 per carat, was a fine gem investment. This started the public stampede for Blue Topaz—long after gemstone cognoscenti had been using them quietly and inexpensively as fine gems in their own right.

While enjoying a higher R.I. than the aquamarine, the Blue Topaz has a somewhat more subtle color intensity but remains virtually indistinguishable to the eye from aqua. Few qualified gemologists would dare to authenticate one stone from the other with a mere "eyeball" guess while a Blue Topaz is being worn in a mounting. They simply look too much alike—although a blue topaz is a bit more slippery to the touch.

A Blue Topaz's and an aquamarine's visual similarity is but one incidence where one genuine gem can successfully hold its own appearance-wise with another. Many such optional opportunities exist —and an appropriate knowledge of colored gems is but an extension of what you already know about gems.

Clarity Isn't That Important . . .

There are different ground rules for colored gems than there are for diamonds. Actually, gemology makes a clear-cut distinction between diamonds and colored gem materials.

For all intents and purposes, any non-diamond is a colored gem material . . . whether it's a colored mineral gem or one of the non-mineral materials such as amber, coral, ivory, etc.

There is a reason for this distinction.

The organization of the colored gem market, from mining to finished product, comes nowhere near the diamond industry. The latter is truly an integrated industry with huge investments in the capital and manpower required to extract the diamonds from the host grounds as well as the organized networks for fashioning and marketing.

In comparison, the mining of colored gems is still in the dark ages, often consisting of little more than open pits or holes where hand labor represents the major element in recovery. Because much less crystallographic knowledge or equipment is required to cut colored gems—even if done poorly or improperly—almost anyone with a cutting wheel of some sort can take up colored gem cutting.

Without a profound knowledge of grain directions you could spend an unsuccessful lifetime trying to grind a diamond; no such grain expertise is needed to grind a colored gem although a trained, knowledgeable lapidary is needed to release a colored gem's beauty through proper cutting—as witnessed by some of the unfortunate "cut(?)" gems occassionally seen.

Also, unlike the diamond, clarity for many colored gems is not so high a virtue. As has been mentioned earlier, inclusions are often quite acceptable in colored gems to a degree that would plunge the price of a diamond into industrial-abrasive categories.

Not only are inclusions acceptable in the colored gem area, but they often have little or no impact on pricing. The ranges of clarity are far less specific than in diamond grading. Most gemologists utilize these broad definitions:

F— Flawless
VLI— Very Lightly Included
LI— Lightly Included
MI— Moderately Included
HI— Heavily Included
VHI— Very Heavily Included

The average range for acceptable clarity grading in the better known colored gems are:

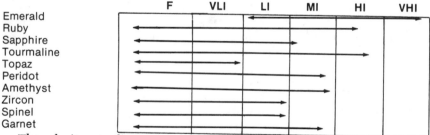

The clarity grading of colored gems is far less standardized than diamonds for a number of reasons . . . most of which relate to the different qualities that enter into the grading of colored gems.

For instance, the deeper and darker color of many colored gems provide an effective cover for many of the inclusions which would be visible in the lighter, more highly transparent gems. Combine the deep color element with a high R.I. in some colored gems, and the brilliance lends additional masking.

Certain of the deeper garnets are often deliberately faceted with what would normally be "fish eye" angles so as to make the final gem shallower, thus allowing light to get through the stone. Otherwise, the gem would simply be too dark to serve acceptably as a gemstone.

This cutting at shallower angles sacrifices some of the gem material's natural brilliance, but in these cases the cut is being made to display color more than brilliance anyway.

Color is a Vital Consideration . . .

Color in a gemstone is perhaps the most fascinating—and complex—quality to grasp. The fact that most gem species occur in various colors catches some people by surprise. To be told that sapphires occur in almost all colors comes as an abrupt awakening to men and women who believe that all sapphires are various shades of blue. To a gemologist, though, a bright red corundum is a ruby—and all other colored corundum is regarded as a sapphire.

It's largely for this reason—and the differential in price between ruby and sapphire—that the cliche developed, "If I'm selling it's a ruby, and if I'm buying it's a sapphire."

When it comes to evaluating a colored gem for its color you should remember some basic guidelines. The three primary color guidelines are:

1) Colors are not a constant and your perception varies with time of day, color conditions, illumination type, etc:

2) Colors in the jewelry trade are not standardized and are, for the most part, a matter of individual interpretation, and,

3) Even subtle differences in color can have an extraordinary impact on price.

Whenever you inspect a colored gem you must keep in mind that your perception of color is dynamic, that it is responsive to a series of elements. Northern daylight is regarded as the standard under which color grading is best accomplished, but even this changes with time of day, sky conditions, etc.

Consequently, you "see" colors slightly different. Under incandescent lighting, there is the ultra violet consideration, and even cool fluorescent lighting has its long wave problem.

Your physical condition likewise is a significant factor.

So realize that the same colored gem you saw yesterday—or only a few hours ago—can appear differently the second time around . . . especially if any conditions other than mere time are involved.

As for the lack of color standard, this shortcoming has proven to be one of the major obstacles in the expansion of the colored gem market. In too many cases, a gem is labeled with a color and people believe that their own impression of this color label represents some sort of standard.

That this kind of thinking can lead to difficulties was made evident in 1979 when a mail order company advertised those famous "bona fide emeralds for sale at only $5 per carat."

Most men and women have a generalized impression of what an emerald looks like . . . a beautiful, dark, lush green gemstone. There is some evidence that many of them had this kind of color standard in mind when they sent off their $5—and received in return a pale, washed out greenish piece of the mineral beryl.

Painfully these non-gem fanciers learned that the lack of color standards allowed this questionable promotion to come off with such success. Emerald is green beryl: the chunks were green beryl, too—a much, much lighter tone of green. (Actually, an emerald's deep color is caused by the influence of chromium in the beryl and when chromium is not present it is more accurate to classify such greenish rocks only as green beryl—so promoting non-chromium bearing green beryl as emerald did, indeed, play on the fringe of truth.)

In the early 80s the Gemological Institute of America took a major step in standardizing color with its introduction of an instrument called the ColorMaster. This device utilizes a patented "color mixer" principle which allows an operator to dial in a precisely calibrated color. Thus, any color—a mixture of colors—can be faithfully and accurately reproduced.

Two rubies, each cut to precise proportions in a round brilliant cut, with equal clarity are priced differently.

One ruby is offered for sale at $3,000 per carat and the other at only $300 per carat. Why the difference? The answer is color difference. the more expensive of the two red gemstones perhaps contains the unique red-purple coloration so characteristic of the term "pigeon blood." Undoubtedly, a touch of brown or gray has influenced the less expensive ruby—and the price plummeted accordingly.

This principle holds true for almost all colored gems. Slight, sometimes nearly imperceptible differences, exert tremendous price impact.

Three factors are concerned when color is being described. The factors are called "HIT."

The letters mean: H—for Hue, described as another word for pure color other than white, gray or black; I-for Intensity, described as the measure of the vividness or dullness of a color, and T-for Tone, described as the lightness or darkness, a basic Hue after white or gray is added.

Thus the Hue of a ruby is red. If it's a bright red it's said to have high Intensity. Should white be added to the Hue it's tone would become progressively more pink until, perhaps, it was no longer a ruby but rather a pink sapphire. If a darker gray is added the tone becomes more of a maroon.

Tourmaline, rhodolite garnet, ruby, red topaz and coral are all red in *Hue*—but each possesses a different Tone. The Intensity of each gem material differs, too.

Looking at gem materials with a blue Hue, there are sapphires, iolite, tourmaline, topaz, aquamarine, zircon. Each differs in Tone, some greatly and some only subtly from others.

The emerald dominates gemstones of a green Hue, but other green gems—of varying Tones—include tourmaline, quartz, garnet, diopside, sapphire, peridot.

In evaluating Intensity, look for the degree of vividness. Don't be misled, either, into thinking that this is a factor only of transparency.

The green jadeite, in the Tone known as Imperial Jade, is translucent but still displays remarkable Intensity as do other tones of jadeite. Of course, transparent peridot, described by some as possessing a "sleepy" green Hue, is noticeably less intense than emerald or green sapphire.

Until a color standard is available to the jewelry industry so that buyers and sellers can communicate accurately, you should expect that most color descriptions will be far short of objectivity. Most efforts to describe color will be, at best, vague and even slightly misleading.

People selling colored gems often fall back on romantic phrases, platitudes, and geographical or romantic references in an effort to match a mental impression of a color quality to an object. You can expect to hear "the color of Columbian Emerald ... a Burmese ruby color ... Kashmir sapphire ...

Columbian emeralds are, admittedly, capable of the finest, purest greeen. The Burmese ruby is famous in the "pigeon blood" Hue. Kashmir sapphire is familiarly described as cornflower blue, usually of fine Intensity, deep Toned and pure Hue.

But all three of these famous descriptions can be extremely misleading. Not every emerald that comes out of Columbia's Muzo mine is of the finest color; some are rather nondescript.

Burmese rubies vary in Tone from the best red to poorly colored stones. Many of the sapphires found in India's Kashmire area were of a fine blue—and many were not.

How do you know then if the colored stone you are evaluating is of a fine color?

A set of comparison stones is the best answer.

Synthetic rubies—regardless of the manufacturing process used—are usually close to the final "pigeon blood" Hues—and can be purchased for less than a dollar.

Synthetic corundum sapphires are "off" slightly in color from the fine blue genuine sapphires. But synthetic blue spinels which are often passed off as synthetic sapphires can be used as an excellent color standard. A Chatham or Gilson synthetic emerald can function as a starting color for fine emeralds.

Using these three synthetics as comparison stones you can then appropriately evaluate almost any ruby, sapphire, or emerald with a reasonable degree of accuracy, judging any gem color as above or below the comparison stone in either Hue, Tone or Intensity.

The problem becomes much more difficult in evaluating color in other gems. Synthetics or imitations aren't all that close to the finer grades of color in the natural gems so a comparison with a synthetic or imitation becomes much less dependable. Only other natural gems—often too difficult to obtain for non-trade people—would serve well—plus continuous experience with the various Hues and Tones. In a pinch, a book containing high-quality full color photographs of superior colored gems will serve you well.

Color Grading is Scaled . . .

Until GIA developed the ColorMaster, efforts to provide an objective color grading system varied in their usefulness, worth and acceptability. Most of these earlier systems were based on a numbering or alphabetical technique which assigned values for the secondary colors content of the primary color plus any influencing.

For example, aquamarines vary in the amount of their blueness from virtually river clear up to the irradiated variety of deep, deep blue called Maxixe. Other gems—such as blue sapphire—run the gamut from very, very slightly blue (almost clear) to black. Amethyst, a purple quartz, goes from almost clear up through slightly pink named ("Rose d'France") to the deeper purples until it is nearly opaque.

Accordingly, the price per carat along these scales varies with the coloring. The colored gem that is almost clear is quite inexpensive. As the material develops a deeper, richer color the price rises steeply—and then begins falling off rapidly as the deepening color becomes overwhelming and the gem turns excessively dark.

In pricing and evaluating colored gems you should keep in mind this hump shaped pricing line when a gem's coloring deviates from the most desirable Tonal scale (which on a scale of 100 is generally with the 35-70 range). (Fig. 7-1).

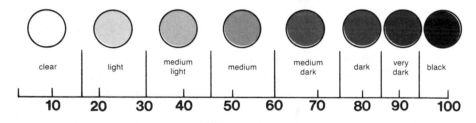

Fig. 7-1 No universally accepted standard currently exists for colored stones. Consequently, most colored stone grading is done along a 0-100 spectrum. Colorless has the lowest (0) rating and the percentage climbs as the primary color increases, until the color progressively dominates to the point of opacity (100). Colored stone pricing generally follows this line with the cheapest carat price at the bottom of the scale, then attaining the highest values in the 35%-70% range, falling off quickly once the commercial color range is passed.

The purity of a gem's color can be influenced significantly by second or third colors. Emerald is often described as slightly bluish green while peridot has an element of yellow in its green.

Ruby reaches its finest color grade when the hint of pink is slightly noticeable.

Generally speaking, though, the addition of gray or brown tends to impair color purity. As you already know, rubies and sapphires are routinely cooked in order to eliminate the brown or gray discoloration. This treatment gives the finished crystal a purer red or blue. In many cases, were not some cosmetic treatment applied the influence of gray or brown would produce a muddy appearing gem. Many of the brown-color influenced red garnets fall into this muddy category.

Cutting Colored Gems For Color . . .

All colored gems are less hard than diamond so here is where will be seen the creative shapes of the gemstone world. Diamonds generally are cut in the round brilliant, a variation of the round brilliant, or in a simple step or "trap" cut shape. Due to the diamond's grain and configuration of the rough pieces it is easier to cut a 4-point diamond (the cube face) in the round; a 3-point diamond (the octahedral face) in a pear or heart shape, and a 2-point cut (the dodecahedral face) in a marquise, baguette or square or emerald cut.

Colored stones—which today are almost always fashioned by using diamond grit on the cutting wheels—have no such limitations. They can be cut in any direction. From strictly a hardness viewpoint, the lapidarist is free to exercise shaping decisions without regard to grain directions. Often the shape and width to depth ratio of the piece of rough is the principal limitation . . . with optics sometimes subordinated in the shaping decision. The fact that many colored stone crystals also vary in directional hardness has little, if any, impact on cutting decisions.

The recovery percentage (the final weight of the finished gem in proportion to the weight of the original piece of rough) will be much higher, of course, if the lapidarist is able to keep the gem outline as close as possible to the outline of the original rough shape (Fig. 7-2), thus minimizing waste.

Step cuts—consisting of straight, rectangular shaped facets—represent the most efficient way to maximize recovery while still cutting properly proportioned gems. Still, odd shaped "custom" cuts are not as popular as traditional shapes.

Because emeralds are customarily cut in an octagon step cut fashion the

**A step cut can follow
the rough's outline**

**Notice how much material must be
cut away when cutting a round**

Fig. 7-2 The closer a gem cutter can stay to the original shape of the rough gem material—other things remaining equal—the higher recovery rate will be achieved. The step or trap cut, obviously, allows a cutter to conform more closely to rough shapes than a pre-conceived standard cut such as a round, pear, oval, etc.

square or rectangular appearance has come to be known as the emerald cut. Step cuts are best for enhancing gem color, particularly light to medium colored gems. Almost all aquamarines are cut in a trap or emerald cut. After all, a lapidarist has reasonable freedom for deepening the cut so light passing through the extra depth will be enriched by whatever existing color the gem material possesses.

Still, there are cutting obligations—severe ones—that a colored gem cutter must observe. Unless the stone's color is excessively deep and a deliberate shallowing is planned, a faceted colored gem must be cut at angles appropriate for the material.

Furthermore, most colored gems display their best optical qualities when cut with the table-to-culet direction in a carefully oriented manner consistent with the gem's crystal axis.

Many times, a superbly executed cut will have a dead, lifeless appearance. A careful examination will show everything in order except for one vital factor: the piece of rough was improperly aligned in accordance with the crystal's optical requirements—and light and color simply couldn't perform to their maximum potential.

Topaz, in any of its tones or hues, is a magnificent performer—when cut so the crystallographic axis lies almost perpendicular to the table facet. The gem will sparkle with color and light. Put an equally well-cut topaz of the same carat, clarity, color where the orientation is away from the crystal's axis direction—and the difference is dramatic.

Just as main pavilion facets are the most critical in diamond cutting, so too are these same facets vital in colored gems. With lower R.I.s, colored gems are quicker to "fish eye." It happens often in colored stones.

The condition can be detected quickly and easily by peering straight down through the table facet where any bottom glassy transparency, as opposed to light reflections, will be immediately obvious. Again, the reasons for this shallowness are many: poorly calibrated cutting equipment, bad cutting techniques, selection of an inappropriate gem shape from a given piece of rough material, deliberate shallowing for light or shallow mounting purposes . . . and, sometimes, a last minute discovery of a value-reducing inclusion that needed to be removed regardless of the optical sacrifice.

Here, briefly, is a step-by-step procedure for evaluating colored gems—a procedure which probably will unveil most of any gem's secrets:

Step One:
Without magnification, look the gem over for consistency of shape, and any obvious optical shortcomings.

Are there any distortions in the shape? If round, is the shape truly round? If rectangular, are the sides truly parallel? If in an octagon shape, check carefully the truncated corners which are sometimes not uniform in length? Is the gem a "fish eye?" Is the gem "bright?"

Turn the gem or the mounting sideways and check the crown and the pavilion ratios. The general proportion is one-third thickness for the crown, and two-thirds thickness for the pavilion (these proportions aren't as critical as diamond and can vary without a value reduction). On a scale of 100, can you assign a color rating?—and what rating is it?

On emerald cuts (or cuts with a line culet vs. a point culet) (Fig. 7-3) check for abrading. Usually, the culet line should be faceted, because the knife edge is easily chipped. Is the culet in the middle? Check the facet rows on step cuts (usually there are three rows on the pavilion and three rows on the crown).

Can you see any obvious inclusions or blemishes? In many colored stones inclusions are quite acceptable—but the light colored stones generally should be Flawless or Very Slightly Included.

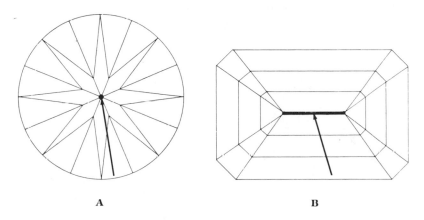

A   B

Fig. 7-3 Not all gems are cut with a point culet such as "A". Some are cut so most of the pavilion main facets can be cut at the proper angle, thus causing a "B" line or knife edge culet. You'll usually see the latter in step or emerald cuts.

Step Two:

Using a 10x loupe, begin a careful examination for clarity, surface finish, cutting accuracy, and setting.

You can't "read" a round colored gem through the table as you can a well proportioned diamond. Diamond proportions can't vary that much; colored gem proportioning can—and does.

But you should see mirror-like reflections from the main pavilion or culet facets. With magnification, look into the gem from a direction perpendicular to the crown and pavilion facets. Turn and twist the gem constantly so that light will play around the inside of the gem. Sometimes a veil or string of bubbles can be overlooked until they're hit just right by the light.

Check carefully the final polishing. If visible, polishing lines appear close together and parallel. This shows the lack of good final finish which can dampen the color and brilliance. Check, too, on step cuts that all facets meet accurately (these cuts all have many 4-corner joins and they should meet precisely). (Fig. 7-4). Are there scratches in the finish?

On step cuts, the girdle should appear uniform in width throughout. If one girdle facet is thicker or thinner than any of the others, check out the adjacent facets (that's where the cutting error will be).

Be certain to inspect carefully around all prongs or bezels. As you know any undue pressure by the stone setter can easily cause a value-reducing chip—and incipient cleavages (promising a much more serious problem later) are often visible.

Tip the stone so light is reflected off its surface uniformly. The light sheen should be consistent all across the facet under magnified inspection. Any appearance change should be reviewed more carefully because it could signify a surface blemish or a split indicating a more serious internal problem. This is often a good way too, of picking up surface shortcomings which have been hidden through oiling.

 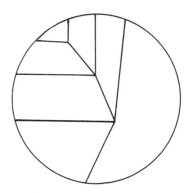

Fig. 7-4 On step or emerald cuts, many of the facet meets are 4-cornered. Here's where you inspect carefully to assure that all the facets are meeting properly.

Step Three:

Know the characteristics of the specific gem you are evaluating.

To assist you with step three, here are a number of the more famous gem stones or families:

BERYL

Emerald—Symbol of immortality and incorruptibility, its deep green is caused by chrome, sometimes vanadium, with the coloring often irregular. Inclusions such as bubbles, cracks, foreign crystals aren't necessarily faults. Usually oiled; sometimes dye is included.

Aquamarine—The gem which preserves marriage and stops wounds from bleeding, aquamarine is the result of heating certain green, brown, and lighter blue beryl to obtain the deeper sea water blue color. The coloring pigment is iron. Flawless or Very Slightly Included grades, with typical inclusions occurring as fine hollow tubes which sometimes reflect light.

Heliodor—A lemon yellow-to-gold beryl caused by uranium oxide, it is called the "Stone of the Sun" and symbolizes durability. Its inclusions are similar to aquamarine and is preferred in upper clarity grades.

Morganite—Soft peach pink-to-near violet, it's color can be improved by heat treating. Coloring is caused by manganese.

CHRYSOBERYL

Transparent Chrysoberyl—In faceted form it appears as bright, flashy golden yellow to green-yellow. Generally of high clarity, big gems are increasingly difficult to obtain.

Alexandrite—Green by daylight, light red by night or artificial light, color change makes it highly desirable. Symbolizes power to make one feel strongly and to reach goals. Sensitive to hard knocks, so check carefully where metal is pushed up against it.

Cat's Eye—Only the cat's eye chrysoberyl can be referred to as "Cat's Eye." Other's must have an additional designation. Honey colored, eye is sharpest of all cat's eyes and has a slight bluish cast.

SPINEL

The most popular color for *spinel* is red (the famous Black Prince Ruby in Great Britain's crown jewels, it has been discovered, is really a red spinel), but it appears in almost all colors—pink, violet, brown, purple, dark green, blue, orange, black, yellow, violet.

Frequently flawless, it looks especially attractive in artifical light. *Spinel*, often found in areas also yielding corundum, has been a somewhat overlooked gem and could be regarded as a "sleeper" for someone wanting a genuine, top quality gem at a bargain price. The reds are already expensive.

TOPAZ

Topaz is said to improve one's psychic abilities and strengthen the body. Best known in the sherry yellow color as Imperial Topaz, *topaz* occurs in such colors as red brown, light blue, pinkish red, and pale green. Be careful with Mexican brown topaz, it fades in sunlight. *Topaz* can be a lively stone, with heat treated pink and irradiated blue topaz catching the public fancy in the early 80s. A distinct cleavage plane makes it sensitive to hard blows. Almost all colors are most desirable as flawless or Very Slightly Included.

Look under reflected surface light for off-color flat appearing platlets on or near the gem's surfaces. They look in relief almost like mica with a chalky or flat-white coloring. Generally, they'll appear over the entire facet surface; they're indications that the facet angle is too close to topaz's natural cleavage plane—which is very difficult to polish.

Colored topaz is usually emerald or scissor cut. Heavily included crystals are often cut en cabochon.

GARNET

Most people tend to think of *garnet* as a rather non-spectacular wine red gem found in old fashioned jewelry.

As the stone which can bring its wearer power, grace and victory, garnet is much more than that; it occurs in many colors, some of which perform splendidly. The green garnet known as *Tsavorite* challenges even the emerald for green magnificence.

Hessonite is a brown honey colored grossular garnet with brilliance and intensity capable of holding its own with any gem.

Almandine, red with a touch of violet, is so rich and deep that it is usually cut shallow or even hollowed out in the bottom to lighten the color. It is sometimes even confused with ruby.

In recent years a find of orange spersartine garnets in Africa were promptly dubbed *"Malaya"* (prounounced ma-lee'-a) garnets and soared quickly in price.

Garnets, coming in various colors and sizes, are available mostly in high clarity grades and are priced from only a few dollars per carat to as high as four figures per carat.

ZIRCON

Zircon developed somewhat of a bad reputation because in its river clear color it was so often used as an imitation diamond. But as the stone which promises riches, wisdom and honor, *zircon* has much to offer including a variety of colors—yellow, orange, green, blue, brown, red.

Blessed with great dispersion and fire, it is brittle and sensitive to hard knocks. You can spot a *zircon* easily by peering down through the table with a loupe and watching for the doubling effect of the facet edges. Found mostly as gray-brown or red-brown stones, *zircon* is often heat treated to produce colorless and blue zircons.

TOURMALINE

The Dutch who imported it from the Mediterranean area in the 1700s call it the "aschentrekker" which means ash puller. And it's true; a *tourmaline* will attract cigarette ashes when heated.

It also attracts gem collectors because of its hard beauty and unmatched array of colors. *Tourmaline* even occurs as a multi-colored gem material one of which is called "watermelon" because it possesses a red interior, a white inner skin, and a green outer skin.

Hard, durable, capable of accepting a bright polish, *tourmaline* is available in violet, blue green, brown, yellow, orange, pink, red, black—and almost all variations inbetween. It's major drawback is a distinct lack of dispersion.

SPODUMENE

Pronounced "spawd-u-meen", this mineral is most noted for it's pink or lavender colored form called *Kunzite,* a majestically beautiful—if fragile—gemstone.

Named after Tiffany & Co.'s George Kunz, it was long thought to occur only in the United States but has recently been found elsewhere. It's value increases as the lilac color deepens.

Kunzite is called a "night stone" for good reason; when exposed to daylight its color fades. Also, it's very sensitive to pressure, shock or impact because of its perfect natural cleavage plane.

When spodumene is colored green—ranging from a near-emerald tone to lighter yellowish-green—it's called *Hiddenite*. Originally found in North Carolina, *Hiddenite* is not plentiful, and is most popular in the U.S. It won't fade like Kunzite—but it has the same cleavage potential.

Both *Kunzite* and *Hiddenite* are available in Flawless or Very Slightly Included clarity grades. You'll sometimes see tube-like inclusions which, depending on their visibility, can impair value.

QUARTZ (Crystal Quartzes)

Smoky Topaz Quartz—Sometimes referred to improperly as "Smoky Topaz" it is quite inexpensive and frequently included with rutile needles. Because of dark color, it's often cut shallow.

Amethyst—As the most valuable stone in the quartz group, *amethyst* supposedly will protect one against drunkeness while calming the over wrought and pacifying the frustrated. In better specimens its color is intensely velvet and not color banded or streaked but rather evenly distributed. A touch of red-violet adds to its value.

It's heat sensitive and can fade if exposed to too high a temperature.

Citrine—*Citrine* is believed to improve psychic abilities and strengthen the body. Most commercial *citrines* are heat-treated amethysts or smokey quartz and you can spot this treatment by the decided red tint; rare natural citrines are pure pale yellow. The trade often—incorrectly—calls them a topaz, usually qualified such as Madeira topaz, bahia topaz, etc.

Prasiolite—By heat-treating amethyst and yellow quartz from the Montezuma deposit in Brazil, a leak-green color is obtained called *Prasiolite*. Some cuttable material is also found in Arizona.

Rose Quartz—Sometimes faceted into a slightly turbid transparent gem, *rose quartz* is generally cut en cabochon as ornamental pieces and beads. The color can fade, and sometimes the material can be cut into a six-rayed star.

Other quartz gem varieties that are inexpensive and used mostly in ornamental jewelry include *Aventurine*—a slightly irridescent green or bold-brown opaque stone; *Prase*—a compact quartz aggregate which is opaque and leak-green in color; *Blue Quartz*—a coarse-grained aggregate (the beautiful transparent type is man-made); *Tigereye*—a well-known gold-yellow or gold-brown banded quartz; *Quartz Cat's Eye*—Because of its honey-like natural color it's often mistaken for true Chrysoberyl "Cat's Eye."

CHALCEDONY (Micro-crystalline quartzes)

A distinction is made between **Crystal** and **Micro-Crystalline** quartzes. In the crystal (macrocrystalline) quartz family are the transparent gems and those with various optical effects such as cat's eye and stars. In the chalcedony (microcrystalline) family are the mostly opaque gem material types such as agate, jasper, carnelian, onyx, sard, chrysoprase—and which are cut en cabochon, into beads or carved.

Some of the chalcedony varieties include: *Carnelian*—a flesh-red to brown-red uniformly colored material and whose brown tints are sometimes exposed to sunlight to obtain a better red tint (for all practical purposes *Sard* has no specific separation from a Carnelian which is also thought to still the blood and soften anger); *Chrysoprase*—the most valuable stone in the chalcedony group, it comes mostly from Australia and when properly polished makes a stunning appearance—as fine as the best Imperial Jade apple green. Color might fade in sunlight but can usually be recovered by moist storage. Makes a superb and inexpensive alternate to fine jade; *Heliotrope*—A dark green material with red spots (once thought to be the blood of Christ so magical powers were attributed to it); *Agates*—Named after the Sicilian river Achates where first found, agates are noted for their unique color patterns and interesting layers which appear often like vari-colored growth lines in a tree trunk . . . often dyed because softer layers absorb more dye thus creating exciting color effects . . . gray agate is soaked in sugar solution and then dipped in sulphuric acid to make *Black Onyx* which occurs naturally as a black chalcedony ... agate is also carefully oriented by carvers so that cameo cutting is possible; *Jasper*—Occurs in many colors and usually striped or spotted, it likes to separate along the color bands ... often dyed blue to make an imitation Lapis Lazuli ...

OPAL

Opal is divided into three groups 1) the opalescent precious opals (best known in the jewelry trade; 2) the yellow-red fire opals, and 3) common opals (colorless and often called potch).

Precious Opal—Two types are available: clear, white or milky opal and the rarer and more expensive black opal. In opals look for complete color coverage and variety of colors. With good opals you never need to "look" for or "search" out color.

Most opal experts agree that you should also be able to see the color pattern when the stone is held at arm's length. The distinct "play of colors" in an opal occur as *pinpoint* (small spots of color), *flash* (as the opal is moved a broad sheet or color flash occurs). The color effect descriptions you'll often hear include *harlequin* (a mosaic of relatively large irregularly shaped color patches) *girasol* (nearly colorless but with a slight bluish sheen and red play of color), and *flame opal* (larger strips or columns of color bands or streaks).

Because opal often is found in thin veins, the use of doublets and triplets (generally with a black back or black cement to simulate black opal) is prevalent. The background for the color play is the value key, whether it's milky white, almost clear transparent (sometimes these gems are called *water* or *jelly opals*), or gray or black. Another precious type, called *matrix opal,* is becoming popular and consists of jelly opal segments in a brown host material.

The best precious opal comes from Australia, but recently some white opal from Brazil has appeared on the market which seems less sensitive to heat and less brittle.

Fire Opal—These are mostly reddish or orange opals—usually transparent. Found principally in Mexico, they can be faceted into rather attractive gems—and are often relatively inexpensive. They're also very sensitive to any stress.

Recently, transparent canary yellow opals have been found in Nevada and are being marketed in the United States. The color is somewhat muddy, though.

Watch our for that word "fire" in fire opal. There is sometimes no fire in an opal sense; fire opals can be single colored as well as possess play of color.

Common Opal—Usually opaque and without play of color, this is the opal usually found in promotions where "true" opal rings are sold at bargain basement prices. Actually, common opal is dull and uninteresting, often useful only for backing on doublets and triplets. If you need to "search out" color, you're probably dealing with common opal.

Addressing opals in general, they are too soft and fragile to make good ring gems. Their great beauty, though, is often too inviting to heed this advice. If you buy an opal ring, plan for careful wear—and try to get some metal in the mounting higher than the opal to serve as a protector against harsh blows.

Opal, the birthstone for October, will bring its bearer good luck, superstition says, and symbolizes loyalty and hope. Most of opal's "bad luck" reputation and abrupt eclipse among non-October wearers can be traced to Sir Walter Scott's novel, "Anne of Geierstein," whose heroine, Lady Hermione, wore a magical opal in her hair. The opal would change its colors to match her wicked moods but disintegrated into a small pile of ashes after Lady Hermione splashed—accidentally—holy water on the opal and then herself collapsed in death—into ashes—in the chapel.

JADE

To many people's surprise, the word "jade" is an all-inclusive term for two different and distinct minerals: *jadeite* and *nephrite*.

Jadeite undoubtedly is the mineral men and women have in mind when they think of Chinese artistry and the luscious apple green translucent type called Imperial Jade. Almost all jade of gem value is *jadeite* which comes in a splendid range of colors, of which Imperial is only one grade.

Actually, Imperial Jade derived its name from the Empress Tzu Hsi, the last of the Chou dynasty (1700B.C.). When Chinese artisans completed a piece of work they were required to offer it first to the Empress. She always selected a specific grade of translucent apple green which came to be known as Imperial (but only to Westerners; in the Orient this color grade is called "Old Mine").

The other jade material—*nephrite*—traces its name to the Spanish conquistadores who called the polished pebbles they found in South America *piedra de ijada,* i.e., stone of the kidneys, and believed it would protect against kidney diseases. In 1863 a Frenchman proved that jade actually consisted of the two different types of mineral.

Nephrite is found almost everywhere in the world. *Jadeite* is found principally in Burma (the most valuable deposits) and in Southern California.

The truth is, most knowledge and understanding of jade remains in the Orient where, unfortunately, the Chinese have treated information as a family secret to be passed on from generation to generation. Some of the world's most superb examples of jade artistry have never been displayed by their private Chinese owners.

While the 4 C's are the vital considerations for diamonds and most colored stones, jade is measured in value according to the "3 T's"—Tone, Translucency, and Texture.

According to jade expert John Ng, president of the Jade N Gem Corporation of California, the definition and use of the 3 T's are as follows:

Tone—As with other gem colors Tone, Hue and Intensity describe any specific color. The finest jadeite colors are "penetrating and vivid *from a distance* . . . pure, evenly distributed, and free of brown or grey tones."

Translucency—This quality should range from near transparent to opaque. The highest quality has a body appearance that resembles honey . . . some say it appears as a watery finish.

Texture—The range is from fine to coarse. Texture is closely related to translucency, with the highest quality appearing clear and free of irregularities. Fine rootlike structures within the stone should contrast or enhance the depth of body color, thus adding to the visual appeal. Dark, irregular specks, clouds or blotches detract from the color and are undesirable.

Here is the Green Jadeite Color Grading Terminology listed by Ng:

U.S. Name	Orient Name
Imperial/Emerald	Old Mine
Glassy	Canary
Apple Green	New Mine
Spinach	Peak Green
Moss-in-snow	Pea Green
Apple Green	Flower Green
—	Melon

Please keep in mind that there are some four or five color grades within each of the above categories—running the scale from acceptable, fair, good, very good to exceptional.

The jadeite characteristics that are regarded as most desirable vs. least desirable are:

More Desirable	Less Desirable
Intense color	Dull color
Even color (single colored stone)	Uneven color
Honey-like transparency	Opacity
Translucency	Cloudy appearance
Watery luster	Dehydrated appearance
Smooth finish	Surface cracks, splits, cleavage
Even texture	Blotchy texture
Vivid root-like structure*	Dull root-like structure*
Pure	Mottled

* Not all jadeite is uni-colored. For example, the Moss-in-Snow is a milky white stone shot through with bands and swirls of intense emerald green. In the better grades, there is a very sharp vivid line of demarcation where the green and white meet, not a dull transitional sort of fading from one color to the other.

Some of the reasons for jade's growing popularity in the Western world is the opening of political relations between China and the West, the ease with which jade can be accessorized, and the remarkable range of color possibilities.

You need to be careful, though. People are faced with a staggering range of jade imitations—serpentine (a mineral occurring in all ranges of green with variable appearance but with irregular little spots and, sometimes, black inclusions), quartz (rose and green quartz, and chrysoprase) plastic, and some ambers.

Also, some jadeites are dyed to kick up their color grades. Occasionally with your loupe magnifier you can spot these attempts which appear as clouds, spots, or cracks of collected dye, fine hair lines of dye along natural veins, and muted root-like structures.

Many of the fake names were included in an earlier chapter but here is a listing of some of the efforts to trade in on the jade reputation:

What It's Called	What It Really Is
Silver Peak Jade	Malachite
Mexican Jade	Green-dyed marble or calcite
Transvaal Jade	Green grossular garnet
Korea Jade	Bowenite (form of serpentine)
Amazon Jade	Green microcline feldspar
American Jade	Green idocrase or grossular garnet
Fukien, Manchurian, or Honan Jade	All are green soapstone
Oregon Jade	Dark-green jasper
Australian Jade	Chrysoprase
Indian Jade	Aventurine
Jasper Jade	Dark-green jasper
Colorado Jade	Green microcline (but nephrite does occur in Colorado and is also called "Colorado Jade")

The distinction between jadeite and nephrite is one for the laboratory. Even experts can be fooled.

But the next time you go into a store and rather attractive but inexpensive green gem jewelry is being sold as "Jade Jewelry" you will probably be dealing with nephrite jade—or, less likely, an imitation. Nephrite jade is quite inexpensive for the most part and can be sold as economically as most of the substitutes.

CORUNDUM

Ruby, the birthstone for July, ranges from a few dollars a carat (for low commercial grades) to the most expensive in the gem world. The most valuable color has a slight touch of violet or pink as a secondary color, with value decreasing as purple or violet influence the intense red hue.

In flawless or very slightly included grades, ruby can run into six figures per carat. The same arch-shaped price experience can be found in star ruby. If diamond is king, ruby is certainly the prince and it was not without reason that a ruby hung from the neck of Aaron by God's command. Very, very rare (and quite expensive) in over 10-carat size.

Sapphire is the name given to any other corundum that is not ruby red in color. The deep, rich blue is the most desired color, and the price drops quickly as the secondary gray or violet penetrates the coloration.

Generally speaking, the finest sapphire blue has little secondary color influence at all—and the price per carat grows quickly as clarity improves. Watch for oiling (as well as for ruby, too) and don't allow yourself to be talked into buying a ruby (at the higher price) when the color is a dark red, similar to most dark red garnets, or a light red; they're sapphires not ruby.

Larger sapphires are not all that rare—but in top color and clarity grades they certainly are rare . . . and expensive.

Padparadscha, technically speaking, is a sapphire. But this bright orange corundum has gained immense popularity in the last decade and the carat price for an intense orange, good clarity gem has soared. To distinguish it from other colored sapphires, the padparadscha has been given its own name.

Even included padparadschas are quite costly.

PEARLS

As one of June's birthstones, the **Pearl** is enjoying a tremendous resurgence in public favor throughout the world—and for good reason. Pearls can be worn under nearly any conditions and their inner radiance symbolizes the fragile and the beautiful.

Gifted with a splendid variety of sizes, colors, styles, and types pearl runs the gamut from the natural Oriental Pearl (named Oriental Pearl not becuase they come from the Orient but because the term "Orient" describes the play of color on or just below the surface of a pearl) to the cultured pearl to the outright imitation.

Oriental Pearls are extremely rare and expensive and cultured pearls from China and Japan currently are moving in to satisfy the demand for more reasonably priced pearls. The beauty of the natural or cultured pearl comes from the pattern of distribution of microscopic crystalline particle of calcium carbonate. When an irritant such as a seed pearl is introduced into the oyster (called innoculating) it immediately begins to deposit in concentric layers a calcareous substance consisting of calcium carbonate and nacre.

Depending on the size of the oyster, the size of the irritant, the temperature of the water, and the length of growing time in the water, a pearl is ultimately produced. The deeper is the nacre layer the more rich looking is the pearl. Pearls with a thin layer tend to have a milky appearance and are usually quite inexpensive.

The deeper nacre layers provide a richer lustre, the name given to the most distinguishing factor of a pearl. Lustre is the deep-seated glow formed by the refraction of light through the crystals and which, prism-like, create iridescent beams of color (called Orient) that give the impression of coming from deep within the pearl. Don't mistake lustre with a mere surface shine which is found on thin coated or imitation pearls.

A quick—and reasonably dependable—test for determining between natural and cultured pearls vs. imitation pearls is called the "tooth test." Merely rub the pearl in question lightly against the cutting edge of one of your teeth. If the pearl offers a grainy, rough feel to the touch, chances are that's the nacre and you are dealing with a "real" nacre coated pearl.

Should the pearl rub smoothly, chances are you are dealing with one of the imitation glass or plastic beads—which are sometimes coated with a pearl-like appearing concoction made from fish scales called **Essence d'orient.** Seldom will fake or imitation pearls offer the grainy sensation when rubbed against a tooth.

In reviewing pearls, you should know that after size Orient is the most important consideration, followed by cleanliness (does the pearl have spots, cracks, chips, discolorations on its surface), color, and shape. To an expert, a pearl can be forgiven many things except the lack of orient—that deep inner glow.

As for pearl color, this is a highly individualized decision. In North America, pink or white tones are most valued while Europeans favor the cream pink colors. In South and Central America, dark gold shades are most favored.

The important thing to remember in selecting pearls is that their color must be compatible with your own skin color. If you possess a florid complexion, certainly pink pearls would not be the most suitable selection.

Also, when you are shopping for pearls it's generally better to have them displayed on a white cloth or even a white tissue. Black tends to be a bit too dramatic when purchasing—although the contrast is dynamic when you're wearing pearls.

Colors can range from peach, pink, to cream and go on to golds, greys, blacks, and purples.

As you know, dyeing pearls is quite common. If you suspect this has been done, a cotton daub on the end of a toothpick which contains fingernail polish remover can be touched near the drill hole. The cotton will usually pick up the dye quickly. Under magnification, concen-

139

trations of dye are also often detectable.

The most popular form of pearl jewelry, of course, is the necklace. These come in the following lengths:

> Choker—about 15 inches long (drops just above the collarbone)
> Princess—18 inches long
> Matinee—20-24 inches long
> Opera—28-30 inches long
> Rope—45 inches or more in length (this length is also called a sautoir or lariat).
> Bib—a necklace containing three or more strands

Freshwater pearls tend to have greater cleanliness than salt water pearls so the smoothness of the surface skin is the critical factor. Think of wrinkles—and the more of these you see the less should be the price. When purchasing round pearls the closer to true round you get the higher is the price.

Shape has little price impact with freshwater pearls. You can obtain baroque, rice, flat or semi-round shapes and the prices shouldn't vary much. Furthermore, fresh water pearls can be conveniently drilled in various directions to achieve different effects.

Because of the differences in shape, fresh water cultured pearls are often priced by weight more than by size which can be difficult to judge. With a round pearl, the most critical factor in pricing is the size with the price increasing at a steepening rate as the diameter increases.

For the most part, a reputable jeweler and your own tooth test and eyes will hold you in good stead when purchasing pearls.

Pearls have been increasing rapidly in price since 1971 and no relief is in sight. This is largely due to the inability of suppliers to expand their production. Japan is currently grappling with a water pollution problem, especially with Japan's Lake Biwa where some of the finest fresh water cultured pearls in the world are cultivated.

China is now beginning to export more and more fresh water cultured pearls (this Chinese marketing approach is currently through Japan and the presence of a label, "Pearls Passed Inspection in Japan," is not necessarily proof that the pearls are from Lake Biwa). An effort was initiated in 1980 to develop a fresh water cultured pearl industry in Tennessee—from where most of the seed pearls for Japan's Lake Biwa have been coming for years.

The big pearls ranging from 10.5mm up to, in rare cases, 20mm, come from the South Seas. Pearls found in Australia tend to have a silvery tone while Burmese pearls exhibit a cream-rose luster. The Tahitian variety tends toward the black.

Alexander may have conquered Persia in search of pearls and Cleopatra may have dissolved two priceless pearls in wine to demonstrate her wealth and love for Marc Anthony. The gates of heaven may be formed by pearls.

And pearls may symbolize love, stimulate the passions, and confer immortality.

All these may or may not be true. But one thing is certain: they probably preceded all other gems as an object of value and beauty—and they are as timeless and beautiful now as when man and woman first saw them as a true miracle of God, made in the body of His own creature.

TANZANITE

You won't find this stone among the birthstones or in the older books on gems and jewelry. Fact is, it's probably illegal, too. *Tanzanite* is less than 20 years old. Discovered in the African nation of Tanzania, it is a heat-treated form of the well-known mineral, zoisite. When heated, zoisite from this particular deposit turns a majestic soft sapphire-blue color of outstanding brilliance and intensity.

Because most of the gem materials leaving Tanzania are smuggled out through the Kenyan border rather than go through the official government export agency, most *Tanzanites* are slightly off-beat in morality.

They're very sensitive. Treat with caution—and wear preferably in earrings or pendants. Avoid putting them in rings . . . where they make magnificent showpieces.

PERIDOT

As the August birthstone, *peridot* is the stone symbolic of the gentle but firm leader and can be expected to provide protection from melancholy and illusion. It's yellow-green or olive green color has a soft, subtle appearance sometimes described as "sleepy" . . . like a very heavy lidded hungry tiger pretending drowziness.

Long the favorite of Egyptian pharaohs and kings, it was first discovered on St. John's Island, a remote island in the Red Sea where unauthorized visitors were put to death. Arizona's Indian lands provide most of the world's top grade peridot rough these days.

Large flawless pieces are rare, but in any size the most sought is the Flawless to Very Slightly Included grades. A brown tinge in the color enhances its value. It has low dispersion or fire but the inner radiance is greatly admired. Be careful with it; it's fragile. As with kings and sleepy appearing tigers you knock peridot around at your own risk. Check prong areas closely for setting damage, and review the polish on all facets. Peridot is sometimes unseemingly obstinate about accepting a fine polish—and cutters occasionally give up in disgust.

TURQUOISE

Named the "Turkish Stone" because the trade route that brought *turquoise* to Europe came via Turkey, *turquoise* is one of the oldest gems, having been found in the tombs of the pyramids. Today, most *turquoise* is treated in some manner, even the most inexpensive pieces.

The best quality turquoise comes from the Nischapur area in northeast

Iran. Labeled *Persian Turquoise* it is found naturally in a pure, dense, even blue color . . . compared to turquoise found elsewhere which contain matrix such as brown gray or black veins.

To stabilize the color turquoise is immersed in oil, paraffin, and even impregnated with plastic. A porous stone, it can be easily color improved with aniline dyes and copper salts. Imitations include dyed chalcedony and dyed howlite.

The porosity and chemical composition present color change problems. Heat will turn its sky blue color to green which is what also happens upon exposure to light, perspiration, oils and cosmetics. That's why most old turquoise has a greenish cast to it. You shouldn't wash your hands while wearing turquoise rings . . . the water gets into the pores, turns it green.

LAPIS LAZULI

A rich blue opaque gem mineral, *Lapis Lazuli* was known as the stone of royalty and ranks with turquoise as one of the oldest gemstones.

The best material sometimes referred to as Persian Lapis comes from the West Hindu Kush mountains of Afghanistan where it has always been mined irregularly under primitive conditions. The Afghanistan and the newly discovered Russian deposits near there (but which have a less intense blue) are identified by the presence of pyrite ("fool's gold") inclusions. A lower grade material, streaked with white calcite, is found in Chile. It's an even blue touched with a slight purple that brings the best price.

Watch out for "German Lapis" or "Swiss Lapis"—they're both jasper dyed with prussian blue. Dyed turquoise—the dye is quite evident under magnification—is also used.

In the best quality, Lapis is an evenly distributed intense deep blue. Enough—but not too much—pyrite spots add value and signify genuineness. Lapis is routinely color improved with dye which a cotton dab with some fingernail polish remover will quickly disclose.

MALACHITE

A copper carbonate, *malachite's* concentric banding of distinctive deep and light green rings makes for a lovely ornamental stone.

Neither hard nor resistant, it is sensitive to heat, acid, ammonia, and hot water. Over time, it will lose some of its high luster which can usually be restored by brisk rubbing with a wool cloth.

In the past, it was a favorite for carving and inlaying, but lately has found use for rings, pendants, and, especially, bead strands. Uni-colored pieces of malachite are very rare, and the bull's eye effect is most popular. It chips easily . . . doesn't like chemicals.

IOLITE

Not a particularly well-known gem, *iolite* is often referred to as a "water sapphire." It occurs in various shades of blue, bearing a close but dark similarity to sapphire. The color is deep and the gem is usually cut shallow to admit sufficient light.

Iolite has strong pleochroism (the color changes when viewed from different directions) so don't be surprised when you turn a sapphire-blue iolite on its side—and it appears straw colored.

SPHENE

Another excellent gem material that is not well known, *sphene* is an extraordinary optical performer—actually rivaling the diamond.

It is found as a yellow, brown or green material in Mexico and in Brazil. Although quite soft by gemstone standards, with care it can make a magnificent pendant stone. Its R.I. of 1.88 to 2.05 approaches diamond in light returning capability. Add to that its intense fire and adamantine luster and you have a truly remarkable gem.

Inclusions are generally acceptable in sphene because the brilliance and fire masks them very effectively. Check around the prongs for setting damage, and try to avoid surface blemishes. Be careful in handling; its softness makes it sensitive.

DIOPSIDE

Many people view the rich, deep green diopside as merely a collector's stone because of its softness and easy cleavage.

Used in a pendant and looked after with a bit more care than usual, the diopside when faceted makes a fine commercial gem. Some material is cut en cabochon and these display both 4 and 6 rayed stars. Faceted, it can challenge a fine emerald in appearance.

Enstatite is closely related to diopside and is also cut en cabochon to display a 4-rayed star. These are sometimes passed off as "Indian Black Star Sapphires." They're soft, split easily—but surprisingly attractive . . . in a pendant. Cheap too.

CHAPTER EIGHT

STYLE: . . . is the Person

Some designers view jewelry as merely an adjunct, an accessory, to attractive costuming.

Maybe so.

Even a cursory examination of literature on dress produces little information on the selection and use of jewelry to achieve certain costuming and cosmetic effects. Most books go to great lengths on advising their readers in such areas as colors, fabrics, and hemlines.

But any recommendation on complete costuming is generally concluded with some debatable last minute thought such as, "and then a nice red pin to add a dash of color."

What an outrageous simplicity! Jewelry is heavy artillery. A gem is an eye catcher—and an eye holder.

More than any other item in your adornment inventory, jewelry represents your own highly personal statement, "This is what I am and it reflects my ideas of value and beauty, my sense of harmony and balance."

Jewelry—unlike clothing—does not hint of "what I want to be."

You either have beautiful, fine jewelry—or you don't. You either wear it tastefully and appropriately—or you don't.

Subject to many exceptions, there are rules of dress; a bright satin cocktail dress may be fine for evening wear but hardly appropriate for a business luncheon.

Jewelry has its rules, too. In business, it's often an advantage to wear little jewelry; a single ring—flat to the finger so as not to draw too much attention—and, if your ears are pierced, single gold posts.

Even when you have a fine jewelry collection you must be careful. The general word of caution is don't wear your most expensive jewels at a first meeting. You're better off in sneaking up on people with fine jewelry, until they know you. That's especially true with diamonds—the detonators.

One highly successful woman, wife of an equally successful business executive in Boston, had an imposing collection of diamond jewelry. In the business circles she and her husband traveled it was appropriate for her to "undim the diamonds." Her friends and associates knew her and accepted the fact that she owned such fine gems.

When her husband was promoted and sent to the mid-West, she un-

Fig. 8-1 Gems are potent. They catch the eye, hold it—and then tell viewers something of the status, power, taste, and value statement of the wearer.

wittingly caused a near-disaster. At a party given by her husband and her, the woman wore a few choice diamonds. From the moment the first guests arrived to welcome the newcomers, she was in trouble.

None of the other woman either had or wore such "rocks." The woman's effort to ingratiate herself with a new round of friends simply failed as the guests interpreted her appearance in the worst possible way—"show off." Recognizing her miscalculation, the woman put her diamonds away—but she had still not totally recovered from the evening even by the time her husband won another promotion back east.

Jewelry is a mere accessory? Not when it can have that kind of impact. If you abruptly enjoy an improvement in your good fortune or lifestyle you can generally adjust your appearance reasonably fast to reflect that change.

You can go out and buy new clothes; fashions change regularly enough and, if in doubt, you can always buy "designer's" clothes. Taste, judgement, or refinement isn't all that vital when going the designer fashion route.

Or, you can go out and buy a new car; they change the styling every year so it's merely a matter of dollars.

But you can't very well go out and buy a new collection of jewelry. It takes time to build a collection which accurately reflects your own constantly developing sense of self and style. Make an obvious mistake with an "eye catcher" and your reputation for "gauche" will stay with you. You need a self-developing sense of appreciation of your own jewelry . . . and that takes time.

After all, the judicious use of jewelry can make you appear younger, older, lighter in skin tone, darker in skin tone, taller, shorter, thinner, heavier.

It isn't necessary to rush out and begin your collection pell mell as did the famous actress Sarah Bernhardt. She was so enamored of diamond jewelry that at the height of her career she simply turned over her Broadway check to her jeweler to pay for her diamonds.

Buy the Better Pieces . . .

Take your time. Work at developing your own style. If big, ostentatious jewels aren't your thing, if you feel uncomfortable with larger pieces, than plan a daintier jewelry style that fits you.

There are always exceptions to any rule in costuming and jewelry, but one guideline for which is heard little criticism is this: buy good jewelry from the beginning.

Please note that no mention is made in this guideline concerning expensive vs. inexpensive, of precious vs. semi-precious. These factors just aren't important. The precious/semi-precious issue is foolish, inconsequential, irrelevant, and inaccurate. With regard to expense, good jewelry is good jewelry—and isn't automatically expensive; it merely reflects sound jewelry judgement by a buyer.

With continuing technological developments, costume jewelry today can match the appearance of fine jewelry pieces so that even an expert has difficulty telling at a glance. Yet costume jewelry can never inspire in a wearer the feeling of total confidence which comes with being adorned by a fine article. The quality workmanship, the enduring beauty and value, the rarity, and the awareness of the genuine are conditions of the mind that can't be measured in dollars and cents.

If you are starting out on your jewelry collection and your budget places emphasis on more vital necessities you would be well served to save up a little at a time and then buy a good piece of jewelry. Then plan for the purchase of the next good item.

Take a good, realistic look at yourself, at those qualities which are relevant to a jewelry collection—your physical appearance, your color and complexion, any particular considerations which might need subtle attention (long fingers, short fingers, round face, long neck, etc.) Write out a long range plan so you'll know what you want in a jewelry collection at the end of three, five, seven, ten years.

Work towards that long range goal.

While building your collection, you needn't back away entirely from costume jewelry. An item here and there can round out your jewelry requirements temporarily, filling in the spots until you can replace them with good pieces.

A fine jewelry collection doesn't need to be a large collection either. A modest number of well-chosen pieces—deliberately picked to afford ver-

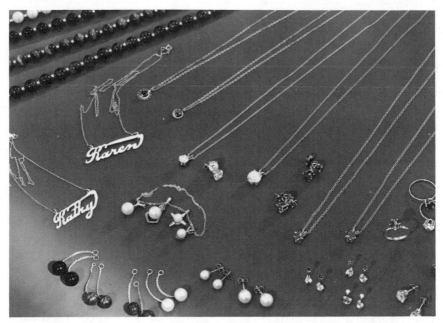

Fig. 8-2 A fine jewelry collection can be low in the number of items but high in quality. Judicious, not necessarily expensive, selection is the key . . . to providing for a flexible and appropriate jewelry collection.

satility—can provide you with enough options to affect a stimulating style . . . one that is you.

Good jewelry has lasting value and beauty and eventually will figure in your selection of costumes as you keep an eye on the mutual harmony of your wardrobe and your jewelry. This, again, makes your jewelry more than a mere accessory—and expands your wardrobe flexibility which is a hallmark of excellence and taste.

Once you begin this kind of comprehensive planning, you are on the way to achieving a unique, individualistic style. And style is the person. Fashions and fashion designers with their expensive names may come and go—but style, like a true work of art, endures.

One merely needs to think of some famous people to draw a mind's eye image of them and their style.

Famous songstress Lena Horne, with her dark good looks, wearing white coral, pale aqua blue and white. Eurasian actress Nancy Kwan, with golden olive skin, dark hair and eyes, wearing scarlet, beige and olive green predominantly, with a careful selection of gold jewelry and pearls.

Earlier, it was mentioned that good jewelry doesn't necessarily mean expensive jewelry. Indeed, fine jewelry pieces can be executed for modest prices—including the precious metals such as gold, silver, platinum which, really, are the sine qua non of fine jewelry.

Popularity and tradition have a significant influence in the price of gems. They obviously account for the sky rocketing price of some gems.

You needn't follow the crowd. Develop your own awareness of the unexplored range of possibilities open to you by selecting fine gems as genuine, valuable but less costly alternatives to the well-known and expensive gems. This way you will build a wonderful collection at a fraction of the cost of many other less informed hasty check writers.

Just as an example: consider, if you will, a fine specimen of the apple-green slightly translucent grade of Jadeite—recognized throughout the world as Imperial Jade—which could easily cost thousands of dollars for a cabachon about the size of your thumb.

Encrust this Imperial Jade cabachon with a row of melee diamonds and you could have an article of jewelry whose cost approaches five figures.

How could you as a gem-aware buyer obtain an equally rich-looking jewelry item? Next, how could you be assured that the alternate piece of jewelry you ultimately select is a fine piece, containing a genuine precious gem? Finally, how could this strategy be achieved at, say, less than 1/10th the cost of a diamond rimmed Jade?

It's really quite simple—and you need to know only about 20 gem varieties to solve this challenge . . . or almost any challenge similar to it.

First, you might have the cabachon cut from Chrysoprase, a bright lustered apple-green micro-crystalline quartz that is often confused with Imperial Jade. Rather than diamonds, the melee could be full cut white Zircons. Zircons have a high refractive index which would give good brilliance and even in an ice white color disperse colors well. Don't be scared away from diamond accents either. As melee they are surprisingly inexpensive—and incomparable.

In a yellow gold setting, you would have a beautiful fine quality genuine alternate—and one that would appreciate in value over the years.

The genuine ruby is rapidly becoming the most expensive gem on earth in comparable size. For many, it's simply out of any reasonable price range in the higher color and clarity grades.

How could you, if you truly wanted a dazzling transparent red faceted gem, add, if not a red king, at least a genuine red prince to your jewelry collections?

Well, good clarity and bright color would be available at a greatly reduced cost to you in a faceted transparent rhodochrosite (this is a relatively soft gemstone so you would need to be careful and have the mounting built up over the gem to protect it against wear), a red spinel, a red garnet, a red beryl, a red topaz, or red tourmaline.

All of these alternate gems differ somewhat from the tone and intensity of the red ruby—but each is a fine, precious red gem and can make a magnificent addition to any quality conscious owner's collection.

Surprisingly often, the intelligent selection of a genuine piece of jewelry isn't that far from the price of the better grades of costume jewelry.

And after investing a substantial amount of your money it is one thing to open your jewelry drawer and find there a collection of costume trinkets, tarnished chains, links, and single earrings.

It's something else entirely to find items of great beauty, enduring quality and appreciating value—and to recognize each piece as a beautiful testament to your own wise and judicious planning and buying.

Perhaps a good question for any jewelry buyer to ask when about to buy a piece of costume jewelry: "Would I buy this particular piece of jewelry if it were real and I could afford it?" If your answer is "no" you might consider letting that purchase await the next customer.

If you're a man buying for yourself—or especially gift buying for a woman—why buy an inexpensive piece of costume jewelry on every occasion? Save up, if you must, and then buy a good piece of enduring value.

A wife will appreciate this—and she'll have something valuable in the end, something into which she can comfortably invest a special sentiment.

Guidelines for Jewelry Selection . . .

Setting down guidelines for anyone to help them select jewelry is at best difficult. There are more exceptions than there are guidelines, and there are as many different criteria for jewelry selection as there are variations in people, each with his or her own build, complexion, coloring—and personality.

Before considering jewelry, you perhaps should review four elements that comprise "total look" costuming:

Color: Tradition and culture have established the appropriate use and meaning of color, as well as people's psychological reaction. Used in accordance with accepted rules, color provides the excitement, the drama of costuming . . . otherwise—(?)

Materials: The kind of material—including texture, appearance and quality—of anything used to adorn a person—likewise conveys a powerful message when used within the confines of certain rules. Tweed and satin carry totally different messages for an onlooker—or wearer.

Cosmetics: Call cosmetics the "eye catchers," the "camouflage," but cosmetics by any other name is still cosmetics . . . that which enhances, controls and leads the onlooker's eye, creates effects, changes and alters the appearance of reality. It's not an afterthought in costuming, but a carefully integrated component.

Style: One might question "style" for being listed along with the other elements of a "TOTAL LOOK" but it is much more than a mental combination of the other three—color, materials, cosmetics. *Style is the Person;* it represents the visual evidence for an individual's realization of costuming. It isn't fashion fads, hemline up today, hemline down tomorrow. Style is that indefinable, enduring quality found in a person's value judgement of dress and demeanor. Without a mature sense of style a man or woman might just as well pull a suit off the discount rack or dash madly to keep up with the dictates of the garus of today's fashion, tomorrow's chic—and yesterday's "out of style."

149

Effects of Color . . .

What makes people so fascinated by gemstones?

Gemstones contain the brightest and most brilliant of nature's colors—and bright colors attract the eyes.

So gems can be used to maneuver other people's eyes, to guide them where you want them to look.

Like to appear thinner? Try darkening the colors of your costume—not just black or somber, but rather dark values. The darker the color the slimmer the figure looks (and that's probably why every woman in the world has an uncompleted wardrobe until she has a basic black dress).

The opposite holds true for someone wanting to appear heavier. The lighter the color, the heavier you look. It's generally recommended that a thin person, wishing to appear heavier, is better off wearing medium-light to light colors. For top heavy types of figures, the darker shades should be above, and the lighter ones below.

As for age and color, light blue is much more youthful looking than dark blue (although baby blue *and* pink are usually too youthful for a mature woman). A surprisingly useful color tactic when going for a younger look is to feature medium color values in the over-all costume while utilizing light color values (light colored gems?) at the neckline.

If for cosmetic reasons you wish to feature a look of maturity, get away from the youthful looking soft bright blues and feature soft *gray blues.*

While the above color generalizations are helpful in achieving over-all impressions, you should guard against giving short shift to any one of the other three total look elements. In too many cases a woman will plan for a careful match of dress, hat and shoes.

Then, almost as an afterthought, she'll throw in one or two pieces of jewelry, grab her handbag, and wonder where the TOTAL LOOK went.

If jewelry is to serve its full function it must be planned just as carefully as the other adornments. Even greater attention should be applied to the selection and placement of jewelry because it has such an enormous impact.

A vivid piece of jewelry—just as a vivid color—should be limited to a single area and probably not repeated. For a balanced TOTAL LOOK you want "eye catchers." What you don't want is too many eye jumps. A pink hat and pink gloves with a black dress is attractive; a pink coral pin, a pink purse and pink shoes, too, is just too much.

As for jewelry, it has the strength to alter radically the look of a dress or suit. When used as an accessory, remember that "access" is not "excess."

Jewels to Enhance the Face . . .

All eyes ultimately lead to the face. Here is the focus of attention.

Nothing serves the purpose better than jewelry in drawing attention to the face and then keeping it there—or leading it away for one cosmetic reason or another.

The rules for enhancing the face with gems and color are usually well understood. A woman with bright blue eyes can enhance their blueness by complementing them with turquoise, blue topaz, aquamarine, or light blue sapphires.

Few can wear bright green jade, chrysophrase, and emeralds better than a woman with red hair and green eyes . . . or just red hair.

Likewise, silver and white gold enhance silver haired individuals. Blondes show best with gold, the yellow Citrine quartz, chrysoberyl (a hard golden yellow gem), or helidor (a yellow beryl).

Dark haired women can lend special drama to their appearance by wearing coral and rubies.

Very bright gems, incidentally, such as rubies, sapphires, coral, and emeralds or tsavorite (a brilliant green garnet the color almost of emerald) are very useful for cosmetizing the apparent color of skin.

Wearing these bright gems in earrings, for instance, gives a white skin a healthier browner look. At the same time, they tend to lighten the color perception of brown or black skin.

The sensors of the eye are overloaded by these bright colors. Inasmuch as color is not a constant this overloading causes the eyes to reverse somewhat for white and black. You can test this yourself if you stare at something intently for about 10 seconds (try it on the U.S. flag with its bright reds and blues) and then shift your gaze quickly to a white or blank wall and stare at a single spot. You'll see an image of the reversed flag imposed on the blank wall.

Selecting, Wearing the Best Piece . . .

Because the face is the center of focus it is in your interest to pay particular attention to the color and style of jewels you wear close to the face.

Facial outlines vary, of course, but most may be classified as round, squarish, oval, or triangular. Each outline offers certain advantages and each has its own limitations. The outlines—with the use of jewels—can be accentuated, modified . . . or the eyes can be drawn away (Fig. 8-3).

Jewels, too, can be used strategically to draw attention away from certain facial characteristics, i.e., large earrings that cover the ear lobes tend to offset a prominent nose with satisfying effect.

Let's take some time to consider the ears. They're vital to the stylish and effective use of jewelry.

For many years, women have believed that long, dangling earrings can be used to achieve a narrowing effect on the face. Right?

Well, maybe not. Long, *thin* earrings are the only ones that have a narrowing effect. As a matter of fact, dangling earrings can be a bit of a problem for the unwary.

For high style, they are nearly the epitome.

But, tear shaped earrings are most suitable for an already narrow face because they make a full face appear even fuller; it's the tear shape that does it. Also, be careful about *long* dangling earrings if you're mature, i.e., you're starting to develop character folds at the corners of your mouth.

Long, dangling earrings that approach the lower chin level tend to

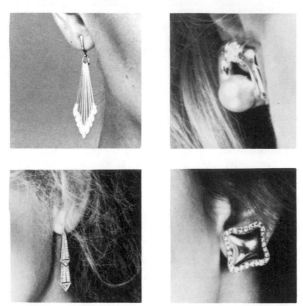

Fig. 8-3 Only long, *thin* dangling earrings create a narrowing effect to the face. Too long earrings may also cause somewhat of a problem for the mature face in that they accentuate "drop lines". Also, large round, button types of pearl earrings are excellent for thin faces but add fullness to a round face. Geometric shaped figures such as diamond shapes, rectangles, squares are rather neutral and somewhat thinning.

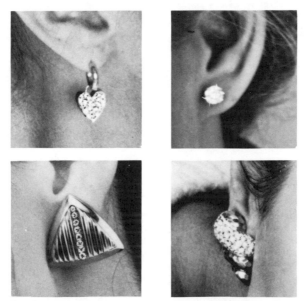

Tear or triangular shaped earrings, close to the ear, are excellent for adding fullness to a narrow face. They may be a bit of a problem for a full face—but used as a drop of dangle can sometimes create the narrowing appearance . . . in cooperation with make-up and hairdo. Stud-set diamond solitaire earrings are still the favorite (right)—and for good reason; they're appropriate for virtually any face under almost any circumstance. Covering the lobe is a favorite technique for downplaying a prominent nose.

152

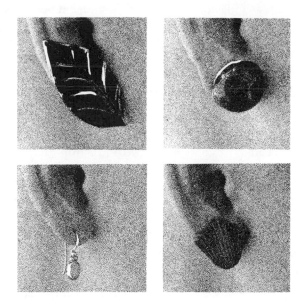

To Add Fullness

Bold, metallic, attention-gathering figures (1) such as "leaves" will create width to a narrow face; so will any kind of button (especially if brightly colored) or pearl (2). Drop or dangle (3) earrings that are *not* narrow or that *do* have a round or tear shape give a fuller look.

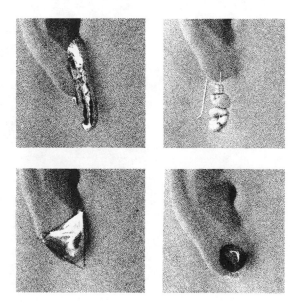

To Reduce Fullness

Long, *narrow* or thin dangling earrings (5) create a more vertical image. A drop of baroque stones on a thin earwire (6) can achieve the same effect. Angular shapes close to the face have a narrowing (7) effect, too.

153

"drop" facial lines—and can make you look older. If you are mature and still want the long dangling earring effect, work for an oval configuration around the face—in other words lead the eyes in an oval path around and below the chin. A pendant or pin can help to accomplish this oval pattern.

While there is truth in the custom of a large woman wearing large and/or heavy (make that *heavier*) jewelry, nevertheless a large, round button-type earring—or a jumbo pearl—is more apt to add fullness to the round face.

You might consider—if your face is round or full—the wearing of oval or rectangular earrings *close to the face*. They add little width impression and give the appearance of greater length to the face.

Pearl earrings on a stud are appropriate for just about any face. While colored earrings will reduce the drabness of a dull or colorless complexion, be wary of pink pearls (or pink anything) near the face if you have a florid complexion. Pink, it's generally agreed, can make such a complexion appear anemic.

It should be remembered that slavish attention to the above observations about earrings would not be in your own best interests. After all, style is often accomplished by the clever breaking of rules.

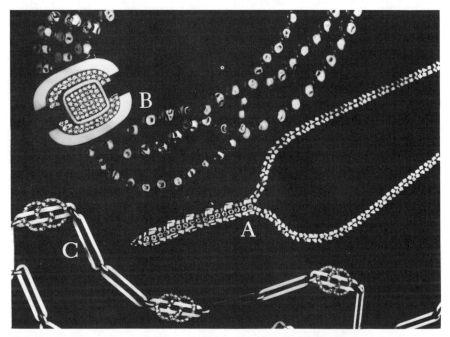

Fig. 8-4/5/6 By using a longer, somewhat tapering line offered by a pendant-type necklace (A), a slimming illusion is created. A choker or short single bead strand (B) will make a neck appear shorter, usually giving an impression of a broader face or fuller face. Type B neckware is usually most effectively worn by those with a slender face and neck; ditto for the short multi-strand necklace. Non-pendant types such as medium length chains or bead strands (C) are neutral or help to provide the desired oval look. They also greatly enhance large and/or tall figures.

Also, the effective use of jewelry depends more on the configuration of your face or body. It depends on your own personality requirements, hair styling, skin coloring, and skin texture.

Extremely long earrings may "drop" your facial lines (if the earring style, placement and texture creates that impression given certain facial lines) and they may add fullness to a truly full face.

But for a very tall, thin figure they might be just what the designer ordered. Long, massive pendant-style earrings conceal the neck—and add width of both space and figure. Costume and hair style would be equally important considerations . . . for long, massive earrings or any other kind.

Addressing the matter of neck adornment, an appropriate pendant or chains are marvelously effective for enhancing—or drawing attention away from—your neck.

The general principle holds that a pendant-style necklace (Fig. 8-4) tends to make a long, tapering line downward, and thus gives a viewer the impression of seeing a neck that seems longer and thinner than it actually is.

Should you wish to effect an apparently shorter neck, try a shorter chain or choker or hoop (fig. 8-5). A chain (Fig. 8-6) is somewhat neutral. Wearing chains of this length does contribute to the desired over-all oval effect.

Perhaps the neck adornment which must be used most judiciously is the choker, or short chained pendant with a gemstone setting.

Again, the integration of a pendant with the style of dress, costume line, hair styling—in short, the complete effect—is the first and most critical consideration. An awareness of the effect created by various pendant styles is useful.

A choker definitely is most effective when worn with a long, slender neck or face because it tends to add fullness to the neck, makes it appear shorter, and broadens slightly facial outlines—especially round or oval faces.

Nor is it true that multistrand chokers will shorten long slender necks better than a single strand or chain/pendant. Multistrands are effective (Fig. 8-7) for slender necks (they are particularly effective for bare necks with costume necklines worn low and away). Should a neck be too long, though, the multistrand choker can draw too much attention, giving an overly long look.

How to get around such a problem if you do have a rather, long thin neck? A high collar—bringing the costume line up off the shoulders and onto the neck)—can make a multistrand useful and effective. It is helpful, too, if the neckline features a dominant flowing line over one side. This neatly breaks up the vertical line from the face to the costume, foreshortening the overall effect (Fig. 8-8).

Getting attention away from the face is rather easily achieved by the use of a pendant type necklace (Fig. 8-9). Many woman use a pendant shape similar to their own facial configuration (with the exception of round

Fig. 8-7/8/9 Effective costuming allows flexibility in jewelry wear. While a multi-strand choker may draw too much attention to a full neck, it can often be worn as a complement to a high collar. A broad, full face and/or neck usually isn't enhanced either by a choker, but can often work if the wearer creates a vertical or oval eye flow, using a low or medium collar (B) which flows one lapel over the other—with perhaps a pen or ornamental design to draw the eye into the much-desired oval sweep. An oval shape or oval cut gem (C) poses the least style problem because—depending on the pendant size—it tends to complement a thin face, slim a round one, and draw attention to the pendant itself, thus creating a vertical eye sweep.

faces) and use color to pull the eye to the pendant.

For contrast and a flair, try a complementary color (colors which are opposite each other on a color wheel). A good example of complementary color use, would be an emerald, Imperial jade or chrysoprase pendant for a red costume or a red-head . . . not too much, though to avoid too much Christmas look.

For a more subtle approach to the same objective, you could select an analogous color (colors which are side by side on the color wheel) for the gem. A good example of this approach would be to wear a yellow or green gemstone with a chartreuse costume—rather than a complementary color such as the purple amethyst (which is, incidentally, stunning). For more on the color wheel, see Fig. 8–13.

For round faced individuals, the style strategy should be somewhat altered. A round facial outline with a short, broad neckline would be best served by a vertical line that draws the eye along a "thinning" route.

Costumes that lie close and flat and high toward the neck often appear to make the neck seem broader, fuller. A short choker or pendant necklace naturally produces a broadening effect. The viewer's eye isn't moving in enough of a vertical plane.

One approach might be oval or rectangular earrings, a prominent collar with one side flowing over the other with a medium drop chain with a square or oval gemstone, not too big if the pendant is to lie flat against the skin. The pendant necklace might be larger if it falls on the outside of the dress or costume.

Some ornamentation on the collar would be a decided asset, such as embroidery or a contrast material in texture or color.

An attractive pin placed in the center chest area helps contribute to the illusion of thinning. A single pin placed to one side is a nice accent too because it establishes a visual point of interest below the face. The costume neckline is equally important. A "V" neckline tends to thin because of the vertical eye movement—but a turtle neck, say, would need a low gem to keep the eye moving down.

While a single pin or clip worn front and center has a slenderizing effect, a moment's reflection on the obvious will remove most doubt that a pair of pins spaced apart offer a broadening effect.

For the most part, pins and clips are worn to break up the eye flow line in costuming. They are strategic pieces and their placement can add a delightful note of panache to costuming.

Survey after survey demonstrate that rings are the most popular pieces of jewelry. They far outsell other kinds of jewelry in total number of pieces sold and in dollars.

It's not difficult to determine why. The hands are always in motion and rings are constantly on display and—when it comes to sparkle—constantly in play.

Ring choices therefore can be most important. A wise choice in a ring can change the apparent look of the entire hand and fingers.

For example, a large emerald ring on the hand of a small woman would definitely give the impression of a forceful personality. Yet, most women with small figures and small hands shy away from a large ring.

Fig. 8-10 A relatively large ring—especially a square or emerald cut—tends to square off the hand, providing a shortened appearance. The same effect can often be achieved by wearing a thinner, horizontal flowing style ring on the ring finger.

By the same token, a large ring—perhaps a button or cluster type—worn on the little finger will give the impression of shortening the hand. Overly long, thin hands are well served by a horizontal style ring (Fig. 8-10) because the change of line direction tends to shorten the fingers.

Long fingers look attractive, too, when wearing a large oval shape, marquise, or emerald-cut shape.

Long fingers are not necessarily slender fingers. Small, light rings are more appropriate for giving strength and additional grace to slender hands and fingers.

If your hands are characterized by short, blunt fingers an elongated ring will give such fingers a decidedly more graceful look. Of course, you should by no means restrict your ring styles to the marquise as shown in the illustration. It would be a good idea though to lean towards a style that gives an elongated appearance. This could be accomplished by select-

Fig. 8-11 Generally speaking, short blunt fingers or a square hand are enhanced by a narrower ring style (A). A large button type (B) is best with large hands and fingers, while a horizontal style (D) gives a fuller look to thin fingers and hands. A small button or gem type (C) flatters thin fingers and hands, too.

ing gems or setting types with long, rectangular cuts, or a series of gems designed to flow along the finger line or at a slight diagonal line (Fig. 8-11).

Large hands and fingers look best with large rings, just as a tall, strong figure is best adorned with heavier styled jewelry. Small rings on large hands and fingers tend to make them appear even bigger.

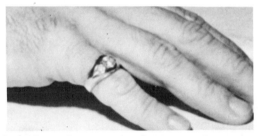

Fig. 8-12 Psychology plays a large part in ring wear. A large emerald cut on a small female hand would hint strongly of an assertive personality because one just isn't customarily supposed to wear a BIG ring or gem on a small hand. A man augments his power-authority impression when he regally consigns an expensive diamond ring to a casual pinkie position. General attitude holds that a man's ring finger is acceptable for wedding bands, school rings, or service/club rings—and diamonds (unless they're in a masonic ring) are seen as a bit "show offy" when worn on the ring finger.

The styles for large hands and fingers could be a button type, or button with supporting accent stones set in an encircling rim (Fig. 8-12).

While it is true that a prominent little finger ring will appear to diminish the length of the hand, if the hand is square, strong—and if the wearer has a forceful personality—a little finger ring will accentuate the appearance of a strong, square hand.

This is a good principle to remember when buying men's rings. A ring—even a large class ring—appears neutral on a man's ring finger. It's traditional, totally acceptable, and carries no particular psychological message for a man to wear a ring on his ring finger.

A diamond ring—or any ring not of a class, lodge, or service type—conveys something else. Diamonds are worn by men who can afford them, who have achieved something in their lives.

When a man wears a diamond on his ring finger he is sending out some pretty powerful signals—and this is especially true if its a masonic ring with a diamond. He is, indeed, rolling out some heavy artillery for anyone with or without a discerning eye to notice.

Let that man place a diamond ring on his little finger, and he loads the message with additional impressions. Given any size to the ring, it will square off the hand, hint of a strong, forceful personality.

But a man, psychologically speaking, who wears a diamond ring on the little finger is signalling a "born to royalty" sign. His highly valuable gem is subjected to much greater danger and he wears his achievements subtly, jauntily.

The chapter would not be complete without some discussion on bracelets. Some designers feel that bracelets are really suitable only for longer, slender arms.

Actually, if you're lucky and have long, slender arms you can get away with almost any choice in bracelet styles, including wearing two or more on each wrist.

If your arms and wrists are plump, it is logical that smaller, thinner bracelets are more becoming. But this is true only if the arm is bare. Given a full arm's length sleeve, a large bracelet can be worn quite stylishly; the appearance of a bare, plump arm doesn't, in this instance, contribute to a viewer's over-all impression of stoutness.

With the heavier wrist or arm it is vital, too, that the bracelet fit loosely. This physical characteristic doesn't lend itself to the tighter style available to the slender armed type; no squeezing or pushing of the skin should be visible or even hinted at.

Jewelry, Costuming and "Total Look" . . .

In everything that has been said in this chapter, the two main principals are: One, the oval is the geometric figure that most closely complements the body shape so viewer eye movements should be directed along this sweeping line, and two, color carries powerful psychological significance and can provide the most powerful cosmetic effect, i.e., the creation of a desired illusion.

Brightly colored earrings can make a dull complexion appear much less drab—and so can color in the costuming. Color imparts dignity, maturity; it makes one's appearance healthier, livelier.

Some people have an innate feel for using color to its full advantage. And some, alas, have the same skills as the husband who is forever selecting the precise wrong necktie to go with his suit.

Telling someone how to dress is the height of presumption. But there are generally accepted rules in color use that can be learned very quickly. This involves use of the traditional color wheel. (Fig. 8-13).

A color wheel is not within the strict province of the artist. It is available for anyone who takes the few minutes time required to learn some of its marvelous secrets.

Look at the color wheel. You need only to pick a color as a starting point. The color directly across the wheel is called the "Complementary

Color" and the colors immediately adjacent to your starting color are referred to as "Analogous Colors" and sometimes as "Harmonious Colors."

It's nice to know that Yellow, Red, and Blue are Primary Colors and that Orange, Green, and Violet are Secondary Colors which result from mixtures of two Primary colors. It's nice—but not necessary to know.

For exceptionally effective color coordination you need only to pick a starting, base color and keep to a Complementary and/or the Analogous colors as shown in a color wheel—and there you have, in very simplified terms to be sure, the magic of color matching.

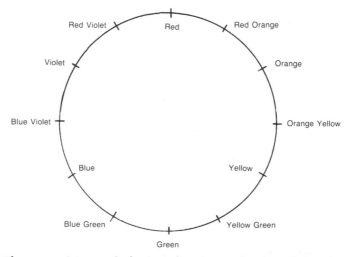

Fig. 8-13 The appropriate use of color is made quite easy by using the standard artist's color wheel. Complementary colors which go together are directly opposite each other on the wheel, while analogous colors which go together are those which are immediately adjacent to the primary or dominant color. It's that simple.

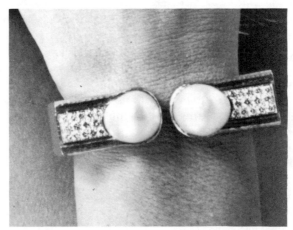

Bracelets, generally should be worn loose fitting. If your wrist or arm is full, it's especially important to avoid tight-fitting bracelets because pinched skin accentuates the fullness.

And what a magic land of gemstone opportunity this knowledge of the color wheel opens up. For any given costume color there is a gemstone color to harmonize or to complement.

Were you to have a beautiful amethyst—a relatively inexpensive gem—pendant and ring, just think of the attractiveness and versatility it would display with a purple or blue-violet costume.

Or swing across the color wheel for a Complementary color—a chartreuse color dress—and you have a dramatic ensemble possibility.

Let's take another example. With a blue dress, you could pick earrings featuring the new orange garnet from Africa, called a Malaya garnet. This would be a dynamic complementary selection. There are, incidentally, orange colored tourmalines and orange colored corundum gems called Padparadschas.

How beautiful would be a blue-eyed woman wearing a turquoise dress with pendant and ring in ruby red, garnet red, tourmaline red, or a brilliant red topaz.

So far, all the emphasis has been placed on single gem or single color jewelry pieces. In building your collection, you should give serious thought to multi-gem pieces.

Diamonds, of course, are the perfect accent stones for any gems. That's why they are used so much in jewelry; their matchless brilliance gives the thrill of richness to almost any jewelry creation.

But for reasons of economy or just good old fashioned design creativity you might reach out for something different and new. For example, a row of fine helidors (brilliant yellow beryl) or small Chrysoberyls (a brilliant yellow gem) could provide for a memorable accenting of such light green gems as the Peridot or a light green tourmaline.

CHAPTER NINE

PRECIOUS GEMS: To Invest or To Adorn

Are diamonds all that good of an investment?

How about colored stones? Are they a good investment, too?

Or should a person purchase gems and jewelry for other reasons? Should gems be limited to beauty . . . to be worn . . . to adorn?

Regardless of the answer to these questions, something quite new has come into the North American gem markets. In the last 10-15 years the traditional marketing concept of "let the customer come to me" has needed to allow room for a brash new upstart marketing approach. That approach can be described as "find a customer and sell him or her."

People on both sides of the gem connection and often with little or no past experience in the gem markets had discovered the gem investment business. As economic conditions throughout the world created an environment for alternative investments as a hedge against an uncertain future, the public began to focus attention on diamonds and on colored stones.

Individuals with sharp, well honed marketing instincts saw the market begin to develop. They responded by coming out after the money-in-hand prospects. The sellers were not—and had no intention of—selling gems as such to anyone; they were selling hopes and fears . . . hedges against the frightening possibility of losing one's hard earned savings.

The idea of storing value in gems or metals perhaps was new in North America, but not in Europe. The latter had had centuries of experience in political and economic catastrophes. Europeans had always stored away some of their net worth in tangibles that could be sold or bartered in an emergency, i.e., diamonds, colored gems, gold, silver, platinum.

As people in North America perceived a worsening world situation they became increasingly receptive to the idea of investing hard dollars in gems. The 1970s and 80s saw a marketing system form quickly to respond as the ready-to-be-convinced buying public hurtled into the gem investment game.

Most of the investors had no knowledge or understanding of gemstones and had even less appreciation of their purpose.

People bought diamonds and then more diamonds. The price per carat soared. For the sellers, it was a bonanza.

And bonanzas have a marvelous talent for attracting certain undesirable elements. Fast-buck operators were quick to join such situations.

162

Fig. 9-1 As economic conditions deteriorate and people move to protect their assets against inflation, investing in collectibles becomes more attractive. It was inevitable that diamonds and colored stones would become part of the money game, along with books, art, stamps, gold and precious metals, etc.

In retrospect, the entry of unethical types was almost inevitable. Retail jewelers, aghast that diamonds and colored gems could be treated in the same commodity sense as pork bellies and sorghum, balked at selling gems like corporate stocks. Since the gem investment market which also required aggressive marketing—going after the prospects where they lived and worked rather than awaiting their arrival in a jewelry store setting —was a "hard sell" type of activity, jewelers allowed a vacuum to occur.

Vacuums in the real world have a very short life. The one in the gem investment business was shorter than most if it even existed at all. Into the market came the so-called "gem investment companies." They set up "boiler room" operations with rows of high-pressure salesmen reciting prepared sales pitches into the telephone to anyone whose name had found its way onto a "prospect" or "pigeon" list.

The salesman—many of whom knew only enough about gems to keep one step ahead of their customers who knew virtually nothing—successfully "fanned up" the national market. To reassure buyers, understandably cautious about sending large amounts of money to peo-

163

ple they didn't know, gem investment companies encouraged the preparation of impressive certificates from gemological laboratories whose purpose was to attest to the quality of the diamonds being proffered. In some cases, diamonds were actually switched. Others ingeniously provided customers with certificates then sealed the "guaranteed to be the same diamond" in plastic with the warning that the guarantee would be broken if the plastic was. When enough victims finally did work up their nerve and break the seal they found all sorts of substitutes. One gem investment house even specialized in sealing man-made Cubic Zirconia stones.

Needless to say, the attorney generals in a number of states were kept quite busy seeking and obtaining indictments and court injunctions against these seedier operatives. At the peak of the activity, traditional jewelers still hadn't leaped into the market.

True, they just didn't know how to sell that way. But they didn't want to learn how either largely on the realistic grounds that a jeweler can't be involved in "sell and get out" type merchandising. He lives among his customers—and sooner or later these customers would want to "cash in" on their sure profits. The dealer, with experience in the jewelry industry, had an instinctive feeling about liquidity—and most of them wanted no part of it.

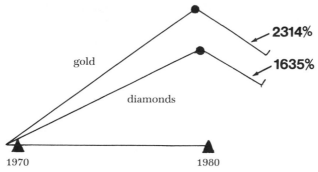

Fig. 9-2 They shouted—those gem investment companies—that diamonds represented the automatic, assured UP . . . but they didn't tell it like it was. Diamonds fluctuate like other commodities and the big price break late in 1980 demonstrated again that investing is risk-taking. Furthermore, gold appreciated more since 1970 than did diamonds—and fell less.

As late as 1980 when the gem investment web began to unravel with new exposures of fraud one after the other the industry was still split. Jewelers, aware of the enormous profits made by the aggressive gem investment group, still withheld their sorely needed expertise and reputations. For the most part they really didn't try to understand or appreciate the investment function.

The investment companies merely saw profit opportunities and took them by building a new market, subordinating the traditional concept of beauty and adornment in favor of the crass utilization of gems as an instrument to profit from contemporary economic problems. They really didn't try to understand or appreciate the adornment function.

Fig. 9-3 The major problem with gem investing is liquidity. You can't sell a gem as quickly, as easily, and at an active market price as you can other collectibles for which a true commodity market exists.

Both sides probably were at fault . . . since each had something worthwhile to contribute to a seriously underserved segment of the gem buying public . . . and both forfeited a meaningful contribution.

Late in 1980 the diamond investment business bit the dust. That's a realistic way of putting it. As a diamond cutter uses various sections of his cast iron cutting wheel for cutting, polishing and touch-down rings, the diamond dust forms into concentric ridges between the rings. The cutter must be careful lest he inadvertently push a diamond into one of these dust banks which would cause a "burn" on the polished diamond surface.

The diamond investment business truly got burned between the end of 1980 and the spring of 1981. The public's diamond buying spree had earlier driven the price of a one-carat D flawless diamond from $2,800 in 1971, to $6,000 by 1976, to $50,000 by 1979, and—then to the peak—to $67,000 in 1980.

Gold was flying high then, too. It had risen to $850 an ounce.

Abruptly, gold plummeted in price—and so did diamond investment prices. By spring of 1981, the same D flawless diamond had a price tag of only $34,000—with no buyers present.

The sales pitch that diamonds always went UP was proven to be no more than promotor's talk. Like other commodities, diamond proved that what goes UP can surely come DOWN. All the gimmicks of the investment companies—the lab certificates, expensive promotional literature, quotations from Encyclopedia Britannica and industry trade organs, long distance telephones, rented name lists—nothing worked.

It had been a good ride. Some of the more honest gem investment companies managed to hang on. But some investment trusts where investors would share in the purchase of a gem inventory for later sale and profit sharing were shelved. Tax shelters, replete with hired appraiser who "kited" the values, had already come under strong attack from the Internal Revenue Service. More and more private investors who wanted to sell their diamonds discovered the lack of liquidity (the ability to sell for cash) that the gem investment companies had earlier poo-poohed. Traditional jewelers got their chance to say, "I told you so."

At the same time, the commercial diamond market softened somewhat. But it certainly experienced no such shake-out as investment diamonds. De Beers withheld flawless rough from its next sight sales in an effort to prop diamond prices—but throughout 1981 the gem investment community laid relatively low.

Economists had little difficulty in explaining what had happened. Interest rates soared to 20% levels and the cost of money was simply too expensive to allow it to be dormant in a diamond—whose principle investment virtue is appreciation, supported by a continuing market keeping carat prices pumped up.

When the big buying came to a sudden halt because investors were no longer willing to forgo the loss of interest, the market bubble collapsed inward—and the price per carat plunged. But primarily for investment diamonds only.

All of these market elements combined to pull diamond investing back

Fig. 9-4 Unless a gem owner can find another private buyer, the usual sales outlet for gems and jewelry is found in the estate jewelry buyer, the francised gem and gold buyers, the itinerent gem buyer, or the local newspaper—if these outlets are interested in anything other than their own prices, i.e., wholesale or under.

to a more realistic and appropriate position in the economic scheme of things.

The "burning" has inspired clearer thinking about diamonds—and colored gems—as investments. It appears the jewelry industry and the gem buying public will be the better for it.

Given this bit of perspective should a person still invest in a diamond or colored stone or precious metal?

Or should a person buy strictly for adornment, knowing that the purchase can have residual value should the need arise?

A hard and fast answer to these questions probably isn't possible or even worthwhile. Every individual has to address that challenge alone.

No one really knows where the pricing line will go in the future for diamonds, colored stones or metals.

The annual output of diamonds in the world is about 40 million carats. In Australia, mining interests there now say the new finds will soon make possible an annual output in Australia alone of 25-35 million carats. If so, what impact will that have on diamonds?

It's reported that the Russians, who cooperate in diamond marketing with the De Beers syndicate, are literally sitting on some 800 diamond-bearing pipes versus the much smaller number of pipes owned or controlled by De Beers. Will the Russians continue to cooperate, or take advantage of their superiority? And do they really HAVE 800 pipes . . . or 80 . . . or 8?

Will racial difficulties in South Africa exert some unfortunate influence on diamond supplies . . . or on gold supplies? How about another big diamond find?

It's even difficult to get industry people to agree on the motives behind De Beers propping up actions. Some see the syndicate trying to re-stimulate diamond investments. Others feel De Beers never has been all that interested in promoting diamond investment and is directing its efforts toward insulating the much larger commercial diamond market from being unduly affected by investment diamond fever.

After all, investment grade diamonds—the famous D flawless-represents only a tiny fraction of annual diamond sales. Buying and selling in this grade is far removed from the reality of the commerical diamond market—which is why the impact on diamond prices in general was so trivial.

One thing does seem reasonably clear from the debacle. The public perhaps won't be so ready to go along with future assurances that diamonds represent the exotic and automatic UP. Purchased or promoted as a commodity, the diamond will, like any other commodity which depends on a market, react to market forces with price responsiveness . . . it will go up *and* down.

There is nothing inherently wrong or unwise about investing in diamonds or colored stones. But it is wise to know you own motives for doing so and to make a clear-cut decision on what your investment goal is.

In any event, the old investor's advice still holds: "Shoeman stick to your best, " i.e., invest in what you know about, the things you understand. Here is a reprint from an actual newspaper story, heralding the investment virtues of a commodity. Only the name of the commodity has been deleted from the re-print. Can you determine what the story is reporting on.

London—If you think _____ are only for certain people you're wrong.

They are also a safe, long-term investment" says Jock Smith, head of the _____ department at Philips auction house in London.

What makes _____ even more attractive as an alternative investment is that they are just about recession proof.

"Provided," cautions Smith, "you go just for the best, and not just in price, but quality as well."

In the past few years _____ have been booming, and although the recession may temper the rate of increase slightly, the auction houses and dealers are fairly confident that this year _____ will once again keep pacè—if not outstrip —double-digit inflations.

Interest in _____ has grown so much that Sotheby's has opened new galleries in London and in New York devoted to _____ as well as other investment collectibles. Last autumn's auction was an excellent one for top-grade _____ with several records being set.

There was more to this article, of course. The excerpt given here provides a good indication of its direction and tone. The marvelous alternative featured was books—but this promotional piece was using the same kind of pitch that can be successfully used with diamonds, colored gems, antique cars, art, autographs, Persian carpets, books, stamps, war souvenirs, Egyptian artifacts—in short, almost any tangible investment.

Was the newspaper story too much different than the thrust shown by some of the following sentences taken from a diamond investment company's direct mail piece:

" . . . if the slide of our dollar isn't stopped soon, or at least slowed down . . . it may be impossible to stop it . . . the flight becomes a stampede . . . paper claims on wealth seek havens of safety . . . collapse of all paper values . . . *open up your mind* to a new type of investment (diamonds) . . . new philosophy of personal and family economic survival . . . survive a possible dollar holocaust . . . even profit from it . . ."

If a potential investor were a bit worried about money matters to begin with, that kind of encouragement should further loosen up the strings on the check book or bank savings deposit.

168

What made some of the higher-pressure sales appeal so appalling perhaps was their assurance that prices on diamonds had enjoyed an unprecedented rise for decades and that this miraculous rise would continue due to the enormous monopolistic strength of the De Beers syndicate. No risk, they said.

DeBeers does exert powerful price influence because of its supply side monopoly and diamond prices have risen generally for decades. But what was largely overlooked was that everything else had risen in price for decades, too, and no monopoly controls public taste—or can force anyone to buy at any price in the short or long run.

As a matter of fact, during all the promotional hoopla associated with building the diamond investment market it was mostly overlooked that gold—the universal medium—performed much better. From 1970 to the gold price peak in 1980, gold appreciated 2,314%. During the same time frame diamonds appreciated only 1,635%.

Whether or not a diamond or colored gem represents a *good* investment is a minor consideration so far as investing is concerned. The real key to your decision is: what do you want your investment to achieve? What is your goal in investing?

Are you afraid that the U.S. dollar and other paper money systems will soon blow up in our faces? Do you wish to reduce your estate's dependancy on paper money or commercial documents? Is a tangible item with bartering capacity superior in case of a crises? Do you need to sneak over the border?

Or do you merely wish to arrange an investment where no management time or attention is required for the portfolio? Do you see the price index of diamonds and colored gems rising faster than the rate of inflation?

Or—and this is perfectly natural and quite understandable—do you wish to invest in a gem to swim with the crowd, to boast of having a chic investment?

Remember, an investment is really a sacrifice. You sacrifice the pleasure of current consumption by pledging your money or capital in the hope of a future profit or interest reward. For the most part, investment in business paper yields up (hopefully) regular dividends as well as, in certain cases, appreciation. Alternative investments, such as tangibles, represent the ambition to buy low and sell dear. You hope to sell the tangible item for a dearer price than you originally paid for it.

Throughout history mankind in almost every culture and civilization had placed value on precious gems and precious metals. Since Egyptian times they have been coveted as symbols of wealth, power, authority and status. Is it any wonder that they have been able to hold value?

Is it any greater wonder that contemporary man and woman find this universal value a vital attribute for a stable, predictable, and desirable investment medium? To an investor who recognizes that the higher the prospect of gain the higher the risk, precious gems could appear as the perfect answer.

They have retained their value through the ages and they are universally accepted and wanted—right? The promotors do have a point: buy some good grade diamonds or precious stones, let them appreciate, and then sell and take the profit.

What could be easier?

Well, perhaps, but there are some other elements that a prudent person might want to consider before rushing pell mell into an investment arena so fraught with potential difficulty.

First, diamonds and precious gems—like any other tangible investment or commodity—must be viewed as speculative. Precious gems and metals may be universally acknowledged value carriers—but specific gems and metals rise and fall in response to public fancy, i.e, demand.

When you buy a diamond or precious stone you are betting on that gem's continued appreciation in value. As such, your money—which could be earning profits or interest in some other kind of investment—is tied up in a non-interest bearing speculation which should, at least, appreciate faster than the going interest rate and, hopefully, will perform better than optional investment opportunities.

Chances are, you may expect to receive little of the non-monetary satisfaction which gives gems their value . . . the enjoyment of wearing a rare, beautiful, durable, and envy-creating wonder of nature. The future, profitable sale of the gem lies in its certificated specifications and it would be unreasonably risky to mount or to wear it as a single bump or chip could drastically reduce its saleability or price.

Second, unless you are wired into the jewelry and gem network it's frankly problematic if you can successfully buy cheap and sell dear. As an individual its' almost certain that you will be buying above the wholesale price—regardless of what the promotors tell you, and it's not unlikely that the buying transaction will be finalized at or near retail.

Thus the initial purchase could put you into an investment disadvantage from which it will be difficult to extricate yourself. If you do buy at retail, the gem would need to double in value before you could hope to break even in selling it back to the trade. Find another private buyer? Yes, that's possible but even here it's unlikely you'll get—or even know—what full retail value is on the gem.

And, if the value of your gem merely doubled and you did manage to sell out on top you must consider the true impact of inflation on your investment while you were awaiting adequate appreciation. Chances are you'd have been a net loser because the purchasing power of the twice-what-you-originally paid money you now hold diminished.

Third, no large, visible buyer and seller market exists for precious gems. It does for gold, as you know, and that's why gold is such a popular investment: you can switch gold for cash anytime, anywhere in the world and buyers and sellers alike are familiar with gold's going price.

With precious gems, you often can't even find a buyer.

The stock exchanges are magnificent examples of an active, almost immediate, and competitive meeting place for buyers and sellers—of stocks and bonds. The commodity exchanges operate in the same mass manner; it's where a seller can find a buyer for his paper at a best price.

No such meeting place of gem buyers and sellers exist *for the individual gemstone investor*. The diamond exchanges in New York, London, Antwerp and Tel Aviv exist for the benefit of industry members—the professional cutters, dealers, etc.

But as an individual with a diamond(s) you'd like to sell, the marketing possibilities are relatively thin and difficult to locate. If you've ever tried to sell a gem or a piece of jewelry you are fully aware of the problems. The situation hasn't changed one iota: liquidity is a massive problem for individuals trying to sell gems. If you are not truly wired into the gemstone marketing apparatus you may expect difficulty.

That's really why diamond and colored gemstone investment decisions require expert opinion. The purchasing of a gem is merely one aspect of the investment process—and it's not the easiest.

See your gem purchase in this light: if you buy the right gem, at the right time, at the right price, then perhaps a market will exist for that gem when you are ready to take your profit. Otherwise—?

Gems may advance in price generally. But within this broad advance there are specific oscillations. Some gems fall from public favor while others climb. Some out of favor, begin a comeback. The market is constantly changing, dynamic, often unpredictable; to stay with it you must remain aware—and that certainly precludes any argument about investing in a gem and then forgetting about it until YOU are ready.

The market for the Big Four has existed for centuries—diamonds, emeralds, rubies and sapphires. It's best to keep investment dollars involved with these four dependables . . . but like the newspaper story on books it's wise only if you've invested in saleable, i.e., top quality merchandise. Price, though, being a function of the market you must decide if your investment will be in top quality expensively large stones (for which a market exists but tends to be somewhat small) as against smaller, less expensive gems (for which a larger market exists). The risks differ along with the profit opportunity because larger quality gems may represent greater profits but could involve heavier losses if you must sell under conditions other than suitable for you. Prices on smaller gems advance and decline as the market shifts, but the swings are less violent. This could mean a longer time to realize your investment goal.

What often happens is that a gem investor, lacking marketing knowledge, goes directly to a jeweler in the naive belief that while some compromise in the price will be necessary the jeweler will at least be an interested, logical outlet. The result varies between a rude awakening about the complexities of gem marketing and suspicion that jewelers are Shylocks waiting in the shadows to take advantage of the unwary.

Jewelers buy gem inventory at or below wholesale whether the item comes from an industry wholesale source or comes in "off the street." They don't need to tie up cash in inventory when a wholesaler is but a telephone call away. Besides, they can get a gem on memo (the wholesaler provides the gem free to the jeweler for a certain time period or until he sells it). Sometimes out of a sense of public relations, compassion, pity, or as a favor they may agree to help sell a gem and "split the profits"—but don't bet on it.

Are diamonds and colored gems a good investment, then?

Yes, but—

You must buy wisely—and low—in the first place. Then economic conditions must remain with you—as with any other kind of tangible investment—and you must sell wisely in the last place. Someone obstensibly made a profit on you initially; can you also perform the great hat trick . . . sell at a profit, too.

That means that between the first and last step you must still be dealing with a gem whose Cut, Clarity, Color and Caratage retains or improves in its marketability.

Colored Stone Selling Muted . . .

The market fanning in colored stones for investment hasn't gathered as much public excitement as diamonds, but the effort has gone on with muted strength and conviction.

As you may have surmised earlier the challenge posed by colored stones involves the same risks as diamonds with one added requirement; you have to pick rising stars. Just letting the gem market index advance for your investment isn't quite enough with colored gems.

Given constantly changing public taste as well as availability, specific colored gem prices are ebbing and flowing as market conditions dictate. Pearls are a good example. Since World War II interest in natural and cultured pearls had remained somewhat dormant as buyer attention focused on other gem materials. In the late 1970s pearls began a powerful resurgence in public favor. As demand increased, so too did pearl prices.

Admittedly, some doubt exists that they'll ever regain the near veneration afforded them by the ancient Romans who restricted their wear or ownership to members of royalty. But pearl prices today are reaching toward astronomical levels—and climbing.

Fine opal was another favorite of ancient royalty. Again the Romans who label opal "cupide paederos" meaning *child beautiful as love* revered opal. Marc Antony so coveted a beautiful opal owned by the Senator Nonius that he gave Nonius an offer he didn't think the latter could refuse: give the opal to Antony or be expelled from Rome. Nonius chose expulsion. Such was the status of the opal.

Then publication of Sir Walter Scott's novel, "Anne of Geierstein," ended opals popularity—and it's never regained its place since. Peridot decorated Pharaoh and palace alike. So highly esteemed was it that adventurers risked death in an effort to raid the mines of St. John's Island. Today peridot is known mostly to gem connoisseuers and those born under the sign of Leo.

Lapis Lazuli, turquoise and amber were the gem materials of royalty. All three have been pushed from their lofty perches. While they are still relatively well-known not one is regarded as a top investment gem.

Modern marketing methods have much to do with swings in public gem buying. Tanzanite won't be found in most older gemological manuals; it's less than 20 years old. But an American gem company introduced it with pizzazz, and the beautiful blue newcomer caught the public's fancy. It climbed swiftly in price.

Garnet, once the rage of Victorian times, has received a couple of commendable value bumps in recent times. The marketing of Tsavolite, the deep emerald green garnet, has sparked interest in garnets. Now the discovery of the orange Malaya has provided additional stimulus.

Blue topaz responded well to a TV mention. Its reputed investment potential and close resemblance to more expensive aquamarine gave it a good price hike. It remains to be seen if either blue topaz or aquamarine will maintain their current growth lines.

Colored gems are mined under primitive conditions and almost invariably in isolated locations. Many of the mines are located in countries where political unrest and revolutions are the order of the day. Under such circumstances existing supplies are constantly threatened. Difficulty in obtaining materials and the very real prospect of a mine being shut off permanently or temporarily—or a new one discovered—provide the delicious tidbits of conversation for gem enthusiasts.

It also provides the wherewithall to promote a gem, issue a strong closing argument on a wavering buyer. Colored gems maybe haven't attracted the high-powered sales talent and promotional investment that spectacularized the diamond craze. But the colored gem investment promotors are still out there hawking this month's latest hot gem item.

If the foregoing treatment of diamond and colored gem investments seems unreasonably harsh and pessimistic, it's only because such a serious involvement requires cold, calculated decision making. The promotors were proven false: diamonds aren't—and never have been—an automatic, monopoly controlled ride to certain profits . . . and colored gems aren't either.

As gemstones, they make beautiful objects. As commodities, they involve risks. In both cases, it behooves a person to know something about them. Purchased wisely they can bring joy and pleasure—or heartbreak and loss.

Gem Investing Takes Planning . . .

Knowing that a gem investment bears some of the opportunities for gain as well as the possibilities for loss as other tangible, valuable investments, you might still want to invest. Is there a way to do it intelligently while steering clear of the charlatans?

The advice here is the same as for other investment schemes: look before you leap. Investigate fully any company or sales person seeking to sell you diamonds and colored gems as investment. The 1980 Diamond Caper helped clean up the situation somewhat—but there is just too much money involved with diamonds to ever keep the corner cutters away.

Have your lawyer or banker investigate fully any prospectus offered you. Then get some truly expert assistance, preferably a qualified gemologist. Inasmuch as it will be virtually impossible for you to pin down precisely what the wholesale price of a given gemstone grade is, get competitive bids on the same stone—and on the same specifications. As you know, a single color or clarity grade can have a significant impact on price . . . so when you price compare make certain the quotations are all on the same set of specifications with no deviation.

Fortunately, more and more reputable jewelers are providing gem investment services to their customers. If you know of a jeweler in your area who provides such a service he or she is infinitely superior to any other. It pays to know with whom you are dealing—and the fact that you will be able to locate that individual or company later.

Liquidity? Don't expect the seller to re-sell the diamond for you later. No one can guarantee either that the gem will be more profitable when ultimately or even if it can be sold. Some of the legitimate diamond investment firms are now setting up marketing programs which work through jewelers, but for the most part jewelers are continuing to resist the investment business. To them, it's such a messy business with far more potential for injuring future customer relations that any profits such selling affords.

If your local jeweler doesn't seem too enthusiastic when you approach him about gem investing, don't be too surprised. He undoubtedly thinks of himself as a jeweler, not an investment counselor.

Talk to the jeweler about adornment and chances are he'll brighten quickly to the task. You'll be talking his language—maybe.

The jewelry industry is currently on a major campaign to bring gemological understanding to the jewelry store. Colored stone sales staggered along for years because the jewelry trade had difficulty selling stones beyond the Big Four. Customers looking for guidance were almost required to bring their own expertise to the jewelry counter.

There is still much to be done before retailers and private buyers alike will have the level of mutual understanding that exists, say, in automobiles, clothes, dry goods, food or furniture. With these kinds of merchandise precious little hard sell is required because buyer and seller alike possess a fund of knowledge and understanding.

Strange, isn't it, that with such luxuries as gems, jewelry, furs, items that truly require a considerable outlay of money the buyer so often must trust the seller's assurances and representations.

By bringing even a modicum of understanding to your gem and jewelry buying you can acquire an extraordinary collection of valuable pieces at a cost that will astonish people. It really is that easy—if you know what you're doing. Nor do you need a deep, lengthy educational commitment in technical jargon and gemological technique.

Let's make the assumption that you would like to possess a wideranging and valuable collection of fine gems with sufficient flexibility to accessorize any color costume in your wardrobe—and any color or costume you're likely to ever add to your wardrobe. That sounds like a reasonable ambition, a first goal.

Let's make a second assumption. That is, you would like to have a collection that will probably increase in value in lockstep with inflation and that, if push comes to shove, you would like to be able to sell for a reasonable amount of cash . . . perhaps even at a profit.

Now for the third assumption. Let's assume that you don't have all the money in the world to spend just on gems and jewelry so you'd like a number of options wherein you may purchase fine, genuine, resaleable stones of nearly equal beauty and durability at a more modest per carat price.

Is this over optimistic? Not really. It's more a matter of knowing what you want and how to obtain it.

Here are two sections dealing with alternate suggestions that you might want to follow to work toward a jewelry/gem collection. The first section for transparent faceted gems will include these color suites: Red, Blue, Green, Yellow, Pink-Lavender, Orange, Brown. The final section will include alternatives on opaque stones generally cut en cabochon.

RED SUITE

1. **Ruby**—prices per carat vary widely, with prices climbing swiftly as clarity improves and color approaches desired red-violet. A hint of brown brings price down quickly.

2. **Rhodocrocite**—Usually a cabochon opaque material but facetable material is brilliant, bright red with little or no secondary colors. Price is quite reasonable. It's quite soft, though, so plan on using it in pendant, or earring. It looks almost identical when cut to the most expensive ruby.

3. **Red Spinel**—Quite expensive and rare. They're gobbled up quickly by gem lovers. They can fool you into thinking ruby; the color is bright, pure.

4. **Red Tourmaline**—Quite moderate in price. The tone is lighter than the bright ruby reds, but it's intense.

5. **Red Topaz**—Moderate in price, with a light, somewhat watery, tone. They tend to be small and somewhat scarce.

6. **Malaya Garnet**—This name usually refers to the orange hue but this spersartine variety of garnet also had a deep, full red. It's not the ruby red—but it is attractive. Sometimes must be cut shallow for best color results. It's much less expensive than orange Malaya.

7. **Rhodolite Garnet**—Another variety of fine, red garnet. They make beautiful gems. With a high R.I. and brilliant intensity.

8. **Red Diamonds**—Yes, they occur naturally. You can also have a genuine diamond irradiated red. The natural fancy is prohibitive in price; the cyclotron-bombed one can be quite modest in price (they look alike).

BLUE SUITE

1. **Sapphire**—The Kashmir blue is the epitome of sapphire blue and prices climb as this is approached. Some of the inkier blues are quite

modest in price, but fine sapphires can be had for a moderate price.

2. **Iolite**—Called the "water sapphire" it can resemble the finest sapphire blue but usually must be cut shallow to do it. Little brilliance or fire, but it's color and finish are very, very attractive. Inexpensive.

3. **Blue Tourmaline**—Called "indicolite" blue tourmaline is quite moderate in price and has a rich, intense blue hue. It takes a fine finish and sometimes seems a bit dark, as if it could have been cut shallower.

4. **Zircon**—Heat treated blue zircon makes a majestic gem. Its high R.I. and great transparency makes for a lively performer. The blue tone is lighter because the crystal has the ability to return so much brilliant white light. Reasonably priced per carat.

5. **Aquamarine**—A sea or sky blue in its best tones, aquamarine is approaching four figures per carat for good color, clarity and size. The lighter "snow blues" are quite inexpensive but you get the blue color flash only intermittently. (Hint: buy the low priced nearly clear aquamarines and then paint the pavilion with a light blue felt tip pen—makes for a sensational looking aqua . . . but be sure to use non-soluble ink).

6. **Blue Topaz**—Blue topaz can be treated to achieve a blue as deep as blue tourmaline, or as light as aquamarine. It's a hard, bright gemstone—and has been rising rapidly in popularity and is still priced reasonably.

7. **Tanzanite**—The heat treated zoizite is a rich, deep almost Kashmire blue color. It's soft and fragile, but its marvelous color and optical snap make it a favorite. Rather expensive—it's one of the best performers for the money.

8. **Diamond**—There are blue diamonds, about one every 100,000. If you want a blue diamond, buy an inexpensive white one and have it irradiated; they're magnificent.

GREEN SUITE

1. **Emeralds**—They're the Queen of Green. Flawed or not, you'll pay dearly for a rich green emerald (the oil comes free). Green beryl is the same mineral—but it's not emerald and should be sold cheap.

2. **Tsavorite**—The famous emerald green garnet—and it truly can hold its own with the Queen. It's expensive, too. More brilliant, greater clarity, hardier than the emerald.

3. **Peridot**—A soft, sometimes described as "sleepy" yellow-green gem, it flows with an inner radiance possessed by few other gems. It's really volcanic glass. Relatively inexpensive, its price climbs quickly with size.

4. **Tourmaline**—Tourmaline comes in many tones of green . . . deep emerald-like green, light green, chrome green. A hard, brilliant, showy gem—especially when cut in the emerald cut. Relatively inexpensive.

5. **Green Sapphire**—Green sapphires often have a strong blue influence in them, but they make a fine, hard, showy gem with good brilliance. Relatively inexpensive as corundum goes.

6. **Hiddenite**—This is the green variety of spodumene. True Hiddenite ranges from emerald green to light green and is truly a spectacular gem. Unfortunately, it is very rare and comes only from North Carolina. They're really collector's items, but green spodumen which doesn't qualify as Hiddenite sometimes shows up on the market. Grab it—it's usually bargain priced for such a showy gem.

7. **Diamond**—Diamond comes naturally in green. It is also irradiated a gentle green tone, somewhat like a beautiful pastel . . . almost peridot tone.

YELLOW SUITE

1. **Helidor**—The yellow or golden beryl is relatively inexpensive and has the same optical characteristics of the aquamarine—if not the color. Helidor is not expensive, but works best in somewhat larger stones.

2. **Chrysoberyl**—Most people think of chrysoberyl only in terms of Cat's Eye. But when transparent and faceted, it makes a beautiful, showy golden-like gem . . . and rather inexpensive. Has a good R.I., which gives it fine brilliance.

3. **Citrine**—It's heat-treated amethyst and one of the most inexpensive gems available. Looks somewhat like Imperial Topaz—but its reddish tint gives it away on the heat treating.

4. **Topaz**—Yellow-orange topaz is popularly known as Imperial Topaz. It's rather expensive and gets more so as the size of the gem increases. Brilliant and showy, it works well in any kind of jewelry setting.

5. **Yellow Sapphire**—More and more yellow sapphire is coming on the market. Relatively inexpensive, it's brilliant and showy like most sapphires.

6. **Labradorite**—Seldom seen in jewelry stores, but it's a straw yellow with surprising and unique optics. This gem could very well be a "sleeper" because most feldspars tend to be cut en cabochon (such as Moonstone). You might have to ask around—but it's very inexpensive (and puzzles even gem experts).

7. **Diamond**—Diamond comes in yellow, too. And, yes, it can be irradiated into a fine yellow fancy.

PINK-LAVENDER SUITE

1. **Amethyst**—As lavender colored quartz, amethyst is quite inexpensive. Tell your jeweler you want man-made amethyst (nobody can tell the difference and this often cuts the price for you). It's lovely in the deeper shades—and goes great with a chartreuse dress.

2. **Kunzite**—The lavender or lilac colored spodumene, it's known as the night stone because its color fades in daylight. In the larger sizes it's stunning —and even fools some into thinking its a diamond because of its awesome clearness. Inexpensive to moderate in price.

3. **Topaz**—Pink topaz is pushing the top of the topaz price scale, as the optical qualities of topaz make this pink stone, even if it is heat treated, an eye catcher. Because topaz is usually a light colored gem, the deeper cuts are every effective for enhancing color.

4. **Tourmaline**—Called Rubillite, pink tourmaline varies in price from included grades to the finer, more flawless levels. Like all tourmaline, it's bright, showy and hard.

5. **Morganite**—Pink beryl, it's a light colored gem which performs optically as·the other light colored beryls—brilliant, flashy, and with an elegant coloration.

6. **Purple Sapphire**—There are numerous tones of purple beryl. Relatively inexpensive, they have good brilliance and clarity and you'll be able to pick from a wide range of cuts.

ORANGE SUITE

1. **Padparadscha**—Don't let the name throw you (pronounced pad-pa-rad-shaw), it's an orange corundum. As the same mineral of rubies and sapphires, the padparadscha is a lighter color stone with great optical qualities and strength. It's quite expensive and somewhat scarce.

2. **Malaya Garnet**—This is one of the newer gemstone finds, an orange garnet, found in Africa. It's orange color is deep, rich and the high optical qualities of spessartine garnet gives it a lively appearance. The price is relatively high, dropping as the gem turns toward the red hue.

3. **Tourmaline**—Orange tourmaline has a color purity that is quite distinctive. It tends to be a bit more expensive than other colored tourmalines, but this reflects the scarcity of orange material as much as anything. Still, it is moderately priced.

4. **Hessonite Garnet**—This is an amber or honey colored grossular garnet with extraordinary brilliance and color. Not only does it have a high R.I. but its dispersion provides excellent fire. It is relatively inexpensive, although some grossular garnets exceed $1,000 a carat.

5. **Topaz**—The orangey dominance of some Imperial type topaz makes for a superb orange gem. Put this stone into a pendant or ring setting with blue sapphires as accent stones and you have something that borders on the incredible. Imperial Topaz is expensive.

BROWN SUITE

1. **Andalusite**—It's not especially well-known so carat prices are still reasonably inexpensive. A hard, sparkly, deep brown gem, andalusite is usually available in one- and two-carat sizes. Large stones are rare. The color, actually, is more of a greenish-brown or a reddish-brown.

2. **Tourmaline**—Brown tourmaline is called *dravite* and is hard and durable. Watch for the cutter's orientation; it's a muddy color if the cutting direction is incorrect, bright and brilliant when aligned properly. Like most tourmalines, dravite is moderately expensive.

3. **Zircon**—When found in the rough most zircon is brown colored. It makes a beautiful gem with brightness and color depth because of its relatively high dispersion and RI. Most brown zircon is heat treated to obtain the more desired blue and clear gems.

4. **Topaz**—Most brown topaz comes from Mexico. Be careful about this material; it tends to fade in daylight. Many cutters allow rough material to

sit in the daylight for a period before cutting. Unfaded material has a decided red-brown cast. Brown topaz is or should be inexpensive.

5. **Smokey Quartz**—Sometimes—and improperly—called smokey topaz, this heat-treated quartz had a decided, deep brown color. The deep color pretty much masks any brilliance or fire—which is pretty low anyway—but the deep color is most desirable.

6. **Spinel**—The color of natural spinel is closer to a reddish-brown, but the gem's superb optical qualities gives it a flashy brilliance. The gem is hard and lovely—and inexpensive. Actually, spinels could be regarded as "sleepers." They occur in many beautiful colors and make fine, durable gemstones.

OPAQUE GEM MATERIALS

The first gemstones of history were the opaque ones. Cleopatra's favorite eye shadow was powdered Lapis Lazuli made into a beautiful blue paste.

Little has changed. They are still favorites. Rather than bedazzle a viewer with optical effects, though, opaque stones gather their value in their interestng textures and color tones.

Who would ever deny the beauty and value of Imperial Jade . . . of a Cat's Eye . . . of the majestic pearl . . . or opal . . . and even of the lesser expensive gem materials such as Lapis, malachite, the various varieties of quartz, and so forth.

Of all the gem materials in nature's inventory none has the general wearability and the ease of accessorizing as jade, pearls, and opal. They not only can hold their own with virtually any costuming demands, but complement fabrics as well.

No gem collection would be truly complete without a number of items featuring opaque gemstones.

Jade leads the field in green opaque gems, of course. But superbly colored jadeite comes in other hues, too, just as outstanding as the green ones. The best known are the lavender, white, brown, mauve, and melon hues.

Interestingly enough, the Chinese believe that white jade brings luck; lavender signifies achievement and fulfillment; red guards one for a long life, while green symbolizes good fortune and the determination to go on in the face of obstacles. Furthermore, jade bracelets show a difference between Western and Chinese preferences. Westerners tend to want hinged jade bracelets, whereas the Chinese want a continuous, solid and multi-hued band of jade—known to the Chinese as a *bi*, or circle of eternity.

If the finer hues of jadeite put a strain on your pocketbook, Chrysophrase makes a magnificent substitute. Its apple green color bears quite a close resemblance to the finest jadeite and the substitute material accepts just as fine a polish. The price of Chrysophrase is considerably below jadeite—but you can fashion from it virtually any piece of jewelry that jadeite would enhance.

Another fine opaque gem material is malachite, a soft, green banded mineral easily fashioned and accessorized.

Lapis, Turquoise, sodalite are three excellent blue opaque gem minerals—and make excellent jewelry. Occasionally, you may find a mineral called Chrysocolla in an intensive blue, but often this material occurs as a blue-green or yellow-green variety.

Red opaque stones include Rhodonite, material which occurs from a rose-red hue to pink and brownish-pink. Black patterns are also prevalent, making an interesting appearance once fashioned and mounted.

Other opaque red stones include ruby, bloodstone, the red and pink corals and massive rhodochrosite—a white and red banded stone of great attraction. Both rhodochrosite and rhodonite are occasionally faceted, but mostly as additions to gem collections. Still, they are not exhorbitantly expensive and their dramatic red hue makes for beautiful gems when they are used in jewelry (preferably in a pendant where they can be well protected by the metal mounting and from the prospect of rough treatment).

This brief summary by no means exhausts the color possibilities in opaque gem materials. Just keep in mind that many of these minerals are sufficiently porous that they readily accept aniline dyes—and, accordingly, the cosmetic opportunities are outstanding.

Almost any color can be provided in an opaque gem. Chalcedony, the quartz variety, is a splendid material for dyeing and it provides many of the brilliant, uniquely fashioned and colored opaque gem materials.

Again, watch out for two-word names to describe any given material, particularly when the first qualifier hints of geography, or when the name is enclosed in quotation marks. For the most part, no fraud is intended in the cosmetics of opaque gems—but you will be happier if you know what you're buying.

CHAPTER TEN

GEMSTONE EXPERTISE: It Really Starts With You

Her concern was understandable.

Her wedding rings contained a splendid 1.73 carat round brilliant diamond that had been her mother's. But the mounting and the stone needed maintenance . . . general cleaning, prongs inspected, and tightened up—that sort of thing.

She had been told that the diamond was of the finest clarity, color, and cut.

Perhaps it was a fine investment grade diamond; perhaps it wasn't. To her it didn't really make all that great of a difference; her mother had given it to her. She had heard that diamonds are sometimes switched by jewelers so, rather than let her diamond out of her sight, she did nothing despite the jeweler's repeated assurances of personal integrity, long held reputation for honesty, etc., etc.

Question? Did she do the right thing by not trusting anyone with her diamond? Answer: She most certainly did do the right thing—providing she didn't wear it while there was a danger of the diamond dropping out of its loose mounting.

Does this imply that you can't trust jewelers because they'll switch your good diamond for a bad one?

No, it doesn't mean that at all. Switching goes on a lot less than most people think. But it has—and does—happen. Once for you is once too many.

In the matter of security, a number of precautions must be taken before you release your gemstones into the custody of someone else. These precautions assure you that the gemstone which comes back to you is the same gem you sent out—and that its physical condition is the same, too.

The diamond ring owner acted wisely in trusting her suspicious instinct because she knew she couldn't recognize her own diamond anyway. If the jewelry store people had exercised any appreciation for her concern they would have followed a reasonable take-in policy and even protected themselves in the process. They would have reviewed the diamond with the owner, pointing out identifying inclusions or marks; they would have noted any obvious damage or dangers such as chips or cleavages that would also have helped identify the stone and protect the jeweler from possible later accusations of damage; they might even have given the ring owner a sketch of the diamond so she could make a comparison when the ring was returned to her.

The jewelers did none of those things and, consequently, didn't deserve the woman's patronage—or trust.

If you own valuable pieces of jewelry and you are afraid to take them to a jeweler for fear of switching, don't fret. You have a lot of company. And they are acting as wisely as you.

You can Protect Yourself . . .

Given your own reluctance to part with your gems and in the absence of any reassurance from a jeweler, is there anything you can do except do nothing? Surprisingly enough, you can provide your own safeguards with little fuss or bother—while providing yourself with documentation that would be valuable for other security situations as well.

Your own gem security system starts with a careful "mapping" of your gems, a copy of which should go immediately into a safety deposit box or some similar secure place. Then when you place your gems into the custody of others you will have a record on hand that will make it virtually impossible for anyone to switch or deny their responsibility for obvious damage.

Any person who knows how to "map" diamonds and colored stones certainly knows how to "read" those same gems through a magnifying loupe, comparing the size, character and location of the sighted inclusions with the "map" diagram of the gem that had been sketched earlier. It's really as simple as that.

Here is how you can go about "mapping" a gem. Trace or draw a diagram of the gem's cut so you have a crown and a pavillion illustration.

Holding a magnifying loupe to the gem, begin the careful search for inclusions or blemishes. Make a small "x" as a starting reference point on the diagram and then use an identifying mark on the gem—or, if mounted, one of the prongs—as the corresponding starting point on the gem itself. This helps you get the gem oriented quicker and with greater accuracy. (Fig. 10-2).

 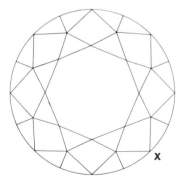

Fig. 10-2 To assure consistency between your drawing and the position of the gem in the setting, scratch or make a small file mark on one of the prongs and then "x" the drawing to indicate a reference point.

Look straight down at the stone first, looking for exterior or surface irregularities which, as you know, are called *blemishes.* Draw or reproduce and locate each blemish that you see. Although a black pen or pencil is adequate, try to follow the GIA policy of a green color as best to indicate surface *blemishes,* with a red color for internal *inclusions.*

Are there any chips on the girdle? Is the shape distorted? How about some abrading on the facet edges? A natural? Inspect each of the eight main crown facets and the adjacent girdle and star facets in turn. When you have finished inspecting the top, turn the gem or mounting over and review the bottom, going all the way around. Again write down in picture form anything unusual you see on the surface.

Next pick up the red pen. Again look down through the table, and carefully sketch or reproduce each inclusion you see—being very careful to mark your sketch with the same line heaviness and length or so to match the actual relationship as it appears in the gem (a very thin pen or pencil is best because you can always retrace a line to make it appear thicker).

The key to "mapping" is to make the sketch as precise a picture of the original as you can possibly make (Fig. 10-3). Don't feel that you must keep and use only the original drawing. When you've finished "mapping" a gem, take a critical look at the completed diagram. Is it as good as you can make it? Does it really need "touching up?" Can you take a look at one line, or spot, and say to yourself, "well, the inclusion (or blemish) isn't actually *that big (or small)* or prominent?" If you can say that about any of the lines, spots, or shadings, you probably should re-do the sketch.

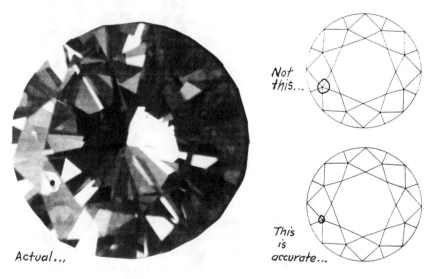

Fig. 10-3 Be very careful in drawing your diagram of imperfections. A slight carbon spot in the actual gem should be accurately reproduced in scale on the drawing. Otherwise, the drawing may be of a clarity rating which appears lower on the scale than the actual condition. If necessary, redraw the diagram so the actual and your drawing faithfully compare.

Tip the gem so that you inspect the interior from a direction perpendicular to the crown and pavillion facets (Fig. 10-4). This permits you to more easily locate the inclusions. Inspect the gem, too, at a right angle to the girdle for marks that you may have missed before—and also as a double check for lasering (Fig. 10-5).

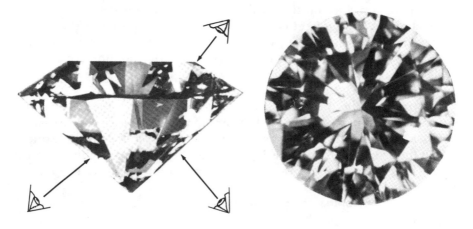

Fig. 10-4 Again, viewing a gemstone perpendicular to the crown main or to the pavilion main facets is best for locating imperfections. Once you locate a flaw, it's a simple matter, if you wish, to tilt the gem and take a look through the table.

Fig. 10-5 Viewing the gem from a side profile with a loupe assures you that you've not missed any imperfections—and gives you a good inspection viewpoint for detecting any lasering that may have been done.

Check carefully around the prongs. Here is where exterior damage is usually inflicted, either in the setting or possibly by bumping. A bench worker very likely may remove your stone to work on it or the mounting and when he replaces it the gem may not be aligned exactly as it was—and the chips *that were there all along* under a prong are now visible AND SOMEBODY GETS ACCUSED OF CAUSING DAMAGE THAT "WASN'T THERE BEFORE."

If you wish—as an extra precaution—try to include key dimensions such as depth, diameter (or width and length if its a step or trap cut). Put in the weight. In other words, fill out your own form (Fig. 10-6) so your gem is as completely identified as possible.

Get it notarized with your signature—and date of inspection—on the form. Make some Xerox copies—and then you're ready to turn your gem

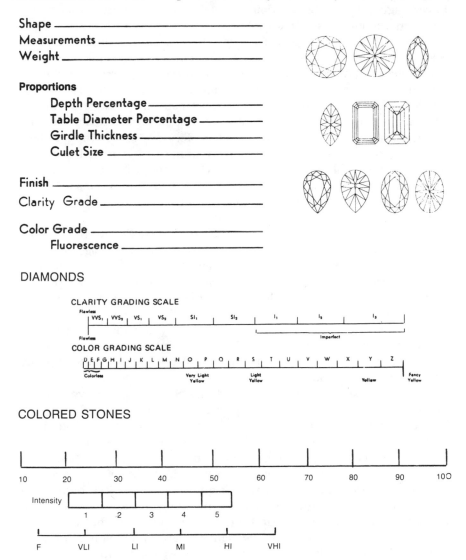

Shape _____

Measurements _____

Weight _____

Proportions

    Depth Percentage _____

    Table Diameter Percentage _____

    Girdle Thickness _____

    Culet Size _____

Finish _____

Clarity Grade _____

Color Grade _____

    Fluorescence _____

DIAMONDS

CLARITY GRADING SCALE

Flawless | VVS₁ | VVS₂ | VS₁ | VS₂ | SI₁ | SI₂ | I₁ | I₂ | I₃

Flawless   Imperfect

COLOR GRADING SCALE

D E F G H I J K L M N O P Q R S T U V W X Y Z

Colorless   Very Light Yellow   Light Yellow   Yellow   Fancy Yellow

COLORED STONES

10   20   30   40   50   60   70   80   90   100

Intensity   1   2   3   4   5

F   VLI   LI   MI   HI   VHI

Fig. 10-6 An Example of an Evaluation/Appraisal Form (You might Xerox this page and use the forms for making and keeping a record of your own gems.)

over to any jeweler regardless of the efficiency of the jeweler's take-in policy because your own record and ability to identify your gem makes a switch virtually impossible.

The security of your gem(s) only begins, though, with the "mapping." You should take one of the copies of your gem diagram to the jeweler and have it signed by the person doing the take-in. Review also what's written on the work or take-in envelope.

In stores where there is a truly professional take-in program, you'll seldom see your diamond—in the absence of a careful inspection —described as a diamond on the envelope; usually the jeweler will write something to the effect, ". . .white stone . . ." or ". . .blue stone . . ." Don't be upset at this display of professionalism; it isn't a set-up for anything other than the jeweler seeking to avoid unnecessary liability. Chances are, when you present a sketch of your gem for the jeweler's signature to confirm the identity of the stone being turned over, the jeweler's loupe will come out quickly. He wants to make certain your stone and drawing matches up. In effect, your own precautions will force a better take-in procedure on the jeweler's part. It might even prompt some indignation.

You should confirm that your personal instructions are written on the work envelope. If your diamond or colored stone has a cleavage or flaw in it, or if there is a possibility that your gem has been color improved by oiling—or for any other reason—you should insist that proper precautions be taken by the jeweler, too. Under these circumstances you wouldn't want your gem cleaned ultra-sonically, or by steam or boiling because the possibilities of damage are simply too great. Have these restrictions written on the envelope prominently; a bench repair worker, not knowing, might toss your gem into one of these cleaning units to everyone's sadness.

When the repair or maintenance work has been completed, you should follow good pick-up procedure. Inspect the gem and the work carefully before leaving the jewelry store. Inquire about anything you don't understand or which looks peculiar. Go over these questions with the jeweler. Just as on take-ins, your stone and "map" should match.

Again, inspect carefully around the prongs. Make certain that the gem matches your diagram in every way—right down to the last tiny chip. If the jeweler has one of the new stereoscopic microscopes on premise, ask to use it for your inspection—and then kick up the magnification to 40x or 50x for a really good look. At the higher magnification you'll be able to locate and check out inclusions. You can't hide prong damage very well from these higher magnifications . . . or the workmanship either . . . but, remember, that microscope will see things your 10x or 15x loupe didn't even hint at.

You should assure yourself that your own diamond has been returned to you in the same quality condition which existed when you gave it up into the jeweler's custody. If not, then you and the jeweler should discuss any difference of opinion—and negotiate some form of restitution. This is where careful take-in procedures pay off . . . after you and the jeweler had agreed on the gem's original condition.

When there is something wrong with your gem—or at least a significant misunderstanding occurs—you should discuss things with the store owner or manager. Sales personnel usually don't carry enough authority to make any settlement arrangement—and often don't have the gemological skill to be able to estimate the severity of cost of any damages anyway.

It takes expert opinion to determine the extent of value loss in a diamond which has just sustained a heavy chip in the girdle, big enough that it distorts the stone's shape. When you are dealing, for instance, with a 2.00 carat diamond with a large chip that extends down into the pavillion what is the loss to you?

If the sales personnel probably can't figure out the extent of loss, who is to say that the jeweler can either? Do you know and can you determine yourself what an equitable settlement would be? Given your own lack of expertise in the matter, you could very well accept a settlement in which you have sacrificed too much . . . or demanded too much?

It's not any easy matter at all—but it's not an unsurmountable one either.

Is there a way to arrive at a fair and equitable resolution? A reputable jeweler will want to do so because, if the settlement doesn't represent an excessive amount, he will probably adjust the loss himself rather than involve his insurance company.

There are two things you must know to settle a gem damage problem, either of which could come first. One, you must know your gem's specifications with regard to clarity, cut, color because any of these key qualities can exert tremendous importance in establishing the price of the stone in question, and two, you must calculate as carefully as possible what the weight loss of the gem would be were it to be recut to remove the chip.

As for clarity, cut, and color hopefully you would already have had the gemstone appraised by a professional. Without such an evaluation there is no reliable way you can know the value of the stone. The jeweler can give you his appraisal but the strict objectivity of such an opinion would be problematic unless that individual was somewhat less than human.

To eliminate the possibility of your own doubts, you would probably be better off obtaining a disinterested third party appraisal. You could also ask the jeweler to obtain a report on the gem from the Gemological Institute of America. Such a GIA evaluation would carry almost unquestioned authority on the adjudged specifications but would not have a price; GIA doesn't give prices.

There are other competent laboratories where the damaged stone could be appraised. Any one of them could also establish the stone's quality so you and the jeweler could work out a mutually acceptable basis for settlement.

The other important piece of information that's needed is: if the stone is re-cut to remove the damage, what will the new weight of the stone be? In short, how much less valuable is your newly cut, smaller gemstone? That might appear to be a very difficult problem, but it isn't. The answer can be calculated very closely for diamonds on standard type cuts.

On standard cut diamonds one can use an instrument called the A.D. Leveridge gage and a small book giving approximate diamond weights and measurements, which is used in conjunction with the gage. (Fig. 10-7). This book contains measurements on all standard cuts together with carat weights for every conceivable set of dimensions. It is a relatively easy matter to measure the dimensions of the diamond as they would exist on the re-cut and then look up the new estimated weight. In this way you could calculate very closely how much material, i.e., weight, would need to be removed from the damaged stone. Most every jeweler has a Leveridge gage or knows where one is available.

Fig. 10-7 The use of a Leveridge gage will be instrumental in estimating the weight of a diamond or colored stone when it is mounted or in estimating weight reduction in re-cutting a damaged gem. In a pinch, a simple micrometer is nearly as accurate.

At this point, the matter would be up to you essentially. Do you take a cash settlement and accept the stone with the damage? Do you insist on the stone being recut and accept some form of restitution for the loss in weight? Do you accept a replacement stone?

Be careful when having the stone replaced. It's a reasonable offer, but you might want to make certain that any replacement stone is at least as valuable as the damaged stone being given up. As you know, a slight change in color—especially with colored stones—or in a clarity grade can produce a considerable change in carat value. You'd want to be assured that the new stone is equal.

Remember, you only have a strong case for restitution if you can *prove* the damage occurred while the stone was in the jeweler's custody and if the treatment of the gem was less than careful. Sometimes a jeweler will note a dangerous condition on take-in and call it to your attention, perhaps refusing to work on the stone unless you excuse the former from responsibility and liability. There must be complete understanding between you and the person handling the original take-in (which is why many jewelers insist on handling take-ins themselves).

It's in your own best interst to try and resolve any problem directly with the jeweler. Any other course such as lawyers, consumer complaint agencies, or jewelry industry trade groups who sometimes involve themselves in consumer-jeweler disputes do offer alternative possibilities—but often leave a residue of ill feeling which neither you nor the jeweler may want.

The Critical Step is Buying Wisely . . .

One of the most dramatic indications that gem buyers feel inadequate about their gem knowledge is the persistence of so-called "getting a second appraisal." There is nothing that sometimes infuriates a jeweler more than to know that a customer who has just purchased a gem has gone as soon as possible to another jeweler for an informal and, hopefully, free quickie appraisal. "Is it a good gem for the money I paid?" customers want to know the second time around.

What sometimes occurs then, the industry refers to as "low balling." That rather disreputable sounding term describes the practice of a jeweler belittling the gem and/or the price paid. The objective of the low balling allegedly sets up an opportunity for the second jeweler to sell the individual the same quality gem at a lower price or a better stone for the same price—at the expense of scuttling the first jeweler's sale.

When a gem buyer has been skillfully "low balled", he or she will presumably return to the first jeweler—and the battle starts. It all generally revolves around which of the two jewelers put the gem's specifications in writing. Truth is, neither seldom do. To avoid being left with the belief that you've paid too much for a gem, that you may have been "taken" in the transaction, just ask the jeweler to warranty the color, clarity, cut and carat in GIA terminology. A reputable jeweler will be glad to; a chiseler will find an excuse not to.

Many jewelers bewail this lack of trust by customers. They discredit some of the certificates that are later issued on stones which they have sold. One association of jewelers has asked its members to refrain from providing people with informal evaluations when buyers are merely using the information to "check up" on the validity of a recent purchase. The general attitude often is, "I know few appraisers who know as much about diamonds and colored stones as I do: I am absolutely honest, so you should accept what I say about a gem because it will give you the comfort of buying here." Fortunately, many jewelers don't feel this way.

Are you, indeed, acting unethically by having your purchase checked by another jeweler? . . . or an appraiser? Does certification of stones create confusion? Is your effort to obtain a second opinion a direct insult to the first jeweler's reputation, long-standing in the community, integrity, gemological knowledge, ad infinitum, ad nauseum?

So long as you—the customer—represent the unknowing side of the transaction formula you should . . . you might even say you have a responsibility . . . do everything you can to assure yourself that the purchase you made was reasonable and fair to you. Nobody likes to be "had." The fact is that today the average diamond buyer—thousands of years after diamonds became fashionable to own and to wear—still doesn't have the slightest idea about diamond grades or values . . . and is still at the mercy of the seller's superior knowledge and representations. This shows that something is seriously amiss.

If all the jewelry industry can do about this information gap is to re-affirm its reputation for honesty, you should quickly remind yourself of the not-altogether invalid saying, "The louder they boast of their honor, the faster you should count the silver."

Can you buy the same gemstone cheaper at the second jeweler? Often you can because the second jeweler now knows what price he has to beat and it's merely a case of reducing his profit mark-up. No wonder they don't want you going down the street! Now, will you get the same gemstone cheaper? Maybe you will and maybe you won't if your knowledge of gems isn't any greater than the first time around. With thousands of combinations to choose from in different clarity, color, make, etc. the second jeweler could easily move a trusting buyer into a cheaper stone at a cheaper price and the buyer probably wouldn't know the difference. What's the alternative at that point? Go on to a third appraiser—and start the whole, tiresome, disappointing process over again or shout, "a pox on all your jewelry houses." If all you're looking for is a lower price you would be well advised to heed the warning of John Ruskin: "There is no product or service that a person can not make a little worse and sell a little cheaper, and the people who shop price only, are this individual's natural prey." Certainly, this can be true with diamonds and colored stones.

So long as buyers are unsure of themselves when buying gemstones the practice of the second appraisal will persist. The practice will also persist until meaningful communication takes place between the salesperson and the buyer i.e, when quality definitions are used that both sides understand and can evaluate.

When you buy a new or used automobile you are aware of the make, model, year number, mileage, general condition, and what accessories are included. You can use this information to compare with another offer —and then make your decision based on reasonable knowledge. Automobile dealers will even write out the specifications so you won't forget a "deal" while you are shopping.

Much of the problem in a jewelry store lies in the lack of useable information. Many stores have their own quality grading systems—and most of these convey romantic impressions, not hard information. An "Excelsior" grade may sound beautiful and top-of-the-line but it explains nothing about clarity grade, color grade, proportions, table size, etc. A salesperson who says this ". . . is our finest diamond . . ." conveys not one iota of information to you. Then you hear the expression ". . . a perfect, blue-white diamond . . ." or some other misleading non-sense—and you should realize that you have heard some beautiful sales-making phrases but no information.

There's nothing wrong with getting a second appraisal from another jeweler . . . but it is inefficient for you the way it's currently done. Here's a better way:

Insist that the salesperson describe a gemstone using definitions which have been used throughout this book, definitions promulgated by the Gemological Institute of America. Throughout North America and much of the world these definitions or terms are universally understood. People who use them to communicate are "on the same wave length." If a salesperson says a diamond is an SI2 with a J color these are two terms which will mean essentially the same thing to everyone familiar with the GIA grading system.

In those cases where a store may have its own individualized labeling system—and there are various, worthwhile reasons for this—you should ask the salesperson to translate any term of definition into its corresponding GIA equivalent. You should insist on this—unequivocally. Nor should you accept an answer which is approximate, such as ". . . well, it's somewhere around an SI or I and/or the color is somewhere between an I and an M. " What kind of nonsense talk is this? You may be assured that the store buyer was much more accurate than this when the diamond came into inventory.

Once you have firm specifications you have a basis for comparison. You may purchase the first gem you see at the asked-for price—or shop other stores, comparing prices FOR THE SAME SET OF SPECIFICATIONS. Remember, an eye-clean stone is one thing—and a stone just as pretty but with one tiny little flaw that you can hardly see is an entirely different matter *and price.*

When you do finally consummate a sale, demand a written warranty on the gem's specifications. As stated earlier, reputable jewelers generally provide this kind of documentation. Pawn shops, discount stores, jewelry departments in large general department stores usually try to avoid this; their salespeople are often badly undertrained and they're a bit jumpy about warranting gemstone quality grades or often in letting anyone know the real level of quality that their high-falutin labels "High Quality, Finest, Superior" truly represent. The old saying, "you get what you pay for, " is true in diamonds and colored stones where a low price invariably buys low grade merchandise.

If you wish, you may then take your purchase to a gemologist or a jewelry store and request a professional, paid for appraisal. You should be advised against going in and showing the stone or jewelry item to a jeweler and asking him, "is this any good? I paid X for it; was it a good buy?" Such an appraisal may cost you nothing—which is an appropriate price for the appraisal you'll get. The few dollars you'll pay for a professionally done appraisal will give you the information—or confirmation—you want or need. If you had dealt with a reputable jeweler who warranted the gem, it is very, very unlikely that the appraisal dealing with the gem's quality will deviate from your warranty specifications.

The key to your own piece of mind, though, is getting your purchase documented with the seller's warranty. If the salesperson says its a G color, then there should be no reluctance to put this into writing.

Appraisals Should Be Done Carefully . . .

In the absence of a reasonable fund of knowledge among the gem buying public, the so-called professional with a loupe to his eye has been vested with the image of almost infinite wisdom about gems. Many people feel they can hand a gem to someone with a loupe and from that individual will flow an unassailable torrent of gemological knowledge, marketing analysis, pricing advice, etc.

This just isn't so.

Only in such professional laboratories as GIA and some of the other better known ones is it possible to obtain the wide range of disciplines necessary to authenticate the world of gems. There exists hundreds of thousands of combinations of different stones, different colors, different clarity grades, different shades of color, different inclusions and degrees of inclusions, in various countries and markets of the world.

Diamonds are unique that they are treated separately from other gems. But the evaluation and pricing of pearls is just as complex and difficult, often requiring a near lifetime to become proficient. It takes a true expert to walk confidently in the world of jade.

How could any single human being command such a constantly changing spectrum? The answer is: there is no such person. Appraising has very definite limits—and much of the price appraising is little more than an approximation. That's why any second appraisal you obtain *should* contain the same quality specifications as the seller's—but might not. And that's why the money appraisal by a second person almost invariably will differ from the first—even if both appraisals are done on the same day. Give the same handful of rubies to five appraisers and you'll get five different value estimates—probably not close together either.

Appraising is not a science; it provides no absolutes such as $2 + 2 = 4$. Gemstone grading terms are defined as precisely as possible but the application of any term is still largely the result of an appraiser's subjective evaluation. Unless an appraiser works daily and consistently with all kinds of gems—a near impossibility even in a laboratory—he or she will suffer a loss in proficiency. After all, despite the GIA's breakthrough ColorMaster, there is still no universally acceptable technique for communicating color differences with each other. If one appraiser says a ruby has a 25% violet influence as a second color, who is to say that another appraiser's calling it 20% purple secondary color is right or wrong—and how would you communicate these different descriptions when a goodly amount of money is involved? It's done every day, yes, but the resolution sometimes distills itself into a quite un-scientific confrontation.

Because of the non-absolute quality of appraisals, you shouldn't be too upset if your confirming appraisal differs in price evaluation from what you originally paid for the gem. A radical difference should be brought to the seller's attention so the latter has the opportunity to accomodate your concern. As you know, an honest difference of value opinion and "low balling" aren't identical—and you can quickly detect the motive of the latter approach.

At the very least, appraising is a somewhat controversial segment of the jewelry industry. The entry requirements involve little more than studying up on gems a bit and then announcing you're in business as a gemologist and appraiser. But it is vital—especially for your protecting your gems' value.

An appraisal form should contain all of the specifications necessary to describe adequately the gem (Fig. 10-8). An appraisal that contains, say, only the weight and the current replacement value, is inadequate. It's fine for the insurance companies who don't mind hazy quality descriptions; they collect the premium based on the insured replacement value and when a loss occurs, can replace your gem with another of the same weight. Inasmuch as gem weight was the only specification, the insuror need not be too concerned with other qualities. As a result you could wind up with a lower quality stone than you had originally, but the insurance company is off the hook because they fulfilled their contractural obligation to you.

Fig. 10-8 For insurance purposes, one of the best pieces of evidence you can present for a loss claim is a simple photograph—preferably a color print—of your jewelry. This is a record or log of various jewelry items and any missing items can be proven by the photograph.

Had your appraisal certificate included clarity, color, measurements, etc. you would be well within your rights to insist on a stone of equal quality—providing, of course, that your insurance policy covered any appreciation in value.

Consider, too, how easy it is to identify a stolen gem at a police station when you already have your documentation—and it matches precisely with a mysteriously familiar looking gem that has been switched to another setting. Your own "mapping" ability is just as valuable . . . and as valid . . . in these cases.

Selling: The Liquidity is Low . . .

Pick up a book on gems and the advice invariably is on buying. You'll find precious little on selling gems. The literature simply doesn't exist.

Unless you are wired into the jewelry industry, selling a gem at or near the accepted retail level is just about impossible. Many have tried; few have succeeded. Indeed, some retailers wish they could sell regularly at top retail.

The investment gem business—whose success depends on the investor ultimately selling a gem at a profit—has floundered and foundered on the problem of liquidity. A gem buying public isn't "in" the gem business even when a substantial number of people buy gems as tangible investments. When they wish to convert their gems into cash, the problem begins in earnest. Gems just aren't that easily and quickly converted—and it takes an awful lot of appreciation to overcome a near-retail purchase price so you can sell off at or near wholesale so as to show a profit. The actuality of buying high and selling low is the complete opposite of investment advice where you're *supposed* to buy cheap and sell high.

Because they can't legally guarantee that they can resell the gem for their customers, the gem investment companies have devised all sorts of promises—most of which have fallen considerably short. Even their promise to try and help you sell—for a small fee—has fallen flat.

So, what do you do when you have a diamond or colored stone that you would like to convert to cash? Is there a market?

The market exists all right. You can find it nearly everyday in the daily newspaper. Many stone dealers, retailers, and parttime precious stone entrepeneurs advertise regularly their readiness to buy your gemstone. Be advised, though, that these individuals *coming after you* are, understandably enough, looking for bargains. They are in the true business of buying low and selling higher. They aren't even especially interested in buying at wholesale prices. But they offer easy convenience; you pay for this.

To your protest, "why I know it's worth more than that." these people have a quick, rehearsed answer, "Of course, it's worth more than I'm offering you. If it wasn't, I wouldn't offer you what I have just offered." What they offer is usually very low, or what they can describe to a colleague as a price where "I stole it." Where you're even more likely to get clipped is the itinerent precious stone and metal buyer who comes into town and holes up for a day or two in a hotel or motel room. His arrival is often preceded by an advertising blitz, offering to buy. Visit these people

194

at your own financial peril; they aren't in business to make friends or lose money. They aren't necessarily crooked. It's just that they turn over money and merchandise quickly—buying from you as low as possible and then bulk selling to gem wholesalers and metal refiners with the difference going into their pockets. But they offer easy convenience; you pay for this.

The firms offering to buy from you aren't crooked either. With their contacts they can buy a gemstone wholesale any time they choose. For you to get these merchants to part with cash you'll need to offer a premium, i.e., sell below wholesale or offer up a "home run ball" by selling off an antique or top quality investment grade stone so inexpensive re-cutting will send the value up into the pricing stratosphere. Before the age of hyper-inflation, high quality diamonds were regularly sold—which is why buying estate jewelry can sometimes be such a lucrative undertaking.

So don't be angry at your local jeweler because he won't buy your gem at top retail; chances are, he's doing you a terrific favor just by offering to buy it at wholesale because at any given time he neither wants nor needs to buy a particular gem. His supplier is a phone call away.

If the trade can provide you with a wholesale price, at best, or considerably below that, at the least, what are your alternatives then? You must go into the gem marketing business. By keeping a few key guidelines in mind, this is not all that hairy of an expedition even for someone who doesn't like the idea of selling or bargaining; it isn't easy or convenient either.

The first thing you'll need is an independent appraisal. Get this done, telling the appraiser that you wish a retail value appraisal because you want to sell the gem. (Obviously the price will differ from an appraisal made for estate purposes, wholesale, investment, etc.).

Before anything else, decide where you will want to meet potential buyers. It's best not to meet them in your home or apartment. Often you can make arrangements to meet them in the appraiser's office or in the jewelry store where the stone was appraised. It could also be in a bank or business office—or even a public place.

Try to avoid a location that's colored yellow or brown because this discourages the color appearance of a diamond. Blue or grey surroundings are excellent; they enhance color. If your gem—especially a diamond—is mounted try to arrange for plenty of incandescent lighting. Such lighting, despite its yellow color content, vastly improves a diamond's sparkle and fire.

If you're using a pad or box to hold the gem or jewelry piece make certain it's black, gray or white. Black is often regarded as the best color for clear stones such as diamonds because it contrasts so well with the color of either gold or platinum while accentuating scintillations and brilliancy. White is best for colored stones.

Dull textured materials will also emphasize the brilliancy and sparkle of diamonds.

Finally, make certain that the gem is clean and the metal, if any, is as highly polished as possible.

Nothing happens until somebody buys something. Therefore, you'll need to develop a prospect list, a series of people who may wish to buy your gem. Without doubt, the most effective way to do this is to run a series of classified advertisements. They are inexpensive and have an unquestioned ability to flush out people wanting things. Check your own newspaper and watch it for a few days.

Most newspapers have classified sections under such titles as "Miscellaneous," "For Sale," "Gems", "Jewlery." You might wish to run a single ad or a series . . . or run your classified ad in more than one section. You can easily get the wording of a classified ad by re-writing those which appeal to you whether they are promoting gems or something else.

The best response seems to come from ads which state clearly the price. Decide if you are firm on a price or if you are willing to negotiate and say so, "$500/Firm," or "$500/Negotiable," or "$500/Make Offer." Frankly, you're probably better off by not offering to negotiate. A simple statement of the amount you want will suffice, and if a buyer insists on negotiating then that's a decision you'll have to make. Include the appraised value, particularly if your selling price is lower to appeal to the bargain hunter.

A display ad? Certainly, if your selling price is high enough to justify that kind of expense. Display ads do pull better and you have more room to describe the item . . . to make your own pitch. You might need some help preparing a display ad—but the added results may be worthwhile.

Don't overlook bulletin boards. A 3x5 card posted on a church or supermarket 'swap 'n shop' bulletin board has pulled off more than one successful gemstone transaction. Is there a bulletin board or newsletter at work? Co-workers are a good source because it means dealing with someone they know.

Ministers represent a good contact, particularly for diamonds. They'll often know of young people in their church who might be in the market for a bargain diamond. You might even respond to some of the gemstone classified ads when someone is trying to move more than a single stone in the same ad. This often indicates some kind of dealer and a commission arrangement can sometimes be negotiated.

Find out if there are any stores in your area which cater to the marriage market. Often these salespeople will agree to mention your *for sale* diamond to customers as a favor but, more often, in return for a slight fee. Ask your friends to keep an eye out for anyone who might be in the market.

If cash is your sole ambition you must simply resolve yourself then to keeping everlastingly at it until you make the sale. Prospecting had been described as 80% of sales success and to make the margin over wholesale you must find a potential buyer and then successfully conclude the sale. Selling isn't easy; it never has been, and it apparently never will be.

As an alternate, though, you might consider barter. In the last 10 years, this non-cash underground economy of trading something valuable you own for something valuable that someone else owns has increased. No money changes hands—but effective bartering can be fun and could also represent a strategy for you to realize a full retail value. Gems and jewelry represent value to everyone and some people would much rather trade with you than spend cash.

If the value of your item isn't too great there is always the possibility of having it sold through a consignment or commission shop, too. These retail outlets specialize in selling items for people—clothes, shoes, furniture, gems, jewelry—on a commission basis. Generally, they are not too effective on high-ticket or expensive items.

As your patience grows thinner in the task of liquidating a single piece or a collection of jewelry just remember: if it was easy everyone would be doing it.

But somewhere out there—as every jeweler will tell you—there is someone who wants the beauty, rarity and the thrill that comes from buying and wearing one of the true wonders of nature—a precious gem. The desire has gone on unabated since civilization began.

So has finding the gems and the owners—and getting them together.

CONCLUSION

In the chapters leading up to this—some final words—you should have developed a background and knowledge about diamonds, colored gems, precious metals that will prove invaluable.

Hopefully, some of the guidelines will provide you with an even deeper appreciation of nature's most precious miracles, while showing you how a fine collection of gems or jewelry items can be the work of a perceptive buyer rather than the mere handwriting of check writing.

At the same time, it is best to keep in mind that few absolutes are available to the gem lover. Beauty, indeed, is in the eye of the beholder and quite often so, too, are the judgements that dictate value.

For example, the ideal cut diamonds—called, as you know, the Tolkowsky or American Ideal Cut—adheres to strict proportioning. But you should keep in mind that a cutter or a cutting factory's designer often makes decisions on what proportions will be used on a piece of rough.

In many cases where the piece of, say, rough diamond is of high clarity and color the decision may be made to cut to the Tolkowsky proportions which, as you know, provide for the maximum amount of brilliance and fire. Given the high cost of rough and the need for the cutter to maximize his recovery rate and carat price, the proportions may be altered.

The ideal cut (See Fig. 11-1) may give the most "life" in a round brilliant diamond. It does not provide the best recovery rate. Consequently, the

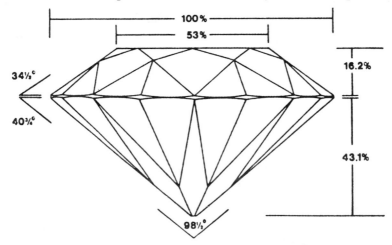

Fig. 11-1 These are the dimensions of the American Ideal Cut, stated as a percentage of the girdle diameter. The crown angle and the pavilion angle are measured from the perpendicular girdle plane. The actual pavilion angle is 40¾°, but for all practical purposes it is considered as 41° . . . and the crown angle is rounded off to 34° usually.

decision may be made to alter the angles somewhat. As a result, you may expect to be exposed to far more diamonds cut with a 55% or wider table.

It's likely that cutters will move close to the Ideal proportions only on the high quality, investment grade stones while going for the best recovery rate on stones of commercial grades.

The Scan D.N. cut (shown in Fig. 11-2) with its 57.5% table shows up in jeweler's stores far more often than does a true American Ideal Cut. Tables with wider tables show up just as often—so be prepared to be viewing diamonds with varying proportions. The variance of the other specifications can be dramatic, too.

Diamond Proportions: Round Brilliant Cuts

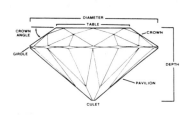

Fig. 11-2

1. DEPTH %	57 TO 63 PERCENT
2. TABLE %	53 TO 65 PERCENT
3. CROWN ANGLE	30-35 DEGREES
4. GIRDLE THICKNESS	1% TO 3% OF TOTAL DEPTH
5. OUT OF ROUNDNESS	SHOULD BE LESS THAN 30%
6. CULET SIZE	SHOULD BE SMALL
7. SYMMETRY	SHOULD BE "GOOD"* AT LEAST
8. POLISH	SHOULD BE "GOOD"* AT LEAST

*Usually graded: Poor, Fair, Good, Excellent

This Matter of Certificates . . .

Toward the end of the 70s, a fifth "C" was added to the famous "Four C's" of gemstones—clarity, color, carat and cut. That fifth "C" is certificate.

We can thank the gem investment companies for this latest wrinkle in gemstone marketing. Because many of the gem sellers were unknown to the gem investors, they needed some warranties or assurances as a wedge to separate the hesitant buyers from the final act of purchasing.

Thus, the well known gem laboratories were called upon to evaluate the various gems—basically diamonds—and issue certificates stipulating the experts' opinions as to the quality specifications of each gem. Certificated stones soon became the byword in gem investments. It didn't take too long for the commercial jewelry industry to catch onto the value of certificates.

Keep in mind the certificates from a reputable gem laboratory are helpful and acknowledged throughout the industry. But also keep in mind that the ratings contained in these certificates are the *considered opinion* of individuals—however well trained—and, as was pointed out earlier, can be challenged. Industry people recognize this . . . and they tend to place the greatest confidence and reliance in the GIA reports.

This is not to disparage other fine gemological laboratories. But a GIA report is most universally accepted by virtually all North American jewelry professionals—and by many overseas as well. Even then, a GIA report can be challenged—and GIA, as evidence of its integrity, prints a disclaimer on its own reports in recognition of the fact that two qualified evaluators looking at the same gemstone can come up with different ratings.

If the ratings of the most imminent laboratories in the world can be questioned you should be somewhat wary of accepting any ratings offered by salespeople REGARDLESS OF THEIR GEMOLOGICAL CREDENTIALS. It's not unusual for a salesperson to give a particular gemstone a favorable interpretation in the interest of selling the stone or in reducing resistance against the asked-for price.

A VS_1 rating sounds much more enticing for a given carat price than does a SI_2 (Fig. 11-3). The number rating technique given in the section on diamonds will provide you with a reasonably accurate and defendable system—and you should stick to your guns when you question a non-warranted rating. Because clarity and color ratings are often controversial you should remember that DEMANDING—not merely asking for—a warranty stating the cut, clarity and color of any purchased gem, especially a diamond, be a part of any transaction.

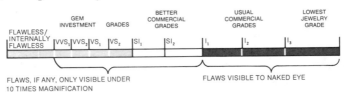

A salestalk goes with the wind. Memories are usually unreliable as to what was said or promised and the conditions under which statements were made are usually viewed as representations. As you know, a written statement by the seller is more of a warranty . . . and protection against excessive claims.

Sometimes, for a variety of reasons a gemstone can adhere reasonably close to the Four C's and still lack that something that many jewelry professionals refer to as "Life." The "Life" of a gemstone involves three major optical contributions: 1) brilliance, or the return of white light; 2) fire, the dispersion of light into its component colors, and 3) scintillation, the twinkling or sparkling largely caused by reflection of light off the gemstone's exterior.

All nine factors given in Fig. 11-2 must be in unison for a gem to possess "Life." Even the diamond—the possessor of the most "Life"—can be a mediocre performer if one of these elements is too far out of step. Just as an example, a diamond could be of extremely fine cut but have a poor polish. This one defect, where light would strike an irregular surface and be diffused rather than reflected consistently, would reduce the beauty visibly.

As anyone knows who has ever seen a drawing of a prism, the more light is bent and the longer distance it travels the more it is dispersed into its component colors. The girdle facets contain much of the light that would normally be lost through the sides of a cut gem, and the crown facets refract or bend the light as it emerges through the crown, causing fire.

But if the gem material itself has an extremely low dispersion index, all the bending in the world won't provide fire. It's this characteristic which distinguishes many of the lesser white, clear gems from the diamond; they simply aren't firey.

With these gems the only major optical contribution of the crown facets are inner light containment and exterior light reflection or scintillation. The small crown facets reflect surface light and when the gem is turned and twisted it provides the sparkling or twinkling effect. Clear, transparent non-diamond gemstones depend more on brilliance and scintillation for their beauty when dispersion isn't available. It's for this reason that colored stones usually will be quicker to reveal poor proportioning than will a diamond.

A moment's review of Fig. 11-3 will disclose the reason for brilliance. When a gem is cut shallow or "fish eyed" there is a leakage of light through the pavilion, creating the easily noticed glassy appearance. Because light is leaking down through the middle, the light rays are not being returned uniformly up through the table and the gem has a decidedly washed-out appearance.

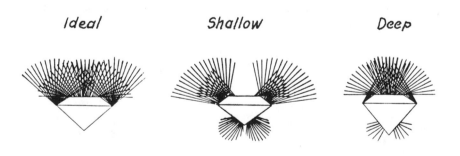

Ideal   *Shallow*   *Deep*

Fig. 11-3 The lines indicate the strength and direction of the light rays. At best, this explanation is theoretical and approximate and is intended only as an indication of what actually happens.

201

When the stone is cut too deeply, there is some light leakage in the pavilion because of the steeper angles. But the angles cause the light to concentrate across the table reflections, turning the gem dark, i.e., masking and losing brilliance.

It's only when the pavilion and crown angles are cut properly for the gem material that the bottom of the gem returns the maximum amount of white light. Thus the light flows brilliantly and proportionately through the table and the crown facets.

A Final Word . . .

Hopefully, the preceding chapters have elevated your interest and knowledge inventory about precious gems and metals.

It's what was intended for this book to accomplish.

In the interest of keeping the book readable and useful to the non-gemologists who simply want to know more about this fascinating subject, the treatment level has consciously avoided perhaps interesting but technical discussions.

The thrust from the beginning has been to provide information which could be immediately useful. Why the star facets are used to return light into the stone while acutally reducing brilliance is a fascinating optical subject that keeps cutters talking to each other for hours. There's some question as to whether the average gem buyer is remotely interested in the trigonometry of light and star facet angles.

I don't think there is much question, though, that a gem buyer is interested in knowing that the star facets and the table facets form a visible line that is useful for approximating the width of the table facet. Or that this information can be used in the determination of an appropriate buying price.

Caveat emptor? . . . let the buyer beware.

Not really. In diamonds, colored stones, precious metals and their combination into jewelry, the philosophy still operates—as it does with any other business: an honest transaction is in the balanced best interests of everyone concerned . . . if not, the transaction should be restructured.

ACKNOWLEDGEMENTS

Diamonds, by Eric Bruton, N.A.G. Press Ltd., London, England, 1970

Diamond Design, by Marcel Tolkowsky (London, 1919)

Diamond Proportion Grading and the New Proportionscope, by Richard T. Liddicoat, Jr., Gems and Gemology, Spring 1967 (GIA)

Diamonair: A new Diamond Substitute, by Robert Crowningshield, Jewelers' Circular Keystone (December, 1969)

A Simple Approach to Detecting Diamond Simulants, by Jill Hobbs, Gems and Gemology, (Spring, 1981)

The Art of Lapidary, by Francis J. Sperisen, The Bruce Publishing Company, New York, 1916

Handbook of Gem Identification, by Richard T. Liddicoat, Jr., GIA, Santa Monica, 1977

Diamonds . . . Famous, Notable and Unique, by Lawrence L. Copeland, GIA Santa Monica, 1974

Gemstones of the World, by Walter Schumann, Sterling Publishing Company, New York, 1977

Jewelers Circular Keystone Magazine, Chilton Publishing Company, Radnor, Pa.

Cultured Pearl Associations of America and Japan

Diamond Information Center, New York, New York

Modern Jeweler Magazine, Kansas City, Mo.

Gems Made by Man, by Kurt Nassau, Chilton Book Company, Radnor, Pa., 1980

Jewelry Manufacture & Repair, by Charles Jarvis, Bonanza Books, New York, New York, 1979

Practical Gem Knowledge, by Charles J. Parsons, Lapidary Journal, Inc., San Diego, Calif. 1969

Gem Cutting, a Lapidary's Manual (2nd Edition), by John Sinkankas, Van Nostrand Reinhold Company, New York, New York, 1962

Diamond Cutting, by Basil Watermeyer, Purnell & Sons SA (PTY) Ltd., Cape Town, South Africa, 1980

Jewelry Making Gems and Minerals, Mentone, Calif.

Gem Identification Course, Gemological Institute of America, Santa Monica, Calif.,

Diamonds Course, Gemological Institute of America, Santa Monica, Calif.

Colored Stones Course, Gemological Institute of America, Santa Monica, Calif.

Analytics Course, by Cap Beesley, American Gemological Laboratory, New York, New York 1979

Mineral Names, What Do They Mean?, by R.S. Mitchell, Van Nostrand Rheinhold Company, New York, New York

Gem Testing, 8th Edition, by B.W. Anderson, Butterworth & Company, London, England

Irradiation-induced Colors in Gemstones, by Kurt Nassau, Lapidary Journal Magazine, Vol. 34, No. 8, 1980

INDEX